Hiking
Grand Canyon Loops

Help Us Keep This Guide Up to Date

Every effort has been made by the author and editors to make this guide as accurate and useful as possible. However, many things can change after a guide is published—trails are rerouted, regulations change, facilities come under new management, etc.

We would love to hear from you concerning your experiences with this guide and how you feel it could be improved and kept up to date. While we may not be able to respond to all comments and suggestions, we'íll take them to heart and we'íll also make certain to share them with the author. Please send your comments and suggestions to the following address:

The Globe Pequot Press
Reader Response/Editorial Department
P.O. Box 480
Guilford, CT 06437

Or you may e-mail us at:

editorial@globe-pequot.com

Thanks for your input, and happy travels!

Hiking
Grand Canyon Loops

Adventures in the Backcountry

George Steck

FALCON®

GUILFORD, CONNECTICUT
AN IMPRINT OF THE GLOBE PEQUOT PRESS

Cover photo: Bruce Grubbs
Maps: Tony Moore
All photos are by the author.
Special thanks to Bruce Grubbs for editorial assistance on this book.

Library of Congress Cataloging-in-Publication Data

Steck, George.
    Hiking Grand Canyon loops / George Steck.— 1st ed.
        p. cm. — (A FalconGuide)
    ISBN 0-7627-1208-2
        1. Hiking—Arizona—Grand Canyon—Guidebooks. 2. Grand Canyon (Ariz.)—
Guidebooks. I. Title. II. Falcon guide.

GV199.42.A72 G7386 2002
917.91'320454—dc21   2001053198

This volume is for two special people who have figured prominently in my Canyon hiking:

To my wife Helen who encouraged my fascination with the Grand Canyon from the very beginning almost forty years ago. She and our children—Mike, Stan, and daughter Ricia, as well as niece Sara and nephew Lee—would join in the two-week Canyon vacation we took each year. Finally, though, Helen's deteriorating kidneys prevented her from direct participation, but her encouragement never wavered. No one should ever underestimate the power and value of encouragement. From the bottom of my heart Helen, thank you.

To my friend, Don Mattox, who asked me on my first Grand Canyon hike back in the mid-1960s. This hike took us on the Old Thunder River Trail and was the beginning of many such explorations. Don is a great companion with an abundance of common sense—and strength. Unfortunately he snores like a steam calliope. But I always felt safe with Don. If anything happened to me, he could just strap both my pack and me to his pack and carry us all out. But that was a long time ago. I don't think he could do that now. Thank you Don, for your company on all those hikes and for your continuing friendship.

Contents

Foreword

Each piece of land calls its own person. There are landscapes on this planet for the timid, the restless, the angry, and the romantic. The earth is probably the one thing that shows more emotion than even the people who live on its surface.

I have watched a man walk this surface, a person whose body and mind seem to be in tandem with a single landscape. George Steck and the Grand Canyon. Strong, lengthy arms and wry observations. A desire for difficulty and for conclusion. Sweet moments of rest and arduous days that seem as if they will not end.

There was a time that George and I walked together, our packs loaded for only a few days of travel. George was seventy-five years old at the time. He took me to one of the countless rims within the Grand Canyon, a place with no established trail, and stood there weaving his arms in the air, telling me of routes he had found in the past, places through the cliffs and inner canyons. His voice did not become sluggish with sentimentality, nor did it express endless knowledge. It was humble. He knew better than to put himself above the Grand Canyon. He led my eyes down from one rock formation to the next, explaining the difficulties of each, where rope might be needed, and where the walking would be easy. Good places to sleep or to set a resupply cache.

Then he put his head down to study the terrain immediately ahead and entered the Grand Canyon.

It is no simple country. There are few trails. Much of it is absolute wilderness, places that will defy any poet. The word beauty is useless here. And if you are looking for a simple guide book, an unenergetic description of how to get from A to B, go elsewhere. The Grand Canyon is made of tales, meals, fresh springs, and nights crazy with stars, not of rote, inflexible instructions.

What is most surprising is that the Grand Canyon is made of routes. In its labyrinth of cliffs and chasms there appears to be no passage, yet there are ways, quiet corridors and scrambles through tumbled boulders. Without these ways, travel is impossible. A person could look down from the towering edge and imagine that the inside of the Grand Canyon is closed. It is not. George has been there. He has followed the narrow catwalks and the hidden inner rims. This book of his is an archive of ways. It will tell you where George has found off-trail possibilities and loops, and tidbits of information that will not only reveal A to B, but might also save your ass. How to get beer from passing raft outfits. The proper way to go looking for drinking water. How to walk with only one boot. An emergency route to and from the river. A field recipe for chili. These are the true routes that are inside of the Grand Canyon.

The Grand Canyon is a vault of stories. When you walk inside of it, you will understand this, passing through animated climaxes, down into subdued undertones in the narrow Redwall canyons, through one transition and transformation after the next. I spend my life walking and writing books about such things, but I must bow here to George Steck, the true master. He tells the story here to all of us, to his apprentices, giving us the information we need to go in and find the Grand Canyon for ourselves. If every guide book were written this way, we would see and comprehend so much more of the wilderness. I promise. So take note. Hug yourself to George's words. And most importantly, go out there. Find this wild thing that the land holds. George has found the first step. The second is yours.

Craig Childs
August 2001
West Elk Mountains, Colorado

Acknowledgments

It is a joy to acknowledge the contributions and companionship of all those who have shared the pleasures and perils of my Grand Canyon wanderings. Of these I particularly wish to acknowledge my debts to Robert Eschka and to Gary Ladd.

To Robert, aka Robert Benson Eschka and who, for the rest of the book shall be known only as Robert, whose solo explorations greatly extended my knowledge of the Canyon. Those readers who use the extended route on the Muav ledges between Knab Creek and Tuckup Canyon described in this book have him to thank—or curse. Thanks, Robert, wherever you are.

To Gary, who has accompanied me on many of the loops in this book. He has also helped me see the Canyon through different eyes—to concentrate less on turret and tower and more on leaf and lichen. For all that and for his sense of humor and his ability to carry a prodigious amount of stuff, some of which is mine, I wish to thank him. Thanks, Gary.

Thanks, too, to those of you readers who have taken the time and trouble to communicate with me over the years. I enjoy the sharing of your experience and I welcome your comments about this guide.

USGS Topographic Maps

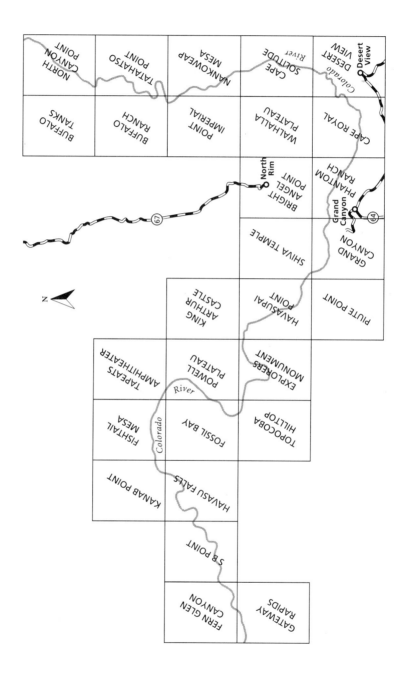

Overview

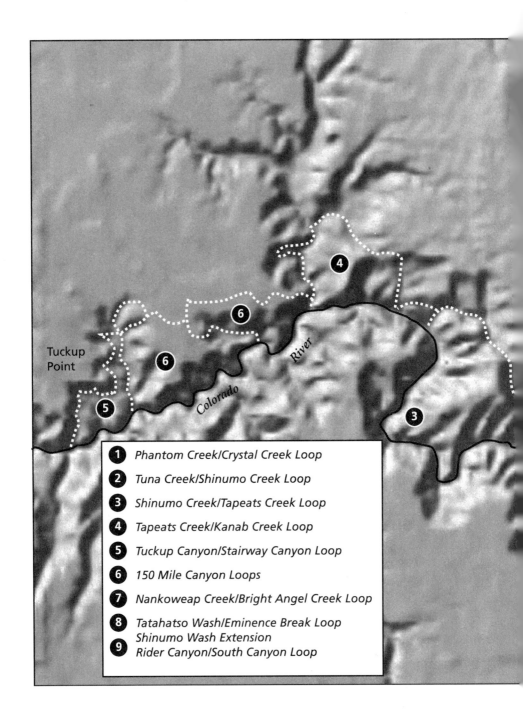

Tuckup Point

Colorado River

1. Phantom Creek/Crystal Creek Loop
2. Tuna Creek/Shinumo Creek Loop
3. Shinumo Creek/Tapeats Creek Loop
4. Tapeats Creek/Kanab Creek Loop
5. Tuckup Canyon/Stairway Canyon Loop
6. 150 Mile Canyon Loops
7. Nankoweap Creek/Bright Angel Creek Loop
8. Tatahatso Wash/Eminence Break Loop
   Shinumo Wash Extension
9. Rider Canyon/South Canyon Loop

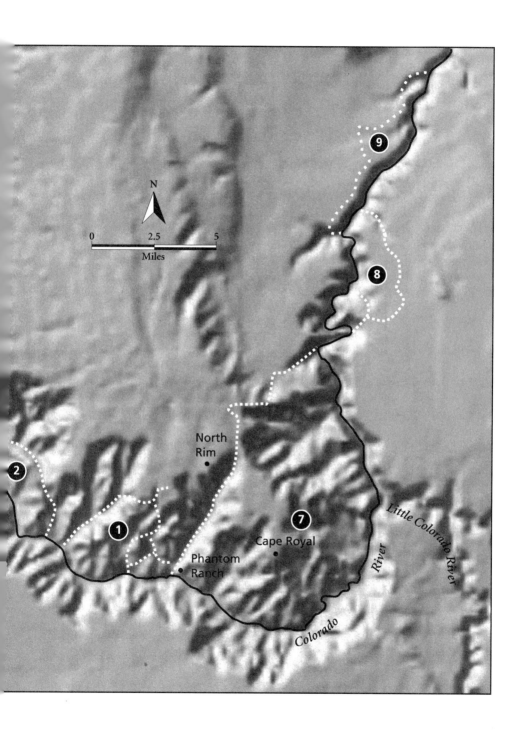

N

0   2.5   5

Miles

9

8

North
Rim

2

1

7

Cape Royal

Phantom
Ranch

Little Colorado River

Colorado River

Colorado

Legend

Paved Road	
State Highway	64
Trailhead	**T**
Main Trail	
Alternative Route	- - - - - - - - - -
Optional Route	··············
Spring	
Campsite	▲
Overhang	▣
Latitude/Longitude	36°07'30"
Compass	N
Scale	0 0.5 1
	Mile

Introduction

Welcome to the pleasures of hiking in the Grand Canyon outback. I use the term outback to denote the bulk of the park—more than 1,000 square miles—where there are no trails except for those created by deer, mountain sheep, and an occasional burro. Ignoring that part of the park with named trails eliminates at one stroke many popular segments of the backcountry—for example, the Nankoweap and Tapeats Use Areas, which contain the Tilted Mesa and Thunder River Trails, respectively. For obvious reasons, it also eliminates almost all of the park south of the Colorado River and upstream of Elves Chasm. It might seem that very little is left, but that is not the case. Most of the wild use areas and some of the primitive ones still remain. This off-trail, inner Canyon backcountry comprises just over half the area of the park.

Although the outback is enormous, it is largely unvisited. The park hosts about 5 million visitors per year, and a typical one stays only a few hours. In once recent year the outback saw just under 900 visitors, and a typical one stayed several days. This is very close to one outback visitor per square mile per year.

If the outback were always filled to the capacity permitted under current Backcountry Management Plan rules, there could be more than 500 campers there every night. These user nights would probably represent about 50,000 people per year, fifty times more than the 1,000, if that, who are actually there.

I have often wondered why the outback is so underutilized. Do misconceptions frighten possible users anyway? Is there a lack of information about this part of the park? Are modern cars unable to get to the roadheads? Is it because foreign visitors don't have the time and domestic ones don't have the interest?

Some of my friends argue that it is lack of information. They feel that the wealth of outback hiking information in Harvey Butchart's book, *Grand Canyon Treks,* is too cryptic for the average hiker. But I disagree. I think the information is there and only appears "too cryptic" because apprehension, spawned by misconception, leads many readers to approach Dr. Butchart's terse and economical style with trepidation instead of confidence.

My view is that despite ample information, potential users are frightened away; that the outback is perceived as inaccessible and hostile and hiking there is so hazardous and painfully difficult that off-trail hikes are, in the words of an eloquent friend and onetime companion, "not to be enjoyed but to be endured." There is, of course, some truth to this—certainly some of the roadheads are almost inaccessible and the hikes are strenuous. But to a large extent hazard, hostility, and struggle are like beauty—they are "in the eye of the beholder." In this book I try to present a more balanced view of the outback.

So what is the attraction of the outback? A few years back I was accompanying a newly minted high school graduate on the Powell Plateau Loop. I asked him if he thought the trip—it was his first—would be any more enjoyable if he had been to the Canyon before. He said something to the effect that if he had been before he probably wouldn't have come again because he would have seen it all the first time. I was astonished, and even a little angry, at his reply. Was he saying I was a slow learner? Perhaps. But whatever he meant, I felt I had to examine my reasons for continuing to return to this special place.

Each person has different reasons. Harvey Butchart once listed seven of his at a talk I attended. High on his list was being first—first to do something, first to know something, first to track down some historical tidbit. In the middle was physical challenge. Aesthetics was near the end.

Those are valid reasons—for him. Here are mine, in approximate order:

1) The Canyon provides physical and mental challenge. And I find the doing of a difficult hike more rewarding than having done it.

2) These hikes glorify essentials—water, in particular, and the individual in possession of a properly functioning body. People sometimes ask me whether, in the midst of such wonder, I feel totally insignificant and inconsequential. The answer is I feel just the opposite. When I can look around and survey that wonder, I feel magnified by knowing that without my brain there is no wonder, and that my body got me there on its own two feet.

3) The Canyon represents a magnificent contradiction. The fossilized beds of ancient oceans surround me, the sculptings of long-ago wind, rain, and River envelop me, yet water is basically absent. Oh, there's a substantial, but often inaccessible, flow in the center, a few trickles scattered here and there, and springs—treasured microcosms—hidden in secret places. But in the main, the Canyon, carved by water from rocks formed in water is now a desert—that is the contradiction.

4) The pure unity of the group under stress.

5) The appearance of wildness—thank the National Park Service and the Backcountry Management Plan for that.

6) And then there is beauty; and don't forget fun.

These are my reasons for returning to the Canyon, again and again, and my goal in presenting these loops is to afford you the same opportunities for enjoyment that I have had.

This book begins by describing four hikes off the North Rim, each approximately a week in duration, which end where they begin. I call them "loop hikes." Taken together they cover the Canyon from Bright Angel Creek on the east to Kanab Creek on the west. Dedicated and energetic hikers with several weeks to spend can even, with the help of caches near rim access points, string these loops together into an extended round-trip excursion from Phantom Ranch.

I then go on to describe four more north-side loops, three covering the region downstream from Kanab Creek to Stairway Canyon, and one covering the region upstream from Bright Angel Creek to Nankoweap Creek. This loop circumambulates Walhalla Plateau. I also include a loop on River left from Shinumo Wash downstream to Eminence Break, which takes you across the top of Redwall Cavern; and another, on River right from Rider Canyon downstream to South Canyon, that takes you to a point almost opposite Redwall Cavern.

I originally intended to conclude this volume with a major loop between Surprise Canyon and 209 Mile Canyon, circumambulating the Shivwits Plateau, but I'm not sure I wish to expend the physical effort required for its documentation. Instead, I will outline its route description, as well as others that might have been included, in a final chapter of possibilities.

Unless you have already hiked in the Grand Canyon, the hikes in this book may be the most physically and mentally demanding ones you have ever taken. This is not an elitist statement; it is the collective opinion of those who have been with me on their first Grand Canyon hike. But despite that assessment, I think any hiker in good condition who is comfortable with off-trail travel can do them. Still, I urge you to hike with at least one companion who has had experience with off-trail hiking in the Grand Canyon. Although I have tried to be sufficiently detailed in my route descriptions to keep you on course, some outback route-finding experience may still be required. But more important, I feel it is critical for at least one member of any hiking group to have had Grand Canyon experience in dealing with heat. Failure to deal with it properly causes more problems throughout the Grand Canyon than anything else. More on this in a moment.

Note also that two of these hikes may be unnerving: the descent of the 150 Mile Canyon, and the optional descent just upstream from Redwall Cavern.

The former requires four short rappels—15 to 25 feet—down over chockstones, but the problem is not so much getting down as in getting back up if an emergency develops before you get to the River. A retreat will require expert climbing skills unless you take out insurance by leaving ropes behind at each rappel site for possible later use. The final—but unnecessary—descent to the beach at the mouth also requires care, and a belay or fixed line is in order. If you do one of the loops that require this descent, it may ease your mind and increase your margin of safety to have a climbing friend with you to supervise the rappels and to set up the belays.

The second, optional, descent near Redwall Cavern is basically a scramble—but if you fall, you're dead. I have been down and back up without a rope and so has my friend, Robert, but to paraphrase Bob Dylan, I'm saner than that now. More recently I went down with ten others using fixed lines set up at the harder parts. One person, with more sense than the rest of us, stayed behind to notify our next of kin.

Besides the occasional climbing peril, there is, as I noted, the ever-present threat of hyperthermia—a malignant overheating of the body. Do not take this threat lightly and be aware that the first casualty of overheating will probably be your judgment. If your party is in a situation where it is at risk for hyperthermia, watch for examples of bad judgment among your companions and have them watch for the same in you. An example of bad judgment, occasioned by ground temperatures in excess of 120 degrees, is described in chapter 7 on the circumambulation of Walhalla Plateau. Fortunately, this lapse did not have serious consequences.

Extremes of heat can kill and so can extremes of cold. The problems posed the body under these two conditions have a certain symmetry, and when I am suffering from the heat, I sometimes think the Grand Canyon and Antarctica are similar places. Before I try to defend that statement, I need to mention a book I think ought to be required reading for hikers in the outback—especially leaders. This remarkable book is *Scott and Amundson* by Roland Huntford. More recently, after the success of a television series *Last Place on Earth,* the title of the book was changed to the name of the series. This book compares and contrasts the physical and psychological profiles of Scott and Amundson, and finds in their personalities and leadership styles the mind-sets that elevated the one and killed the other.

Let me quote a passage in which Huntford is describing the difficulties of travel in Antarctica. "The dangers are impersonal. . . . It is a clinical environment, where a man survives by his own intelligence and foresight. . . . " This sentence clearly describes both environments. In Antarctica the danger is cold; in the Grand Canyon, heat. In each case the danger is clinical—almost mathematical. If you must go 13 miles to your next food and fuel cache and you can only go 11, you die, as did Scott. So, too, if you must go 8 miles to your next water source but, because of the heat, you can only go 6, you are similarly dead. A "Scott"—mad dogs and Englishmen and all that—might feel he ought to be able to force that final 2 miles. An "Amundson," on the other hand, would probably have taken out insurance by putting in an extra water cache beforehand.

There are many passages in the Huntford book that, though written about Antarctica, apply equally well to the Grand Canyon during the summer if you change words like snow, ice, and cold to sand, rock, and hot. My symmetry is not perfect, however. I have not found an Antarctic equivalent for the temperature-moderating effect of darkness. In the Grand Canyon, even if you fry during the day, you can usually be comfortable at night. In Antarctica the cold is unrelenting.

Another quote. This time Huntford is quoting Amundson. "The wildness of the landscape from above is indescribable. Pit after pit, crevasse after crevasse, and huge blocks of ice scattered helter skelter. It was easy to see that here Nature was at her mightiest." A little farther on Amundson is quoted as saying that seeing his tent far below "in the midst of this chaos," gave him a feeling of "strength and power." Change crevasse to chasm and ice to the Supai formation and I could be somewhere in the lower Supai looking down on my tarp tent on top of the Redwall.

The Grand Canyon is something different to each of its visitors, and I have told you something of what it means to me. Doing any of the loops I offer in this volume will give you the chance of finding out much more about what it means to you. There is an enormous amount of rugged and remote Canyon to be enjoyed and I hope that the hikes I describe here will help you participate in its enjoyment.

WARNING

More and more often, bodies of hikers and climbers are being found in adventure settings, including the Grand Canyon, with a guidebook or photocopied pages thereof in their possession. This coincidence does not mean that guidebooks account for increasing use of remote areas where help is a long way off. Hikers traveling alone in the remote Grand Canyon backcountry—what I call the outback—are particularly at risk because even a sprained ankle, a benign injury under ordinary circumstances, can be fatal if it keeps you from needed water.

Park rangers at Grand Canyon expect one or two accidental deaths per year in the outback—usually the result of heatstroke, dehydration, or falling. Obviously, hiking in the outback can be hazardous to your health; this book describes hikes in just these risky places—so be careful.

The purpose of this book is to facilitate, not to discourage. I have the same purpose in writing it as Goossen did in writing the book with the intriguing title *Navajo Made Easier*—I want to make it easier for hikers to enjoy the Grand Canyon outback. However, I have the same problem Goossen had: I cannot make it easy. Similarly, I can try to make the hikes safer, but I cannot make them safe.

The hikes described in this book are for experienced Grand Canyon hikers. At least someone in your hiking party should have prior experience hiking in the area. Not only do I assume experience, but I also assume you will be in adequate physical condition. Be aware that these hikes are hard. For some newcomers to the Grand Canyon outback who are otherwise experienced backpackers and who may run marathons, these may be the hardest hikes ever taken.

How to Use This Guide

A general statement of condition and/or attitude:
"Them that die'll be the lucky ones."
LONG JOHN SILVER

PERMITS

A permit is required for all overnight use below the rim in Grand Canyon National Park (GCNP). You obtain one by either: (1) going to a Backcountry Information Center on either the North or South Rims, (2) sending a permit request to the Backcountry Information Center, P.O. Box 129, Grand Canyon, AZ 86023. Call (928) 638–7875 weekdays 1:00 to 5:00 P.M. (Mountain Standard Time) for information or for the Trip Planning Packet, or (3) faxing a permit request to (928) 638–2125. Permits cannot be obtained over the phone. There is a non-refundable fee of $10.00 per permit plus $5.00 per person per night camped below the rim and $5.00 per group per night camped above the rim. There is a one-year frequent hiker permit that costs $25 and waives the $10 per permit fee. Permits for exploring caves are also required.

Hikers on the east side of the River in Marble Canyon need two permits from the Navajo Parks and Recreation Department in addition to the one required by the park service. There are fees for these Navajo permits. A handout titled *Navajo Parks and Recreation Department 2001 Backcountry Use Information* lists them as:

Backcountry Use Fee —$5.00 per person

Camping Fee—$5.00 per person per night

The handout goes on to describe how to obtain backcountry use and camping permits:

You may wish to write or visit the following locations for obtaining Backcountry Use and Camping permits. The permits can be obtained throughout the year during office hours at three locations.

Cameron Visitor Center, P.O. Box 549, Cameron, AZ 86020. The visitor center is located at the junction of Highway 89 and Highway 64 in Cameron, AZ.

Tuba City Community Center, P.O. Box 216, Tuba City, AZ 86045.

Parks and Recreation Department, P.O. Box 308, Window Rock, AZ 86515.

The office hours at these three locations are from 8:00 A.M. to 5:00 P.M. Monday through Friday. The handout also includes the following paragraph:

Requests by mail/telephone: Upon receiving the Backcountry Use and Camping Permits, complete both permits and return all copies by mail with payment. The Department will process permits and return top copies of each permit. Mailout permits require three weeks to process so advance planning of your hiking trip is suggested.

Another quote from the handout is appropriate:

Consumption/possession of alcoholic beverages or illegal drugs prohibited.

The Navajo regulations differ from the national park ones in that important respect. For more information about hiking here, visit www.navajo nationparks.org.

USE AREAS

Trails Illustrated Grand Canyon National Park Map is useful for preparing your request for a reservation. The backcountry is divided into eighty-seven use areas, and each use area is allowed only so many parties (one to six people) and/or groups (seven to eleven people) per night. On any day of any month, reservations can be made for the remainder of that month and for all of the next four months. A request for a reservation should give the number of people and list the designator of the use areas in which you wish to camp each night. Don't forget to request a reservation for nights spent at the roadhead at the beginning or end of a hike.

BACKPACKING RULES

Besides the rules you might expect, here are two you might not: (1) no cooking fires and no campfires; in other words, no fires, period; and (2) carry out your used toilet paper—it helps to have a plastic bag reserved for this purpose. The second rule prevents the visual pollution of partially buried toilet paper, and the two together should prevent a toilet paper fire like one at Deer Creek that burned several acres and destroyed several big cottonwoods.

MAPS

Everyone who comes to the Grand Canyon to hike should have the appropriate U.S. Geological Survey (USGS) 7.5-minute quadrangle maps, or at least its older cousin, the GCNP map. It should be noted, however, that this large map, despite its seemingly all-encompassing title, includes only a little more than half the park. It should also be noted that this map is no longer printed.

USGS Maps

The USGS has either mapped, or is mapping, parts of the Grand Canyon to five different scales. These five scales are: The old 1:62500 maps, which are now out of print. 2) The 1:24000 maps. The entire Grand Canyon National Park is now mapped to a scale of 1:24000. These are the now familiar 7.5-minute maps; the USGS calls these maps its Primary Map Series.

In addition, the United States has been partially mapped to a scale of 1:50000. These maps cover the same area as the 15-minute maps and are in the same messy folded format as the 1:10000 maps. If the Grand Canyon were ever mapped to this scale, it would become the map of choice, having, as it does, a scale between those of the 7.5-minute and 15-minute maps. I generally preferred the 15-minute map over the 7.5-minute—it is smaller and you do not need as many. In my opinion, the fifteen-minute map rarely gives too little information, and the 7.5-minute map almost always gives too much.

A set of 1:50000 Grand Canyon maps would perhaps overcome the deficiencies of both. The ones I have seen still have 80-foot contours, which is too bad—50-foot contours would be nice.

3) The 1:100000 maps. These are called the 100K maps or metric maps. They have a contour interval of 50 meters.

4) The 1:2500000 maps. Four of these maps will cover all of the Grand Canyon. A raised relief form of these maps is produced and sold by Hubbard Scientific, P.O. Box 2121, Fort Collins, CO 80522; (800) 446–8767, www.shnta.com.

5) The 1:48000 maps. Though these three maps contain information not on later ones, they are mainly of historical interest. Two are the famous East Half and West Half maps of GCNP prepared from surveys done in 1902 and 1923. The latest edition is that of 1927, though it was reprinted as late as 1961. The third map is the Grand Canyon National Monument map. All have a contour interval of 50 feet. All three maps are out of print. USGS maps are available from local outdoor shops, the Grand Canyon Association (see below), and directly from USGS Information Services, Box 25286, Denver, CO 80225; (800) 275–8747; www.mapping.usgs.gov.

Fault Map

Another useful map is The Geological Map of the Grand Canyon, also affectionately known as the "Fault Map." It is published by the Grand Canyon Association (P.O. Box 399, Grand Canyon, AZ 86023; 928–638–2841; www.grandcanyon.org) and shows what strata can be seen and where the faults are. Faults often provide hiking and/or climbing routes through cliff systems that would otherwise be impassable. Be careful using this map however. A handful of faults are in error, especially in the eastern canyon. Besides its notable virtues, the map is exquisitely beautiful.

Plastic Park Map

Also helpful is a map first sold in 1987 that is a modification of the big GCNP map. In effect, the park map has been cut in half and reduced in size slightly (the new scale is approximately 1:73530, but the contour interval remains 80 feet); each half is printed on opposite sides of a sheet of waterproof, tearproof plastic roughly 2 by 3 feet in size. Its title is Grand Canyon National Park. It is copyrighted by Trails Illustrated and published by National Geographic Maps (www.maps/nationalgeographic.com/trails; 800–962–1643). Besides being almost indestructible, it has the very useful feature of having the use areas outlined in gray. This is a better map for trip planning than the one that comes in the Trip Planning Packet.

Washburn Map

Other maps deserve honorable mention. One is the 1978 Heart of the Grand Canyon, published by the National Geographic Society in collaboration with Bradford Washburn at the Boston Museum of Science. A version of it—abbreviated a little in the east–west direction—was an insert in the July 1978 issue of *National Geographic*. Its scale is 1:24000 and it extends from the Grand Canyon Village on the South Rim to the campground on the North Rim, and from Grapevine Creek on the east almost to Crystal Creek on the west. It has 100-foot contours and is shaded. A story is appropriate here. Mapmakers are perceived to be meticulous, fussy people capable of great attention to detail. I can only presume that Dr. Washburn is such a person. In any case, imagine his consternation and dismay upon discovering that one of the benchmarks on the South Rim that he relied on in producing his map was in error by almost 2 feet. This error was created sometime between 1934 and 1971 when some park employee(s) were told to build a wall over the existing benchmark. Rather than covering it up, these workmen chose to remove it and place it on top of the wall—which was approximately 2 feet high. This illegal resetting of the benchmark was not discovered until 1979—a year after Washburn's map had been published. As a result of this error, Washburn has written, "many, but not all, of the elevations on the map should be increased by 1.972 feet." This map is available from National Geographic Maps (see page 8).

3-D Map
Especially deserving of honorable mention are anaglyphic maps. An anaglyphic map is a topographic map with two sets of contours in different colors—one set for each eye. Each contour in a set is displaced by an amount proportional to its elevation—one set displaced to the left for the right eye and one to the right for the left eye. When you look at the map through appropriately colored lenses, you see a remarkably realistic three-dimensional relief map.

One such map, prepared in Germany, appears in the book *Grand Canyon* by E.A. Heiniger and published in 1975 by Robert B. Luce Co., Inc. It covered about the same area as the National Geographic map at a scale of 1:62500 with 200-foot contours.

Another anaglyphic map of the entire Grand Canyon was published in 1988 by Cygnus Graphic. Order from R. L. Smith, Box 10264, Phoenix, AZ 85064. The scale is 1:300000, and the contour interval is 400 feet.

Forest Map
I must mention one final map. This is the Kaibab National Forest map (North Kaibab Ranger District), which shows all the forest roads and their designations. It is a great help in getting to remote roadheads and is available at the Jacob Lake Store (ask the cashier), at the nearby Kaibab Visitor Center, and at the forest service ranger station in Fredonia, Arizona, and from USDA Forest Service, Visitor Information Center, 333 Broadway SE, Albuquerque, NM 87102, (505) 842–3292.

ROUTE DETAILS

Each route description in this book has an accompanying map that shows the route with a solid line, alternate routings with dashed lines, and optional day hikes with dotted lines. Possible campsites are shown with small teepees; useful springs and sheltering overhangs are shown with an "S" and "O," respectively.

Why Have Maps?

I have received several complaints about the maps included in previous editions of this book. This leads me to consider the question: "why have maps at all?"

I think it is a good idea to have a map showing an entire hike. In the case of the ones I describe, it accentuates their loop nature, and if you can infer geology from contours, you can appreciate how the route handles the different formations. But these maps are only an adjunct to the words—a summary. It is not my intention for them to stand alone; basically, the role of a map is to get you close enough to where you are supposed to be that the route becomes obvious. If a conflict arises between what you see and what I write, then you must believe what you see. If a conflict arises between what I write and what the map shows, then you probably should believe what I write. In either case I would appreciate knowing you had a problem. You should always carry the USGS 7.5-minute quads for your hike, since these maps show far more detail than can be reproduced in a book. You will need this detail to find the routes described here.

LOOP DIFFICULTY

I have decided not to give an index of loop difficulty because all the loops are difficult in one way or another. Moreover, difficulties are sometimes in the eyes of the beholder and can depend on variables like weather or river flow. Besides, a hike is often easier the second time you take it than it was the first. I intend, though, to mention objective difficulties, such as long days away from water, when the occasion arises.

Expectations

Psychological difficulties attending Grand Canyon hiking are at least as important as physical ones. Here is one reason why this can be so. Have you ever said or heard said: "This hike was much harder than I expected," or, perhaps, "This hike was much hotter than I expected."

Your enjoyment of a hike can be strongly influenced by what you expect it to be. If reality roughly conforms to your expectations, you are a happy camper. If not, you're not. If the weather is very hot and you expected it to be very hot, you are better off psychologically than if the heat came as a complete surprise. The same reasoning applies to many adjectives.

If we agree that having a happy hike requires a match between expectation and reality, then it is reasonable to ask a guidebook to provide appropriate expectations for the hikes it describes. This is not easy to do. For example, if I say a particular hike is "hard," or even "very hard," I am not being very helpful because the expectation created is tied to your experience, not mine. Once I had occasion to ask some fourth-graders what they thought mathematicians did all day. One small voice piped up with, "Long division?" The boy knew mathematicians did difficult things, and long division was the most difficult thing he could imagine. The same problem faces the reader of a guidebook. It is hard to imagine a hike substantially harder than the hardest one you have experienced.

In this volume I try to create appropriate expectations through anecdotes relating personal experiences—especially regarding the effects of heat. Two such stories appear, for instance, under The Inner Canyon Is Hot on page 23.

HIKING TIMES

A table of hiking times between segments of a loop is given for each loop. I have chosen to give these times (which include rest stops but not lunch, and which are rounded to the nearest fifteen minutes) rather than distances because I consider them more informative. I feel it is more important to know how far away water is in time than how far away it is in miles. If I need them, I can estimate distances from a map. Another reason times are more important than distances is that there are some places in the Canyon where it may take me two and a half hours to go a mile, and there are others where I can zip along a burro trail and complete a mile in twenty minutes.

I was in my late fifties before I began collecting routes and hiking times and thought of writing a book such as this, and although I have slowed down in recent years, I still think the times I give are average for an experienced off-trail Grand Canyon hiker in good condition. Some can certainly go a good deal faster and some will want to go slower, but remember that a group travels only as fast as its slowest member. To calibrate yourself, I suggest a preliminary comparison of your times to mine and adjusting mine accordingly.

Allow Time for Route Finding

I have received a variety of comments about the hiking times given in previous editions of this book. About a third of the people said their times were usually within five to ten minutes of those given. The rest said their times were somewhat longer—sometimes considerably longer than mine. The discrepancy was usually the result of my having ignored the time required for route finding—or their having ignored the effect of a slow companion.

When I began noting hiking times, it was usually on routes I had traveled before, so I knew where I was going. As a result, I did not have to spend time trying to figure out which way to go. Such times have not been tallied and I am sorry for difficulties caused by the omission. But I see no way to correct it—and am not doing so in this edition—except to suggest that sometimes it may be appropriate to add 10 or 15 percent to the given hiking times to allow for route finding.

CAMPSITES

Some of the locations in the hiking times tables are good campsites. They are designated by the "teepee" symbol, **▲**.

Listing some campsites is not to disparage others. Most outback camping is "at large"—you may camp where you choose as long as you are more than 100 feet from water sources. If you find a good place, use it.

GRAND CANYON TRAILS

Bill Hall, Boucher, Bright Angel, Hermit, Horsethief, North Bass, Old Hance, Thunder River, Tilted Mesa—these are some of the names given to Canyon trails. Collectively they evoke memories—some tragic—of other times and the people who lived them. Bill Hall, for example, was a young North Rim ranger who was killed in 1979 in one car wreck while en route to another. But history is only one aspect of the concept of trail. Except for the Bright Angel and the North and South Kaibab Trails, which are the only ones routinely maintained, all the named trails in the Canyon are either rarely maintained, unmaintained, or abandoned. In one recent year there were 30.7 miles of maintained trails and more than 400 miles of all the other kinds.

What Is a Trail?

What is a *trail?* The word connotes a certain ease of travel. But there is a great difference between hiking on the Bright Angel Trail and hiking on the Horsethief Trail. The first is a Canyon equivalent of Interstate 40 complete with flashy sports cars, convoys of semis, and even an occasional cop. The second, after almost a hundred years of abandonment, is a route marked only by a few horseshoes, a few pans, a coffeepot, and the rusted-out skeletons of a few tin cans. So the concept of trail has both interest and relevance.

The Trail as History

For the most part the "trails" taking you off the North Rim to the edge of what I call the outback are either historical artifacts or game trails. The first trails into the Canyon were game trails, and when the ancient inhabitants of the Canyon began using them, they made some modest improvements— like leaning a log against a cliff or piling up stones at a useful spot. But I doubt that much else was done. Neither bare feet, nor even feet with moccasins, could scuff out much of a trail bed. That would come later, when prospectors, miners, and cowboys ventured into the area.

Most of the named trails that exist today as something more than just a route were built by miners to get their ore to the rim and by cowboys to get their stock to good grazing. The remnants of their constructed trails into the Canyon abound and are silent witness to the enormous amounts of time and energy these people had. The North Bass Trail, when you can find it, is such a testimonial. Besides the Horsethief Trail, whose users probably didn't have much time for construction, cowboys built several trails into the area west of Kanab Creek. Few are in good-enough condition for hikers today, let alone cattle or horses. I have mentioned the fancifully named Horsethief Trail. According to legend, horse thieves would steal horses in Arizona, drive them into and across the Canyon and sell them in Utah or Colorado. Then they would reverse the process, stealing in the north and selling in the south. But not everyone agrees there ever was such an activity. While in the park library trying to find out exactly where the trail crossed the River, I found copies of several articles about the Horsethief Trail as well as a copy of a newspaper article saying that all the horse stealing nonsense was a myth.

That may be, but later one of the rangers in resource management told me about some pages in George Wharton James's book *In and Around the Grand Canyon.* There, James describes a trip W. W. Bass made down the Tanner Trail in March 1886. He found a camp, in the upper part of the trail, with bedding, weapons, and saddles. Soon after, he met the owners of this gear "watering eighteen horses, which had just undergone the suspicious operation of 'changing the brands.'" Bass and his companions pretended they didn't know what was going on and went on down to the River. Fearing for their own horses, which they had left on the rim, they returned for them two days later. They had been stolen. After reaching civilization, they read that "eighteen valuable horses had been stolen from Albuquerque, and . . . the thieves had been traced as far west as the Little Colorado, and there lost sight of."

I live in Albuquerque and searched the microfilm library at the local newspaper for the months of January, February, and March 1886 looking for an account of eighteen horses being stolen. I found accounts of stolen hogs and stolen chickens, but no stolen horses. The closest I came to anything pertinent was finding that a Texas Ranger killed some horsethieves near Holbrook on February 6.

The Trail as Property

One interesting sidelight of "the trail as history" is "the trail as property." Mining laws of the Old West gave a miner sole rights to the use of any trail he built to his mine. When the railroad began bringing tourists to the Grand Canyon in 1901, "ownership" of trails became a better source of income than the mines they served. Pete Berry recorded his trail to a small mine at Indian Garden as a toll road in 1891. This was a predecessor to the now familiar Bright Angel Trail. Berry extended the trail to the river in 1899 by a route quite different from the current one.

After Berry received a five-year extension of his Bright Angel Trail rights, Ralph Cameron bought him out. This was 1901, the year the railroad arrived, and there was money to be made. The fee charged for using this "Old" Bright Angel Trail was $1.00 per head, and by 1915 Cameron was "mining" the trail for $20,000 per year. But he did very little to maintain it, and various agencies that in turn had jurisdiction over the South Rim area resented Cameron's exploitation. They sought remedy in the courts, to no avail. The battle was still being waged in 1919 when the National Park Service assumed jurisdiction.

Cameron was elected to the U.S. Senate in 1920, and, in 1922, got a measure of revenge by having operating funds for Grand Canyon National Park eliminated from the Department of the Interior appropriation. Also in 1922, possibly seeking some revenge of its own, the National Park Service began building the South Kaibab Trail to compete with Cameron's trail. I think Coconino County had Cameron's rights by then, but such was Cameron's political power that he was still collecting his dollar per head. In 1925 the Kaibab Trail was finished; in 1926 Cameron lost his bid for reelection; and on May 22, 1928, the park service finally acquired the long-sought deed to the Old Bright Angel Trail.

A recent Grand Canyon National Park calendar (copyright Ken Sanders and Dream Garden Press) has a pertinent entry for September 27. It says, in effect, that in 1924 park rangers and an attorney made a surprise visit to Indian Garden to check up on Cameron's activities. They found several gallons of mash ready for distillation. Within weeks the park service had taken control of Indian Garden.

Game Trails

The most extensive network of trails in the Canyon today has been created by animals—deer, mountain sheep, and until they were eradicated(?), burros. Always be on the lookout for game trails—they often appear when you most need them. When you find one, you will discover that even the skimpiest can sometimes double your speed—especially in difficult places. Not only do they give you something a little flatter to walk on, but they also give you steadier footing. Their effect is so dramatic that I have often been led to speculate about a mathematical definition of *trail*. I haven't anything world shaking to offer, but I do know the concept involves more than just the area around your feet.

The Trail as Minimum Energy Trajectory

Often in following a deer trail, I find it goes up steeply and over a high "pass" when I would just as soon keep contouring. Deer aren't stupid, so why this seemingly unnecessary work? I think the answer is that it actually takes less energy to go up and over and back down than it does to go all the way around. I call such trails "minimum energy trajectories." The notion is important. In contouring around, I am inevitably faced with the dilemma of whether to contour into the head of a drainage and then back out or to climb down to the bed and then back up. Ninety-five percent of the time I go down and then back up. The rest of the time I don't and wish I had. A 1989 trip along the Tonto between Trinity and Crystal Creeks gave an excellent example of this minimum energy concept.

I was plodding along with a companion about twenty minutes behind the main group, and we started following a deer trail. Ahead of us a ridge bulged out toward the River and the trail began climbing up to it. Once there, the trail climbed higher to head out a drainage, aiming for a saddle on a still-higher ridge. I expected the trail to go down from the saddle, but it didn't. It disappeared, but following my rule—"look above you for lost trails"—we found it above us. It continued climbing to yet another ridge. By now we were several hundred feet above the rest of the group, and if we had gone down we would have been only a few minutes behind. However, we had committed so much time and energy to following this game trail that we decided to follow it some more. When the trail finally descended, we were a little ahead of the group and enjoyed the luxury of waiting for them.

The point is that by expending all that energy going up, we were following a shorter path than the others. And we also had the advantage of following a trail that, rudimentary as it was, still helped us go slightly faster than the others. Making up that twenty minutes showed me that this trail, at least, might qualify as a "minimum energy trajectory."

This Is a Trail

So what is a trail? Basically, it's a track that gets you from one place to another more easily than if it weren't there. All trails were probably game trails originally. Some, like the Bright Angel Trail, became an Indian trail and then a major park highway. Some, like the South Bass, Tanner, and Old Hance Trails, were built by miners to move ore. Some, like the Tuckup and Horsethief Trails, were built by cowboys to move stock. Some, like the North Bass Trail, were built by entrepreneurs in the tourist business to move dudes.

All now move hikers and some, in fact, are being maintained by hikers. Twenty years ago the Tilted Mesa Trail was barely even a route and was hard to follow. Now it is easy to follow. More and more, abandoned trails are being resurrected as more and more hikers use them for access to increasingly distant places.

GEOLOGY

It is instructive as well as helpful to know the sequence of geological strata in the Canyon. In what follows, the structure designations are C = cliff, L = ledge, S = slope. Structure is important—cliffs usually mean trouble, ledges sometimes mean shelter, and slopes always mean easy route finding.

Stratum	Color	Ht. (ft)	Age (M yrs)	Structure
Kaibab Limestone	grayish white	300	250	C
Toroweap Limestone	grayish white	200	260	C L
Coconino Sandstone	creamy white	300	270	C
Hermit Shale	deep red	300	280	S
Supai Group	deep red	600	300	C L S
Redwall Limestone	gray stained red	600	330	C
Muav Limestone	gray with yellow	500	330	C L
Bright Angel Shale	blue green	300	540	S
Tapeats Sandstone	dark brown	100	550	C L
Vishnu Schist	black with mica	1,200	2,000	L S

A backcountry ranger once taught me a memory aid to order the strata from top to bottom: "Know The Canyon's History. Study Rocks Made By Time." You must add the V for Vishnu yourself. Creating your own sentences may help you remember the order better. For example, "Kick The Can Hard. Some Rogue May Bring Along The Vodka." If you keep track of the strata, you can notice, for example, that the Bright Angel Shale and the Tapeats are going under water as you go downstream from Deer Creek toward Kanab Creek. This is bad news, because hiking on the Tapeats is usually fairly easy.

The dark rocks of the Vishnu Schist are the roots of ancient mountains that geologists think may have been 20,000 feet high. After a billion years these mountains were worn down flat and the Grand Canyon Supergroup and later the Tapeats laid down on top of them.

A featured loop in this book, the Walhalla Plateau Loop, takes you into formations that are part of the Supergroup, aka the Grand Canyon Series, between the Tapeats and the Vishnu Schist in age. They are the oldest sedimentary rocks in the Canyon and from the top down, they are:

Stratum	Color	Ht (ft)	Age (M yrs)	Structure
Dox Sandstone	red, purple, brown	2,000	>1100	S
Shinumo Quartzite	red, purple, white	1,200	>1100	C
Hakatai Shale	reddish orange	800	>1100	S
Bass Conglomerate	grayish green (columnar jointing)	250	>1100	CL

The Bass sets on top of the Vishnu Schist. My mnemonic for remembering these layers, made up as I type this, is: "**D**rink **S**ix **Q**uarts of **H**ome **B**rew **V**ery **S**lowly." If it bothers you that the words "Shale" and "Conglomerate" are not accounted for, make up your own.

Tonto

The Tonto Platform—or just Tonto—is the plateau top of the Tapeats Sandstone. The line of contact between the Tapeats and the Vishnu Schist is called the Great Unconformity. It is hard to believe a billion years of geology has been there and vanished.

Supai Group

As you might guess from the structure of the Supai, it is composed of sandstones, limestones, and shales. The three main cliffs are sandstones, the slopes are shales, and scattered through it all are layers of limestone.

The Supai, too, is made up of four sets of similar strata, and Gary Ladd has shared with me the following mnemonic for remembering their order—"**Whatta Man Wes Is**." He credits Jeff Gurley, a boatman who worked for Expeditions, Inc., for passing on this morsel. From the bottom up, the associated layers are: Watahomigi, Manakacha, Wescogame, and Esplanade.

The first three of these words are Havasupai family names, and the fourth describes a broad expanse of good hiking.

Coconino Sandstone

The Coconino is an aeolian formation—a petrified sand dune. You can see the layering of the windblown sand and how some layers meet others at an angle.

Oceans and Strata Deposition

Oceans have come and gone many times over the area known as Grand Canyon. Imagine the ocean deepening over a point on an ancient shoreline—the word is *transgression*. The first thing to accumulate there is sand. Whether windblown or waterborne, it is too heavy to be carried out to sea and collects as a sediment. Next, as the water deepens at our location, the finer silts that are carried out to sea begin to collect. Finally, in deeper water yet, limestones precipitate out and settle to the bottom. When an ocean withdraws from an area, this time the word is *regression*; the process of deposition is reversed.

According to Collier's book (see Books on page 45), limestones form at the rate of 400 feet per million years; shales at the rate of 2,000 feet per million years; and sandstones at the rate of 1,000 feet per million years. Thus deposition of 600 feet of Redwall would take about 1.5 million years and 100 feet of Tapeats about 100,000 years. So all the sedimentary deposits were laid down in about 5 million years. Since the Tapeats is about 500 million years old, it would appear that the Grand Canyon region was above water for 99 percent of the last 500 million years.

Pangea

Something else occurred to me only when I read of it in Redfern's book (see Books). Because the breakup of the supercontinent Pangea began about 200 million years ago and because the youngest stratum is older than that, it follows that all the Canyon strata were laid down before the breakup. When you look at the Canyon you are seeing a groove in a piece of an ancient supercontinent that broke off and drifted a great distance. But remember that the grooving is recent. It took about 5 million years, beginning about 10 million years ago.

OFFBEAT SCIENCE AT THE GRAND CANYON

When you see the Grand Canyon and say "wow," the response is not intellectual, it is emotional. To this day, after many decades, whenever I see the Canyon after an absence, sensory input overwhelms the rational and, I must admit, I still say "wow." I am a reasoning man, but reason does not govern this first response. There are only impacts of highlights and shadow and assaults of the twin beauties of form and color.

However, when emotion wanes and reason reemerges, the topic for consideration is most apt to be geology—where did this stuff come from and what does it mean? If not geology, then perhaps geomorphology—how did the Canyon get this way? Or perhaps archaeology—did anybody ever live here? If you are an appropriate specialist, then perhaps you see the Canyon through the eyes of a life scientist—how do plants and animals adapt to life in such an apparently hostile environment? There is an abundance of interesting detail to be thought about and an abundance of science to be studied. Of the many, I am going to discuss only three esoteric items that caught my attention when I learned of them. One has to do with drying mud, another with moving water, and the last with agave spirals. In a later section I will discuss a related topic, the energy costs of hiking. This, of course, is of intense practical (in addition to scientific) interest to hikers!

Drying Mudflats

Decades ago I read an article—possibly in *The New Scientist*—about how cracks in a drying mudflat tend to meet at right angles. I like facts like that—succinct, surprising, and easy to verify, and I did so at my first opportunity. Side canyons that experience heavy loads of clay and silt during flash floods will have many small gooey mudflats in various stages of desiccation. As predicted, I found most cracks met others at right angles—even if an errant crack had to make a sudden course change at the last minute.

For years I had been meaning to track down the reference to find out why this happens, but never did. In the fall of 1991, however, a companion on a repeat of the Kanab/Thunder River Loop, Larry Giacomino, to whom I had pointed out the phenomenon, sent me a copy of *Pacific Discovery*, summer 1991. In it was an article by Raymond Pestrong on nature's predilection for the hexagon because, of all the plane-filling tiles—triangles, squares, hexagons—the hexagon has the least perimeter per unit area of tile. Thus, bees need less wax if they make their combs in the shape of hexagons rather than squares or triangles. This article also included a discussion of the formation of cracks in various materials.

Basically, there are two mechanisms of crack formation. If a homogeneous, elastic material, like basalt, cools uniformly then a system of cracks can form almost all at once. As solidification takes place around randomly placed centers of crystallization, there is shrinkage and cracks begin to form between these centers. A crack propagates faster and faster until a critical velocity is reached, and then it branches at 120 degrees. Why 120 degrees? The end result of all the cracking is to divide up the plane into regions corresponding to crystallization centers, and with branching at 120 degrees the total length of crack will be smaller than if the branching were some other angle. Looking at it another way, by branching at 120 degrees, the crack system is beginning to cover the most area for the least effort.

The cracking of mudflats is another matter. Here, ideally, you start with a nonhomogenous, plastic material, like mud. As the surface dries and shrinks, tensions build up; eventually, somewhere, the tension is too much and a crack forms. At this time the stress perpendicular to the crack is greatly reduced near the crack—zero at the edge—while the stress parallel to the crack is not changed very much. As a result, the gradient—"the fall line," so to speak—is at right angles to the crack. A second crack approaching the first will tend to align itself with the gradient—much as a rolling rock aligns itself with the fall line on a hillside—and thus intersect it at right angles. It is also interesting to note that when two cracks meet this way, it implies one precedes the other.

Colorado River Rapids

While it is interesting that something as ordinary as a mudflat drying lazily in the sun must keep its eye on the mathematics, I find it extraordinary that something as chaotic and churning as rapids must do the same. The remarks that follow represent my understanding of work done by Susan Kieffer, formerly of the U.S. Geological Survey, Flagstaff. In particular, I am guided by her report "The Rapids and Waves of the Colorado River, Grand Canyon, Arizona," *USGS Open-File Report 87-096* (1987).

About the River
First, some statistics. There are 277 miles of Colorado River within the borders

18

of Grand Canyon National Park. In that distance the River falls approximately 1,900 feet and, according to Kieffer, more than 80 percent of that drop is in individual rapids—161 of them by one person's count. Kieffer also notes that 50 percent of the drop is in 9 percent of the distance. What these numbers mean is that the River is a great aquatic staircase whose "treads"—the parts between the rapids—have a gentle slope of 2 to 3 feet per mile and whose "risers"—the rapids—have a more rollicking slope of up to 50 feet per mile.

In 1965, after Glen Canyon Dam was in place but before the diversion tunnels were closed, measurements were made by Luna Leopold on depth and velocity. At that time, when the flow was 48,500 cubic feet per second (cfs), the average depth was 40 feet and the average width was 220 feet. Typical velocities were 7 feet per second (4.8 mph) between rapids and 11 feet per second (7.5 mph) in rapids. (You may remember from a long-ago physics class that 88 feet per second equals 60 mph, so that 1 mph is just about 1.5 feet per second.)

Where Rapids Form
Most rapids form at the mouths of tributary drainages—particularly those along faults. These side canyons are often steep and, because the energy per unit cross section of flow varies as the cube of the velocity and the velocity varies as the square root of the slope, even modest flash floods can carry impressive amounts of material out into the River to form a debris fan. I'm reminded of the ancient paradox, "Can God make a rock so big he can't move it?" I can't answer that, but flooding in steep side canyons can put rocks in the River that are so big the River can't move them until it floods in turn. According to Kieffer, stream velocities of 9, 11, and 13 meters per second are sufficient to move boulders 2, 3, and 4 meters in diameter, respectively.

How Rapids Form
Debris fans deposited by extra-large flash floods in a tributary canyon can extend across the River, damming it and forming a pond until flow over the dam can begin eroding it and forming a channel. Widening of that channel will proceed from time to time as the River floods. That process of deposition, erosion, and main-channel flooding evidently reaches an equilibrium when the width of the rapid is about one-half the width of the River above the rapid—this is the constriction—and Kieffer reports that twenty-five of the fifty-nine largest debris fans (42 percent) produce constrictions very close to one-half. Well, enough of statistics. Now it's on to the physics.

The Hydraulics of Rapids
Before we can discuss the hydraulics of rapids, we need two *concepts—Froude number* and *hydraulic jump.* William Froude was a nineteenth century English naval architect who developed formulae relating the performance of a ship model to that of the real thing; his name is given to a number that is a kind of watery analogue to Mach number. The Froude number of a body of moving water is the ratio of the speed of the water to the associated critical velocity, and the critical velocity is the square root of the product of depth of flow and the gravitational constant.

This critical velocity is the speed at which waves travel under the influence of gravity alone. If I throw a rock in a stream and the splash waves can travel upstream against the flow, then the flow velocity is less than the wave, or critical, velocity and the Froude number is less than one. When the Froude number is less than one, the flow is said to be subcritical, and what happens downstream can influence what happens upstream. If the Froude number exceeds one, then what happens downstream cannot influence what happens upstream.

For example, imagine a small rock suddenly appearing on the bed of a slowly moving subcritical flow. The disturbance produced by this change in the bottom travels upstream against the current at the critical velocity, and the flow adjusts smoothly to the change. Now imagine the rock's becoming larger and larger. The same thing happens—the flow adjusts smoothly to the change, though there may be a smooth wave forming over the rock. If the rock continues to grow, eventually the water flowing over the rock will become supercritical because the depth of flow over the rock is much less now and its corresponding critical velocity is now less than the speed of flow so the Froude number exceeds unity. On the downstream side of the rock, the depth suddenly increases, the critical velocity suddenly increases, the Froude number slips below unity again and the flow returns to subcritical through what is called a hydraulic jump. This is the back curling wave associated with the rock and the height of the wave depends on what the Froude number of the flow over the rock has been.

Conservation Laws
There are two conservation laws that govern what happens to water flowing in an open channel like a river. First, the flow through every cross section is the same. Second, the energy of flow in every cross section is the same. In other words, both mass and energy are conserved. The first law means that when water goes faster than average in the middle of the river, it must go slower than average at the edges—perhaps even to the point of going upstream in an eddy. The second law means the excess potential energy the water has above a rapid must be dissipated in the rapid until the flow below it is pretty much like the flow above it. A hydraulic jump is just one way in which excess energy can be dissipated.

If my hypothetical rock continues to grow—so it sticks above the water—waves associated with the disturbance once again travel upstream and the flow once again adjusts smoothly to the rock. The exception is that the viscosity of the water typically causes a cushion of water in front of the rock and an eddy—bounded by "horseshoe" vortices—to form behind the rock. Kayakers often use such eddies as places to rest and they also—the better ones, anyway—use the upstream side of a hydraulic jump as a playground and "surf" on it.

To my way of thinking, a rapid is only a huge energy dissipation machine—whether it's by hydraulic jumps of various kinds, by eddies, by friction, or whatever. Since the roles of these varying energy-dissipation mechanisms are different in different parts of a rapid, it helps to think of a rapid in four parts: the pond at the top, the "tongue" leading into the constriction, the chaotic flow through the constriction, and the tailwave runout at the bottom.

The Pond

Even the ponding dissipates some energy. The Colorado River is somewhat deeper at the head of a rapid than elsewhere, and it follows from the hydraulics that the depth of the water at the top of the tongue is about two-thirds of the depth in the pool. This would seem to imply that the process of water entry into the tongue is skimming off two-thirds of the flow. But the bottom third must go somewhere. This requirement creates a circulation in the pond—i.e., some water moves upstream—and this takes energy.

The Tongue

Next comes the tongue. This is the smooth flow between the oblique waves branching out from the shore. The equations involved make the Froude number at the top of the tongue close to unity. Kieffer reports that the sine of the angle these oblique waves make with the flow is the reciprocal of the Froude number. Their height also increases with Froude number. Hence, for Froude numbers of 1, 1.414, or 2, the corresponding angle is 90, 45, or 30 degrees. There may also be smooth, nonbreaking rollers on the tongue at right angles to the flow. These are considered undular hydraulic jumps and are unrelated to the topography of the bed.

The Constriction

The region of strongly breaking waves in the narrowest part of the channel convergence below the end of the tongue is the main part of the rapid. Here, the configuration of the channel dictates what happens—jumps, haystacks, waves. Sometimes big boulders are involved, sometimes not. The foaming of the water plays an major role, too. Kieffer reports that "An important aspect of the strongly breaking waves is their foaming and entrainment of air. This plays a significant role in energy dissipation in the wave, e.g., can account for several tens of percent to nearly all of the required energy loss in the jump (Lighthill 1978)." The reference does not explain how this entrainment dissipates energy, but the process of compressing the air, and holding it under water for a time, may account for some of it.

The Runout

When the constriction begins to widen, a narrow jet of fast water often continues on. Data suggest that the jet keeps a constant diameter for several constriction widths downstream. The jet creates an instance of the requirement that water must move upstream along the edges to balance fast moving water in the center in order to "conserve mass." There are usually large circulation eddies below a rapid, and an inattentive boatman may get caught by one and spend much time and energy in the process of escaping. Sometimes the boundary between the jet and the eddy—an eddy fence—is dangerous and can upset a small boat. Kieffer reports in 1983 that an eddy fence in the middle of Crystal Rapids at the Slate Creek eddy was 10 to 12 feet high. Tail-waves—hydraulic jumps—eventually match the jet to downstream conditions, and the River continues on its way below the rapid pretty much as it was doing above it.

This has been a cursory and incomplete account of what happens in a rapid and why, and I hope those readers who find interest in making sense out of such a messy business will read the Kieffer reference. Years ago I listened to a Stanford mathematician talk about "hearing" the shape of a drum—about how to analyze sound waves to infer the shape of the object producing them. I don't know enough yet to infer the shape of the bottom of the River from the nature of a rapid, but I am beginning to believe that it just might be possible to do so.

Phyllotaxis

The third, and last, bit of science I want to offer is really more in the nature of a tidbit. It concerns the way plant branches and such are arrayed around a stem. First, though, you need a little background.

Around A.D. 1200, Leonardo da Pisa—aka Fibonacci—wrote about the sequence of numbers that bears his name. The Fibonacci sequence begins with two 1s, and each number that follows is the sum of the two previous numbers. Thus, the first ten Fibonacci numbers are 1, 1, 2, 3, 5, 8, 13, 21, 34, and 55. These numbers are closely related to spirals, and they crop up in many places—the stock market, the Golden Rectangle, the search pattern for hunting a submarine, the arrangement of florets on a sunflower blossom.

Fibonacci's original context concerned counting the number of pairs of rabbits in an enclosure at the end of each month under a certain breeding schedule: The breeding starts with a single adult male-female pair, which produces a male-female pair at the end of every month; each new pair matures after two months, producing a male-female pair then and every month thereafter. The question is "How many pairs of rabbits will be in the enclosure at the end of a year?" This sequence is of such interest that there is a special mathematical journal, *The Fibonacci Quarterly*, devoted to its study.

Pineapples and Pinecones

The next time you are in a supermarket, find a pineapple and notice the spirals formed by its bumps. If you hold it with the bottom resting on your hand, you can count eight shallow spirals winding around to the left and thirteen steep spirals winding around to the right. These two integers are consecutive Fibonacci numbers. The next time you are on the rim of the Grand Canyon, find a pinecone and do the same with it as you did with the pineapple. You will find five shallow spirals to the left and eight steep ones to the right. The spiraling location of palm fronds around a palm tree is another example—again, two consecutive Fibonacci numbers. This phenomenon of the numbers of opposing spirals being consecutive Fibonacci numbers is common in the plant kingdom and is called phyllotaxis. The only reason I have found offered for this intrusion of the Fibonacci sequence into botany is that it provides minimal shading of lower branches by upper ones. I consider this a weak reason; the only one that will satisfy me is one that involves the definition of the sequence.

My least favorite plant in the Canyon is the agave (see page 29 for a discussion of the dangers of its sharp spines), and it is easy to spot the two opposing sets of spirals surrounding the core of that vicious plant. Many times I have tried to count them, but they were too well defended and I kept losing track. Once, however, I found a dead agave, breached its defenses and counted twenty-one shallow spirals. If I had had more time and some help, I bet I could have counted thirty-four steep ones.

This ends my discussion of science at Grand Canyon. However, a scientist sees science everywhere. There is always a "why" or "how" lurking in the oddest places. Science is not only a profession, it is a way of relating to your environment, and I hope these pages will help you understand what might otherwise have gone zipping by unnoticed.

THE INNER CANYON IS HOT

Spring and fall are both good times for hiking in the Canyon, but I prefer fall because the weather is more stable. In early spring (March/April) it can seem to be boiling one day and freezing the next. In fact, I remember one Easter when we fried one day and had a blizzard the next.

Temperatures (°F) and Rainfall (inches) at Phantom Ranch

	J	F	M	A	M	J	J	A	S	O	N	D
Maximum	72	82	88	98	109	114	119	120	108	102	84	70
Ave. Max.	56	62	71	82	92	101	106	103	97	84	68	57
Ave. Min.	36	42	48	56	63	72	78	75	69	58	46	37
Minimum	26	31	32	27	46	61	62	59	49	41	31	30
Ave. Rainfall	0.7	0.8	0.8	0.5	0.4	0.3	0.8	1.4	1.0	0.7	0.4	0.9

Never underestimate the debilitating effects of heat. A battle with heat in mid-June 1989, which I describe at greater length in chapter 7 on the circumambulation of Walhalla Plateau, taught me three things about heat. First, a shade temperature of 110 degrees in late morning may rise to 115 degrees or more by midafternoon. Allow at least a quart of water per hour for travel under these conditions and remember gaining elevation means slower travel which means more time per mile and, hence, more water per mile.

Second, prolonged travel at air temperatures of 115 degrees or more causes lapses in judgment, even if you are properly hydrated. You may do things, like hallucinate or jump down a 10-foot cliff, that you would not do under ordinary circumstances. This is because the command center—the brain—is overheated. Sweating helps cool the brain a little, but a small towel or bandanna on the head with, say, half a cup of water on it will provide vital additional cooling that may be enough to allow you to look around for an alternative before jumping off that cliff.

Third, the effects of overheating can persist for days. I write in chapter 4 about a young man who almost died of heatstroke. He was told he would be sensitized to heat for the rest of his life. Apparently something similar, but not so lasting, is also true for heat exhaustion.

CRITTERS

Hikers in the Grand Canyon should expect to interact with several species of animals. The ones I will comment on specifically are: rattlesnakes, scorpions, mice, ringtails, ravens, and ants. I have some further things to say on other canyon adversaries.

Rattlesnakes

First, I must say that any rattlesnake bite is potentially life-threatening; I advise all Grand Canyon hikers to decide beforehand what they will do should a rattlesnake bite occur. Second, I must add that my experience over many years of Canyon hiking shows the risk of a rattlesnake bite to be small; though the National Park Service reports one or two snake bites each year. Third, I have concluded that a rattlesnake bite is rarely fatal to a healthy adult.

This view is supported by the following data—and the nineteen deaths from snakebite reported in New Mexico over the years 1931–1972 (Native American deaths from snakebites were not reported), fourteen were ten years old or younger and three were seventy or older. This means only about 10 percent of the fatalities were between ten and seventy years of age. Further, in October 1987 the *Albuquerque Journal* said there are about 7,000 venomous snakebites per year in the United States, with an average of twenty deaths per year; another reference adds that most of the dead are children.

Grand Canyon rattlesnakes are said to be "rare and retiring." I'm not sure what that means, but I expect to see one or two during a week's trip—although I once saw ten in one day. A snake may rattle if you come on it when it is warm, but in the cool of early morning they often don't. At such a time all the hikers in my group may file past a rattlesnake, and only one of us sees it. I hate to think how often this happens and nobody sees it.

Snakebite Treatment

Granting that the risk of being bitten is small, what do you do if, against all odds, you are bitten? First, you observe that even if you are bitten, there is a one in five chance that the snake did not inject any venom—remember, venom is primarily for getting food and not for defense.

I recently wrote to Dr. Willis Wingert, a USC professor of pediatrics and emergency medicine, and asked what he would recommend for a rattlesnake bite in the backcountry of the Grand Canyon where it might be several days before a victim could get help. He replied as follows:

My advice for a person who is in a remote area and is bitten by a rattlesnake is to remain quiet, splint the bitten extremity (stick and cloth or a pillow splint), drink large quantities of any fluid except alcohol, and send a companion to hike out for helicopter rescue. Cutting, sucking, tourniquets, and freezing will not prevent the absorption of venom. It is doubtful that sucking could remove any significant amount of venom. These methods only complicate the problem by damaging tissue (which is already poisoned), introducing infection into the wound and pos-

sibly causing severe hemorrhage. A snakebitten victim doesn't need these additional problems. I reassure you that you have hours to get help. Of course, the sooner treatment is started the better, but even severely bitten victims survive twenty-four to forty-eight hours.

It is crucial that a snake bite victim not try to hike out. See the Emergency section on page 30 for information on getting help for the victim.

Dr. Wingert went on to recommend hiking with a walking stick for probing ahead; your stick "finds" the snake before your leg does. I appreciated that suggestion because I've always used one.

I would like to add to my discussion of snakebite by calling attention to the Sawyer First Aid Extractor Kit. This kit has a powerful suction device and several cups for controlling the area over which the suction is applied. The idea is to try to suck venom out without any prior cutting. I carry one of these kits even though I have never had occasion to use it. It measures 4.5 by 7 inches and weighs 3 ounces. It is available from some outdoor equipment mail-order catalogs.

I will close my discussion of rattlesnakes on a somber note. Even if we agree that rattlesnake bites are rarely fatal, I must remind you that their venom is a poison that destroys tissue. This means that although you probably won't die, you might lose a few fingers or toes or possibly a limb.

When the venom causes swelling, the muscle swells within its sheath, and the blood vessels within the muscle are constricted as if with an internal tourniquet. Gangrene may result.

Scorpions

While no companion of mine has been bitten by a snake, I have had two companions stung by scorpions. Scorpions hunt at night and don't usually wander around during the day. For some sobering excitement, try hiking at night with an ultraviolet light—scorpions fluoresce under UV light. Watch out, though, when a hard rain floods their hiding places and they come out in great numbers. We counted more than twenty scorpions in a very small area after such a rain. A companion, walking barefoot over the slab rock, stepped on one of these. This became a serious medical emergency when the young lady developed a severely depressed respiratory reflex and had to be evacuated. She almost died of that scorpion sting.

My nephew, on the other hand, was stung on the elbow and only had numbness, preceded by a tingling sensation, travel up his arm. He was sure he would die when that numbness reached his heart but, fortunately, he fell asleep before that happened. His pulse and respiration remained good through the night; by morning he was okay, except his arm was "all-a-tingle."

My advice about scorpions: Wear shoes at night and after a rain, and be careful about turning over rocks.

Ringtails

Ring-tailed cats, more accurately called cacomistles, are a frequent pest—particularly at Deer Creek. They are nocturnal, omnivorous, and fearless. A friend took a flash picture of one fighting over possession of his pack, and my nephew made a mistake trying to pull one out of his pack by the tail. They are also strong—able to carry of pound loaves of pumpernickel. They scamper around on cliff faces and make a chittering noise somewhat like that of a chipmunk. But they have a problem with overhangs, so you can hang up your food under one, but far enough from the wall so they can't reach it.

The ringtail's packrat mentality presents a dilemma. Should pack pockets be left open so a nocturnal marauder in search of food does not make holes in your pack, or should the pockets be closed to protect the inedible items inside from pilferage? My view is to leave the pockets open and protect the food by storing it in a pot or by hanging it from something.

Ravens

According to Scandinavian mythology, when Odin sits on his throne, the ravens Hugin and Munin, representing thought and memory, sit on his shoulders. Every day they fly over the whole world and report back on what they have seen. As a result, ravens are sometimes called "the eyes of Odin." I always have enjoyed watching ravens. I think the reason is that they almost always seem to be in pairs, and I like thinking that an intelligent bird like a raven can desire and appreciate companionship. I once watched a pair of ravens engaged in a variety of acrobatics—I particularly remember their climbing high and then diving—and I couldn't help feeling that this was play; they were having fun. Unfortunately, these thoughts are probably only anthropomorphisms on a grand scale.

Ravens as Pests

But ravens can also be pests. A pair watched us at Deer Creek one morning as we were breakfasting, and I thought I had better protect my pack before we took off on a day hike. I closed the pockets and tied down the straps and put it on its back in a small space under an overhang. When we returned I found that someone or something had pulled open the zippers and scattered the contents of the pockets. I have to admit I did not see the ravens do this, but nothing was stolen except edibles. Mice couldn't do it, and ringtails probably couldn't either. But ravens have the intelligence and the dexterity. So enjoy the ravens, but be wary.

Mice

I have a stressful relationship with mice. They are almost everywhere in the Canyon, and there are very smart mice at some places. At least I used to think so until I was told that what I took for intelligence was just instinct. The foraging habits of the genus *Peromyscus* take them up trees and out branches and down whatever they find there. Thus, instinct and not learned response has led them to climb down the cord I use to suspend my food. But what is it that leads them to gnaw through the cord, dropping the food to the ground? Luck? My son claims this has happened to him.

The Mouse as Adversary

I have spent considerable time and energy trying to best the lowly mouse, and at the moment the score is "Mice 513, Steck 0." One night I thought I would surely outwit them if I balanced my bags of food on the top of my aluminum alloy ski-pole walking stick. I awoke during the night, saw my food outlined against the moonlit sky, and thought smugly, "At last, I have outwitted them this time." Then I noticed a small bump on top of the food. I didn't pay any attention until the bump moved. I sat up quickly, and the bump ran down my ski pole. Not "carefully climbed" down the ski pole, but "ran" down—headfirst. I had suddenly been transformed from the outwitter to the outwitee.

For the next few minutes I watched many mice run up and down my ski pole many times. I found out in the morning that mice are also very picky eaters. They ate everything out of my bags of mixed nuts except the peanuts.

At the moment I have only one surefire way of keeping my food for my own use—I put it in a pot, put the lid on, and weight it down with stones.

But I still have hopes of outwitting them. As an experiment I once bought some stainless-steel screening—like window screen, but made of stainless steel. I assumed that mice, and maybe even rock squirrels and ringtails, couldn't chew through it. I cut a piece about a foot on a side and put all kinds of goodies on it—nuts, chunks of granola, raisins, M&Ms. Then I folded the screen over and stapled the sides together. I took this purse of tasty tidbits with me on a trip to Hermit Camp and left it out during the night.

The next morning I found tooth marks all over the thing—but the contents were intact. I took pleasure in the thought of all the frustration I had created and decided to leave it out the next night, too. That was a mistake; the rock squirrels took it to the shop for further study. I only hope that to this day their nest is filled with delicious but unattainable aromas. I think the experiment was a success, but I have not yet made a stainless-steel screen liner with metal zipper closures for my backpack—just lazy, I guess. Or perhaps I'm afraid something big will haul my pack off to the shop for further study.

I have five other ideas to use when the need arises. The first is to slip an 8-inch section of stainless-steel tubing onto the ski pole. I don't think a mouse can run up stainless steel. Second, take my 10-inch pot lid and drill a ⅛-inch hole in the center. Then I feed one end of a 6-foot piece of nylon cord with a knot in the middle through the hole. When I tie that end to a branch and tie my food to the other, I have the food suspended below a lid. Any mouse coming down the cord to the lid and walking out on it will tip the lid, sending the marauder tumbling to the ground. Cynics say I will send the mouse tumbling down on my food. Ha! What do they know?

Third, recalling *Never Cry Wolf* and Farley Mowat's attempt to modify wolf behavior by urinating across their trail, I thought perhaps putting my pack within a circle of urine might define my territory and keep mice at bay. It appears to work. I had no trouble with mice the two times I tried it. The principal defect in my scheme is related to the availability of sufficient fluid. To conserve liquid on the second night, I tried to make the circle as small as possible. Unfortunately, in doing so I got rather more on my pack than on the ground.

Fourth, I use the mouse's own sense of smell to confuse it by putting the next day's breakfast in my boot and cramming all my dirty smelly socks on top of it. This has never failed; however, the volume of food protected is small. The same principle is being applied when I wrap food in my smelly, sweaty shirt and leave it in my pack.

Fifth, I have heard indirectly that one reader used heavy canvas sacks as food bags. They were apparently of such a size and weight that mice could not get their teeth in position to begin a hole.

If none of these ideas work, I have still another. I put out a small dish of Everclear during the night. In the morning I can pick up the comatose bodies and dispose of them in any way I see fit.

Ants

I don't worry much about ants. It is hard to get rid of the tiny black ones once they invade your pack, but they are more an aesthetic pain than anything else. And the red ones, with a bite you can't soon forget, have the happy habit of going to bed when it gets dark. Still, ants are interesting.

I studied red ants at length once when I had hundreds of maggots to dispose of. I was on my through-Canyon hike and had just retrieved a cache I had hidden along Tapeats Creek. Through a tactical error committed at home while packing the food containers, I had allowed moths to contaminate them; when the cache was opened, it was crawling with moth larvae. I was uncivilized enough to want revenge, so I picked the larvae out of the food and put them by a nearby anthill. The ants quickly swarmed over them and, one by one, hauled the wriggly things below ground.

It was apparently a mixed blessing, because several hours later I glanced at the anthill and saw larvae scattered about. As I watched, more were hauled out. They were still alive though somewhat subdued. I can only guess what went on underground. Did the larvae thrash about too much and begin breaking up the furniture? Did the larvae fight back and bite off a few ant legs? Did the ants eat one and find that it tasted terrible? I'll never know, but I am still curious.

On another afternoon I gave some ants a large peanut. With great industry and greater stupidity, they moved it to the edge of the clearing where their hole was. To my delight the peanut got away from its handlers and rolled down on the hole, blocking it completely. I watched that anthill closely as the afternoon passed to see what the final outcome might be. Then it was margarita time, and then it was dinnertime, so it was almost dark before I took another look.

To my surprise both the peanut and the ant hole were gone. There was still a bare patch of ground, though it seemed less bare than before, but there was no hole. All I saw were five ants moving a few small stones around, seemingly at random. A little later they, too, were gone. Rising especially early the next morning, I found that the five ants were back and beginning to open the hole. In about an hour the colony was functioning normally again. It would seem that when red ants go to bed, they pull their hole in after them.

Agave Spines

While rattlesnakes and scorpions are potentially a serious threat, they are not high on my list of dangers. What is highest is not even animal; it is vegetable. The agave cactus has done more harm to me and my friends than any other living thing in the Canyon.

Every time a person stumbles, he unconsciously throws out an arm to catch or steady himself. Most of the time nothing serious happens, but every once in a while he flings his hand onto an agave spine, which enters deeply and breaks off. Surgery is usually required to get it out.

I once had to abort a trip when a ⅝-inch piece broke off in my hand. It had gone into a tendon, and I couldn't move my fingers. I might have saved the trip—and $800—if I had remembered the small pair of pliers I have in my cook-kit for stove repairs. There was a chance I could have grabbed the end of the spine with them.

Two other friends have scars on their hands from similar experiences, so beware the agave. It has beautiful blossoms and very sharp teeth.

Cactus Spines

Cactus-spine splinters are frequent nuisances. I use scissors and tweezers more often than I use a knife. The tweezers are for medium-sized cactus spines. Big ones that you can get a hold on are pulled out with your fingers; small fuzzy ones are pulled off with adhesive tape.

It is not a good idea to try to pull cactus spines out right away. It is better to wait ten to fifteen minutes. During that time fluids gather at the site and the spines slide out much more easily.

Cholla Problems

In the western Grand Canyon, the teddy bear cholla is a common problem. On rare occasions the ordinary cholla poses a similar problem elsewhere. Thumb-sized segments of cholla cover the ground in some places, and every once in a while your boot will pick up one on the inside of the sole as the foot is planted. When the boot moves forward, the cholla can transfer from the sole to your leg. The spines have a fishhook at the end and are most difficult to remove. You must have either a heavy glove or, best, a comb. Place the teeth of the comb among the spines near the skin and pull the cholla bud off. You will be surprised at how far out the skin comes before the spines pull loose.

Man-eating Limestone

Another unlikely villain, this time mineral, is "carnivorous" limestone. When limestone weathers in the rain, a sinister two-dimensional saw-blade effect is produced, not unlike the rock being covered with shark teeth. Throw your hand out onto this kind of rock and you will live to regret it.

Except for the possibility of polluted water, the Canyon backcountry is a healthy place—most cuts and scrapes heal without treatment. Unfortunately, the same cannot be said for a well-populated place like Phantom Ranch.

ACCIDENTS

Over the last twenty years my companions and I have accumulated more than 2,500 person days of off-trail hiking in the Grand Canyon backcountry. The only mishaps have been two badly twisted ankles, one cut hand, and two scorpion stings. I have already described my problems with scorpions, and the hand, cut by a sharp piece of schist, healed rapidly with the help of some butterfly stitches. The strained ankles were potentially more serious—no ankle, no walk. It is interesting and instructive that both ankles were injured on the first day of a hike.

Twisted Ankle

My treatment for a twisted ankle is this: Make camp, leave the boot on, loosen the laces, and take something for the pain. The next day you can lighten the victim's load and give her a walking stick if she doesn't already have one. When this happened to me, I moved slowly, but at least I could move.

Be aware, however, that my suggestion is counter to Red Cross first-aid protocol, which recommends treating all ankle injuries as fractures. Their treatment obviously does not allow walking. If you think your ankle might be broken, then treat it as broken and stay off of it.

Emergency

I urge you to carry a signal mirror and know how to use it. In addition, you can use your sleeping bag and your ground cloth (folded into a strip) to put out international distress signals: X means "unable to proceed," I means "need a doctor," F means "need food and water." If you can get to the river, you will find boat parties anxious to help, if they can. If they can't, they can at least carry a message to the outside.

If you signal for help, put up a streamer that will tell the helicopter pilot about wind conditions and, if necessary, clear a flat place to land. Don't approach the helicopter until told to by the pilot.

FOOD

Don't carry too much. It makes sense to carry extra food for emergencies, but don't overdo it. It doesn't make sense to carry out several pounds of it because you overestimated your needs. By the end of a trip, I am sometimes made to feel like "a lion in a den of Daniels"—to use a quote from the famous New Mexico writer Gene Rhodes—when oversupplied companions try to foist off extra food on me in the name of kindness.

How much food is needed? By food I mean all consumables except alcohol. To answer this question, let's look at the caloric requirements of hiking.

An article in *Backpacker* magazine recently caught my eye: Cindy Ross's "Food for the Long Haul," subtitled "An Exclusive Study of Long-Distance Hiker Eating Habits." It reviewed a master's thesis by Karen Lutz. Being a sometime long-distance hiker myself, I was intrigued.

It is not my purpose here to review the Lutz thesis—Cindy Ross has done a fine job of that. Rather I want to review the field of inquiry into which such a thesis fits. I will follow Lutz's chapter, "Review of the Literature," and list those statements that interest me. Those who wish the exact reference for these statements will have to read the Lutz thesis.

Estimating Energy Costs of Backpacking

- Body weight is the best predictor of the energy costs of walking. Knowing age, sex, height, and resting metabolism adds nothing significant.

- The weight of a backpack can be added to body weight if less than sixty-six pounds and if carried on the torso.

- The energy cost per pound of carrying a load, such as boots, on the feet is 4.2 times the energy cost of carrying zero load at 2.4 miles per hour. The corresponding factors at higher speeds are: 5.8 at 2.9 miles per hour and 6.3 at 3.4 miles per hour. The corresponding factor for carrying loads on the head is 1.2 for all speeds.

- The energy cost per pound for carrying loads from 70 to 150 pounds at a given speed is independent of load, but the cost per pound goes up as speed goes up.

- In studying the relationship between load and speed, it was found that well-motivated individuals will self-regulate their energy expenditure to about 425 Calories per hour. (I am using *Calories* with a capital C to represent 1,000 *calories*. A calorie with a small c represents the energy required to raise the temperature of 1 gram of water from 14.5 to 15.5 degrees Centigrade.)

- Leg and foot length are relevant to the energy expenditure of walking; however, step frequency and weight are more important than stature and age.

- Stature is important for endurance.

- Terrain is important. Researchers who studied walking at two speeds with three loads through loose sand, swampy bog, heavy brush, light brush, on a dirt road, and on a paved road found the coefficients of terrain difficulty to be independent of both speed and load. These coefficients were: 2.1, 1.8, 1.5, 1.2, 1.1, and 1.0, respectively.

- Grade is important. Energy cost graphed as a function of grade increases faster than a straight line. The cost of walking downhill is greater than that of walking on the level, presumably because the back and legs are working to resist gravity.

- In studying six males carrying three loads at six different speeds, researchers found the energy expended (in watts) was:
  $$E = 1.5\,W + 2.0\,(W+L)(L/W)^2 + n(W+L)[1.5V^2 + .35VG]$$
  where: E = energy expenditure, watts
  (Note: 1 watt = 0.86 Calories/hour)
  W = subject weight, kg
  L = external load, kg

V = walking speed, m/sec

G = grade, %—G must be non-negative

n = terrain factor, defined as 1.0 for a treadmill

The Institute for Health Maintenance in Albuquerque, New Mexico, has a table of caloric requirements for various activities. Here are pertinent entries:

Resting: 0.5 cal/lb/hr = H x (W + P) Calories per day

W = your weight in pounds

H = number of hours spent hiking (don't count rests)

P = weight of your pack in pounds

For example, a 180-pound man with a 40-pound pack hiking for six hours a day needs roughly 12 x 180 + 6 (180 + 40) = 3,480 Cal/day

The above formula with n = 2 and V = .5 m/sec yields a multiplier of 1.67 Cal/lb/hr leading to a requirement of 4,360 Cal/day. (I have added in the resting metabolism rate of 12 Cal/pound/day.) Even this may be too small because Lutz reports an average of close to 5000 Cal/day for her seven Appalachian Trail hikers.

Nutritional Considerations

- 50–55 percent of calories should be from carbohydrates

  35 percent of calories should be from fat

  12 percent of calories should be from protein.

- Rest and mild exercise burn fats and carbohydrates for fuel in approximately equal amounts. The more aerobic the exercise, the greater the percentage of carbohydrates burned, until at maximum aerobic capacity only carbohydrates are burned.

- There is general agreement that a greater than normal amount of protein is not needed even under conditions of heavy physical work.

- With inadequate calories in the diet, the rate of weight loss is large at first and then decreases as the body becomes more efficient and the basal metabolism decreases. (Personal note: The same kind of phenomenon was true for me with respect to losing salt in sweat. During the first week of a multiweek hike, my sweat was very salty, but by the third week there was much less salt in it. My body had apparently adapted to the heat and learned how to conserve salt.)

- Energy output is improved by having five meals per day rather than the standard three—especially in demanding situations. Hikers accomplish this by continual snacking.

If you have persevered through my review of Lutz's review, you will notice several statements that are, by now, almost clichés. For example, the excessive penalty paid for wearing heavy boots; the self-regulation of energy expenditure; the body's adjusting to an inadequate diet by becoming more efficient; the benefits in having midmorning and midafternoon snacks. These considerations may not be of vital importance on a short trip—up to ten days, say—but they should be factored in for longer trips. You may have noticed, however, that experienced backpackers are always snacking—preferably on something salty.

Translating Requirements into Food

The following table of Calories per ounce for various camping foods is derived from *Nutritive Value of American Foods,* Agriculture Handbook 456, U.S. Department of Agriculture, 1975:

water-packed tuna	40
oil-packed tuna, cheese spread, dried fruits	80
lentils, rice, spaghetti, ramen, dried nonfat milk, beans, Gatorade	100
cereal, hard candy, cheddar cheese	110
granola bars, salami	125
peanuts, cashews	165
almonds, walnuts	180
pecans, liquid margarine	200

Some fatty foods, like oil-packed tuna and salami, are lower in Calories than you expect because they still contain a lot of water. Correcting these Calories for percent water gives 160 Calories per ounce for oil-packed tuna and 185 calories per ounce for salami.

Precooked Meals

I am a devotee of precooked meals and am using this opportunity to publicize them. Making a pre-cooked meal consists of cooking meats, pastas, beans, rice, potatoes, lentils, and so on, and then dehydrating them. The advantages of such a meal are that it is quickly prepared, since it is ready to eat upon rehydration—which, presumably, it has been doing all afternoon; and much less fuel need be carried since heating food until it is warm enough to eat requires less than half the fuel required to cook it. And don't overlook the possibility of not heating the dinner at all.

I use a dehydrator made years ago from a kit my daughter gave me for Christmas. I later made eight replicas and gave six away as presents, so I now have a total of three. I often have all three going at once. Other people I know use dehydrators they have bought either from a store or a catalog. A close friend built a box with a stack of screen-lined trays inside and used a hair dryer to blow warm air through the stack. Still others—who live in dry climates—use the sun. An oven can be used in an emergency, but leave the door slightly open to allow circulation. Buffet-style food warmers can also be used.

Even though there are many ways to extract water from food, there is only one way to get it back in. For some foods, particularly meats, this rehydration process can take some time. I generally begin it at lunch by adding water to cover the contents of whatever Ziploc bag the food is in. During the afternoon I check what is happening every once in a while, and add a little more water if what I have already put in has all been absorbed. Don't worry about using too much, because you'll probably need it anyway at suppertime to create a dinner of the proper consistency.

Nine Dinners for Eight
Despite my feelings that what you eat is your own business, I am including some recipes in this book. Eight are no-cook dinners. The ninth, a spaghetti dinner involving ramen, does require cooking the ramen, but that takes only two or three minutes and doesn't really need boiling water.

All of these recipes are designed to feed eight. They produce about sixteen cups of stuff—two cups apiece, and in its dehydrated form an entrée will weigh about five or six ounces per person. A complete dinner will also include one and a half ounces of some hors d'oeuvre like nuts or corn nuts—to go with the margaritas—and about one and a half ounces of a dessert like cookies or candy or Swiss Miss.

Buy extra-lean ground beef for use in this type of cooking; fat can easily turn rancid, even in dehydrated foods.

One point to remember is that the smell of food (especially spices) escapes through Ziploc bags, attracting mice and other critters. One possible solution is to assign responsibility to each member of your party to protect a portion of the food. The most effective approach is to store food inside a lidded pot with a heavy rock on top. Wrapping smelly, sweaty clothes around the bags of food can also help.

It will assist the cleanup crew if those meals that use powdered milk have the milk added after the pot is removed from the heat. Otherwise, the milk will burn to the bottom.

In the recipes I use the following abbreviations:
    T = Tablespoon
    t = teaspoon
    oz = ounce
    pkg = package

Chicken Chili

    16 oz dehydrated kidney and/or pinto beans.
    One 15-ounce can of beans yields about 3 ounces of dehydrated beans.
    8 oz dehydrated cooked chicken breasts

Raw chicken cooks and dehydrates at about 4.5 to 1; so ending up with 8 ounces of dehydrated chicken requires starting with about 4.5 times 8 = 36 ounces of raw chicken.

    8 chicken bouillon cubes
    ½ cup onion flakes
    1.5 T garlic powder
    2 t cumin powder

2 t oregano
2 t coriander powder
½ cup red chili powder
1 ea 26 oz can whole green chilis.

Contents of can will dehydrate to about 1.5 ounces. Then fragment to mimic chopped green chilis.

¼ cup tomato crystals

Tomato crystals are available from some backpacking catalogs, but you can also use dehydrated tomato sauce. Tomato sauce dehydrates to a gum that will stick together in a lump unless you treat it like fruit leather and roll it up in a thin sheet of plastic wrap. Two 15-ounce cans of tomato sauce dehydrate to 3.7 ounces of tomato leather. Probably one can of sauce may substitute for the ¼ cup of tomato crystals. Tomato paste is hard to dry in a thin sheet so I don't use it.

8 tomatoes
Cut tomatoes lengthwise into ⅛ths and dry.

Combine all ingredients and rehydrate.

Spiraloni Salad

Because this uses fresh chopped vegetables that have not been dehydrated, we usually eat it the first day of a trip.

2 lbs chopped vegetables

I like to use cauliflower, broccoli, carrots, celery, and purple cabbage—a colorful combination.

20 oz spiraloni, cooked and then dehydrated.
8 oz salad dressing (use something in a plastic bottle)
1 can specialty item—garbanzo beans, artichoke hearts, etc., drain off
   excess water
2 cups croutons

Combine vegetables, spiraloni, salad dressing, and canned item (minus excess water) to rehydrate; when you're ready to eat, add croutons, toss, and serve.

Pasta with Corned Beef and Barbecue Sauce

30 oz spiraloni, cooked and then dehydrated
12 oz canned corned beef, in can (not dehydrated)

When you're ready to use this, shred it with a fork before mixing with the other ingredients.

18 oz barbecue sauce (use something in a plastic bottle)
1 5-oz bottle Pickapeppa Sauce

I transfer this specialty sauce to a plastic container.

Combine all ingredients and rehydrate.

Chili

> 24 oz dehydrated kidney and/or pinto beans
> Dehydrate eight 15-ounce can of beans.
> 8 oz dehydrated cooked ground beef with onions

Start with 1.5 pounds very lean ground beef and two medium onions. Sauté onions in water and add meat. Cook, drain off any excess fat, then dehydrate.

> ¾ cup tomato crystals

See comment under Chicken Chili

> ¼ cup red chili powder
> ¼ cup onion flakes
> 4 t cumin powder
> 4 t oregano
> 1 T garlic powder

Combine all ingredients and rehydrate.

Cashew Curry

> 14 oz rice—cooked and then dehydrated
> 2 cups powdered milk
> 8 oz Parmesan cheese
> 1 pound cashews
> 2 ½-ounce packages Butter Buds
> 8 t curry powder
> 4 t black pepper
> 1 t garlic powder
> 8 oz chopped dried fruit

Dehydrate the dried fruit additionally.

Combine all ingredients except powdered milk, Parmesan cheese, and cashews, and rehydrate. Add cashews when you begin warming it up. When the mixture is hot, remove it from the heat, stir in the powdered milk and Parmesan cheese, and serve.

Macaroni and Cheese with Tuna and Green Chilis

> 4 7¼-oz packages macaroni and cheese

Cook macaroni and dehydrate.

> 2 6½-oz cans water-packed tuna (do not dehydrate)
> 1 26-oz can whole green chilis

Contents of can will dehydrate to about 1.5 ounces. Then fragment to mimic chopped green chilies.

Ramen with Spaghetti Sauce

2 3-oz packages spaghetti sauce mix
8 oz dehydrated cooked ground beef with onions and seasonings

To make the 8 ounce dehydrated meat, start with:
1½ pounds very lean ground beef
1 medium onion, chopped
1 T Spice Island Spaghetti Sauce Seasoning (SSS)
1 T garlic powder

Sauté onion in water and add meat with garlic and Spice Island SSS. Cook, drain off any excess fat, then dehydrate.

4 oz tomato crystals

See comment under Chicken Chili.

1 4-oz package Parmesan cheese
7 3-oz packages ramen noodles (without seasoning packets)

To rehydrate spaghetti sauce, combine the packets of seasoning, the dehydrated beef and onions, and the tomato crystals (or dehydrated sauce) and add water. Warm up at suppertime.

Cook the noodles separately in almost boiling water till done; drain, cover with sauce, and garnish with Parmesan cheese.

Potato Soup

4 4 1/2-oz packages Betty Crocker Julienne Potatoes

Cook potatoes and dehydrate. Save seasonings.

2 heaping cups powdered milk
1 cup dry minced onions
8 feet Italian Swiss Colony Salami Stick (approx. 10 oz)

Cut into ¼-inch lengths.

1 heaping cup Potato Buds
1.5 T garlic powder
4 bay leaves
4½-oz packages Butter Buds

Combine all ingredients except powdered milk, and rehydrate. After you have finished warming it up, remove from heat, stir in the powdered milk, and serve.

Lentil Stew

4 cups rinsed lentils
4 bay leaves
2 medium onions, chopped
½ cup vegetable oil
2 large celery stalks and leaves, chopped
2 large carrots, coarsely grated
2 medium zucchinis, coarsely grated
5 cloves garlic, mashed
¼ cup minced parsley
2 t thyme
3 cups tomato or V-8 juice, or 1 6-oz can tomato paste
½ cup red wine vinegar
2 t salt

Preparing before the trip:

Bring 3 quarts of water to a boil and add lentils and bay leaves. Simmer until almost cooked. Sauté onions in oil until softened and add celery, carrot, zucchini, garlic, parsley, and seasonings. Sauté mix until softened and add to cooked lentils with tomato juice and vinegar. Salt to taste and simmer until done. Remove the bay leaves before serving.

To dehydrate, line a cookie tray with plastic wrap and pour in the finished stew. Dehydrate in an oven on its lowest setting (leaving the door slightly open to allow steam to escape), until it looks like dried mud. Then transfer it to the dehydrator by turning it upside down into the dehydrator tray and peeling off the plastic wrap.

To rehydrate, just add water. At suppertime, heat and serve.

Look Ma, No Stove

You can have good dinners without a stove by cooking, and dehydrating, them at home. Since the meal is ready to eat when it rehydrates, let it do so in a dark pot in the sun. You will have a warm meal, maybe even a hot one, without a stove.

The Sierra Club plans on using one quart of stove fuel for every sixteen person days. This allows for cooking both breakfast and dinner. My commissary allows only for the cooking of dinner. Eliminating the need to cook breakfast reduces the fuel requirements by half, and using only dinners that have been precooked and then dehydrated reduces the fuel needs by another half. This means eight people on an eight day hike would need only one quart of fuel. A big saving comes in not having to boil any water, but this is no great sacrifice in the Grand Canyon in summer.

WATER

I sweat a lot, and having run out of water twice, I am sensitive to the water problem. I believe if you don't have some left when you make camp you didn't start with enough. I seldom leave a water source without half a gallon in my pack, and even then I would first inhaust almost to the point of gurgling when I walk. I like the word inhaust. I found it in a *Readers' Digest* article on camels that inhaust thirty gallons at a whack. A kind of opposite to exhaust.

Water Needs
There are three reasons for taking a lot of water. One, you dehydrate faster than you expect in the hot, dry environment of the Grand Canyon—remember that Lake Mead loses fifteen vertical feet of water every year to evaporation. Two, anything you eat, like lunch, requires water to process. Three, your water needs increase substantially if you have any kind of accident. It may only slow you down or force you into a bivouac but, at worst, it might force you into an evacuation—all away from water.

Use Small Containers
I recommend carrying your water in several small containers rather than in one or two large ones. If one cracks or ruptures—in a fall, for example—you haven't lost as much. I use half-gallon plastic milk/juice containers and carry a spare cap. I also carry a third cap, which I have perforated for use as an improvised showerhead when sun-warmed water is available. If additional carrying capacity is needed try putting a Ziploc bag full of water in a pot.

Drink Your Water
And drink your water. This may sound strange, but people have died of dehydration with water in their packs. The fact is that dehydration often occurs faster than your efforts to rehydrate can counter it. It takes time for swallowed water to get to the tissues. Besides maintaining proper electrolyte levels, use of an additive like Gatorade or ERG will also help water be absorbed more quickly. Continual consumption of water is important because a little dehydration causes a substantial loss of physical function. Additives are useful, too, as a consumption aid—the water tastes so good you drink more. More important, additives can replenish lost electrolytes—particularly sodium. Rescue rangers are noting many cases of "water intoxication," in which hikers are so depleted of sodium that they act drunk. This is caused by drinking but not eating. Snacking on salty nuts is a great way to get sodium into the body; I sometimes add a salt tablet to half a gallon of water.

Drink Mix
The current formula for my very popular drink mix is: Lemon-Lime Gatorade for 24 quarts—1 package iced tea mix for 12 quarts—1 cup Lemon-lime Crystal Light for 16 quarts—8 cuplets Tang for 6 quarts—1 jar. Mix well and use 1 ounce in a quart of water.

Heat Cramps
Heat cramps are a symptom of electrolyte imbalance. When they occur, stop for a rest and drink some of your mix. If it does not contain electrolytes, then add a salt tablet to each quart. Try to get the kind of salt tablet that

contains potassium. In an emergency I have licked the sweat off my arms. My rule is: If salt tastes good, I probably need some.

Purify Water

Water is purified in three ways. In order of effectiveness, these are: boiling, filtering, and the adding of chemicals.

The National Park Service still recommends boiling for at least ten minutes as the only way to purify water. However, recent medical studies indicate that *Giardia* cysts are killed at temperatures below the boiling point of water—140 to 150 degrees for one minute. This means that just bringing water to a boil is more than sufficient to kill *Giardia* cysts. I have also found that boiling helps clear up dirty water by creating a scum that can be scraped off.

Filters are popular, and there are several on the market. I have used both the Katadyn and First Need and am reluctant to recommend either because they clog so easily in dirty pothole water; the Katadyn filter can be removed for cleaning, but in one case I was doing that every three strokes. The Katadyn weighs 24 ounces, and 24 ounces of fuel will boil a lot of water. So my advice is this: If you're willing to carry the water you need and forgo the freedom of purifying a cup when you want one, then carry extra fuel and forget the filter.

My recipe, somewhat simplified, for chemical purification is: 25cc of a saturated water solution of iodine per half gallon of water. I use a little more if the water being purified is cold or cloudy. Let it sit for at least thirty minutes, or up to an hour if the water is cold. Overnight is best.

Exploring

If you have a choice, explore for a new route *from* water and not to water. For example, if you are searching for a route through the Redwall in Haunted Canyon, start from the stream at the bottom. Do not come down from the rim and contour into Haunted Canyon looking for a way down. You may not find one before you run out of water.

Eddy Combing

Look for beverages in cans in eddies below a rapid. Look also where driftwood has collected at higher water. I have probably found ninety-nine cans of beer, and once a friend found a can of Tuborg Gold high up in a tamarisk. On my through-Canyon hike, we stumbled on a cache of twenty-four cases. A note attached to the cache said, "Hi Steve, Ralph, Bill et al, this is for you." Since my brother, who was with us, is named Al, it was obvious we were included in the invitation.

How Much Water

How much water is enough? It is useful to think of water consumption in the same terms as a car's gasoline consumption; that is, in miles per gallon. An air force survival manual I have says you will be lucky to get 10 miles per gallon in a desert environment. I have used a quart per hour when it is 110 in the shade—about 4 miles per gallon—but that's extreme. I think 10 miles per gallon is about right. For trips taken at sensible times, a gallon should get you from one night's water to the next. Half a gallon may do in cool weather.

HEALTHY FEET

Heat and moisture are hazardous to the health of my feet. I take my boots off when I rest and let them and my feet and socks dry. If the socks don't dry enough, I change them.

Although the trend is toward lighter boots for off-trail hiking, I am old-fashioned and prefer a leather boot with good ankle support and a stitched sole. Two weak-ankled companions, with many miles under their soles, use a light boot with a thin, laced, inner canvas "sock" with steel ankle supports. Still others, who carry superheavy packs, get by somehow with only jogging shoes—sometimes with toes worn and side seams split. Because ankles and, to a lesser extent, knees are skeletal weak points, care must be taken to protect them. So wear light boots if you must, but be prepared to fall rather than putting sudden awkward stresses on an ankle or knee.

Off-trail hiking causes a different pattern of boot wear. Some good advice for preparing new leather boots for rough use was given to me by a back-country ranger: Fill the toe seam across the front of the boot with epoxy cement before you do anything else to them.

I still believe in my Red Wing Voyagers but I am also greatly astonished at the performance of lightweight shoes and boots. Two accomplished companions do well with Hi-Tec Sierra Lites, another companion did the very difficult 150 Mile/Tuckup Loop in a dilapidated old pair of running shoes and I did well recently with one boot and one ancient Sears sneaker. The flash flood that I will describe in a moment stole some of my gear, including both boots. After 2 miles of trying to digest them, it gave one back.

The thievery took place the first night of a twelve day hike and until the recovery of one boot, I was wearing both sneakers and wondering if they would hold out for twelve days. After regaining one boot, I had to worry only about one sneaker and the possibility, when it gave out, of wearing my right sneaker on the left foot. To my surprise, the sneaker looked almost as good at the end of the trip as it had at the beginning. I think this was partly due to my trying to take as much of the stress of hiking on my booted foot as I could.

Despite the good showing that lightweight boots, sneakers, and running shoes have made, let me insert some words of caution. Lightweight boots don't wear as well as heavier ones. One user of Hi-Tec Sierra Lites—just mentioned—has a cobbler reinforce all stitching on a new pair, and even then it lasts only for two weeks of off-trail hiking. One pair of cheap lightweight boots began delaminating the first day, and one sole was completely off by the third day. However, with tape and some use of sneakers, these boots got their wearer up the Tanner Trail—much to my surprise and relief. On another occasion, the same thing happened, though it took a little longer. This time the remedy was wire, an awl, and some glue called Barge. The repair was good enough to get the person out.

The bottom line is: Wear what you will, but be sure you paid enough for it at the beginning.

So much for boots. Now for something about socks.

Is Cotton Bad for Feet?

An article for runners by Bob Julyan that appeared in the *Albuquerque Journal* was titled "Pickin' Cotton Not Best Way to Treat Feet." The author described research done at the California College of Podiatric Medicine that involved sixty runners and 800 runs of approximately fifty minutes each. The conclusion was that acrylic socks were best at getting rid of moisture and preventing blisters. The runners who used cotton socks had not only more blisters but also bigger ones. Strangely enough, socks of an acrylic-cotton blend were even worse than cotton ones.

FLASH FLOODS

In the twenty-five years I have been exploring the Grand Canyon, I have encountered only five flash floods. If I also count two that were in the Glen Canyon area, the total goes up to seven. That is roughly one encounter every four years. That isn't very many, but sometimes one can be too many.

The first one I remember was at Clear Creek. We were camped in a good place more than 10 feet above where it would run. We were inconvenienced, however, because we had neglected to fill up with good water before the yucky stuff came through. This is the second rule of dealing with flash floods: "When one is likely, fill your water containers." The first one is: "Get out of the way."

One of the prettiest encounters was just downstream of the Tuckup Redwall narrows. We had intended to camp near the Cottonwood junction, but the rain was so intense after we entered the narrows, that we retreated to a break where talus was abundant and escape possible. We climbed up to a bench 10 feet or so above the drainage and set up our shelters—but did not unpack our packs. We could go higher, but this was the highest flat place. We waited—and the rain stopped. With a sudden roar, a waterfall poured over the Redwall opposite. In another half hour the main bed flashed. Suddenly, there was 3 feet of water where there previously had been none. When it went down a little, we unpacked and set up camp. A foot of water was still flowing the next morning, so a lot of water had been involved.

I write at some length about a dramatic encounter with a flash flood in section 1 of chapter 6 in SOB Canyon. We were absolutely and totally safe; nevertheless, the excitement and drama were extreme.

I remember a flood in the tributary of Kanab Creek leading to the Esplanade near Scotty's Castle. We were on the last week of a six week hike from Lees Ferry to Lava Falls. The last four days would be on the Esplanade between Kanab and Tuckup, and the flood meant an abundance of water without having to carry it. This encounter is written up in section 3 of chapter 6.

Finally, there is an encounter I would like to forget. I ignored Rule One and came close to being washed away. I was so comfortable that my brain was able to lull me into a false sense of security. Only the thought that I might miss something when Mike called out, "Here comes the water," caused me to scramble out of my sleeping bag, put on my sneakers, and take two steps before I was knee deep in water. I estimate the elapsed time from Mike's call to my second step was twenty seconds. I describe this encounter in considerable detail in the recapitulation of the Shinumo Creek/Tapeats Creek Loop in chapter 3.

For a long time, artificial flash floods of the Colorado River occurred due to releases from Glen Canyon Dam. This is not so much of a problem anymore. At press time, an Environmental Impact Study is being made to assess the effect of flow variation on beach erosion. It is possible this study will result in permanent changes to the discharge pattern from the dam. For example, it is possible that flows will be kept more nearly constant with changes being made only gradually.

MISCELLANY

Sunburn
Sunburned skin doesn't sweat well. I use a long-sleeved shirt and a long-billed visor over a bandanna on my balding head. I should use a sunscreen. Long pants are useful for brush.

Shelter
An overhang is the most satisfying shelter for me, and during the years when rain seemed to be rarer than it is now, especially in the fall, it was sometimes the only shelter I had. More recently, I have begun taking a 10-by-10-foot tarp. Originally, I strung it up with a variety of long lines, but the water tended to puddle and start leaks. Now I use it in a sort of half cylinder. First, I rig a taut line between two walking sticks. Then I bend an 11-foot lightweight folding aluminum tent pole and hold it in an arc with string. This arc is tied at right angles to the taut line and helps support it. The tarp is put over the entire thing.

The supporting arc creates the feeling of considerably more room than you would have with just a triangular cross section, and stakes keep everything tight. The result is an effective freestanding tentlike structure, roomy for four and adequate for five if you scrunch together a little. My pack remains outside with a garbage bag over it. One night it drizzled for almost eight hours straight and the only water problem we had was due to water leaking in from the uphill side of the structure. The total weight for this shelter for five is 2.5 pounds.

Walking Stick (lost)
As you can tell, I am a great believer in walking sticks, and after the flash flood stole mine I was lucky to borrow one from someone who uses two. Fortunately, walking sticks are at least as inedible as boots, and mine was found by my companions about 2.5 miles from where it was stolen. It was jammed in among rocks at a 45-degree angle. Initial attempts to remove it were unsuccessful, and thoughts of the Arthurian legend concerning Excalibur came to mind. Ultimately, though, Gary Ladd succeeded in extracting it.

Faint Trail
If you are following a faint trail and lose it, the chances are it went up and you didn't. Look for it above you.

Waistband

I unfasten my waistband when I cross a deep or fast-moving stream, whether wading in the water or walking on a log. That way, I can shuck my pack more quickly if I fall in. I follow this rule even when traversing a cliff above the river.

The Game of What If?

The game of "what if?" is a game all can play. Many things can go wrong during a hike, and which of these many mishaps you choose to protect yourself against depends on your temperament. My wife, for example, considers mainly medical problems; once she was able to save a life by producing epinephrine to treat anaphylaxis. I, on the other hand, consider mainly mechanical problems—equipment failures. Two of my "what ifs?" are the following:

I carry a spare set of shoulder straps attached to the large stuff bag I have for my sleeping bag. Thus, the stuff bag doubles as a day pack. I also take a spare clevis and spare clevis pins and lock rings. The pins and lock rings are stored in unused holes on my pack frame.

CHOOSE YOUR COMPANIONS WITH CARE

Choose your companion(s) with care. This may sound like a strange comment, but the psychology of off-trail hiking in the Canyon is at least as important as the physiology. I remember one youngster who was so upset about not being on a trail that I built ducks (cairns) as I went along to give him the illusion of a trail. The ducks were removed by his father, hiking last. These hikes are not to be taken lightly. If you are the leader, think carefully about taking people you don't know.

There are at least three things to consider. First, is the potential companion physically capable of backcountry hiking? It is hard to imagine more difficult hiking anywhere in the United States, and in my opinion the principal reason for this is the urgent need to reach water within a certain length of time. Sometimes this requirement makes for long and very difficult days.

Second, many people who are capable of difficult Grand Canyon hiking just don't like the indefiniteness of cross-country travel—they are never completely at ease with their surroundings. Usually they aren't as perceptive as a young companion who explained after a trip was over that he didn't feel comfortable during the hike until he had made the conscious decision to trust me—he realized he no longer had control of his own destiny and that I, as leader, had it instead. Some strong-minded, independent people cannot give up that sense of control. They are difficult to have along on a trip.

Third, avoid having a group whose members have widely disparate hiking and climbing skills unless the leader is prepared to travel only as fast as the slowest member. It may also be helpful to have companions who are capable of dealing with emergencies.

Something that happened to some friends—thank God it didn't happen to me—illustrates this perfectly. It was a hike off Atoka Point for members of the New Mexico Mountain Club, and a long first day of sidehilling through heavy brush made it especially difficult. Once down by the River, one mountain-climber type decided he had had enough and wanted up and out. He could not find the way he had come; other efforts to get out were thwarted by Redwall cliffs. He left the group and, although his progress for the next days paralleled the group's and he was sometimes heard, he was not seen. He reappeared when the group reached the rim. This is an extreme example, but it shows what can happen to someone hiking in the Grand Canyon whose behavior on other hikes and climbs seemed normal.

A friend of a friend can sometimes mean trouble. One seriously thought his friend was trying to kill him, and his friendship with my friend ended as a result. Another was disturbed by a downclimb in a steep ravine, and I told him to take a cord and lower his pack; instead, he threw it off the cliff. It fell 10 feet and rolled and bounced another 15. Fortunately, nothing was broken. I think he hoped something would break so he could go back.

I was talking to the another friend of a friend after a long day on the "freefall" shortcut into Nankoweap and noticed that his shoulders didn't look symmetrical. I asked about it and found he had a Harrington rod in his back. These rods are imbedded under the skin along the spine to correct severe curvature of the spine: The vertebrae are clamped to it. The top of the rod is anchored to the lower neck, the bottom to the pelvis. The wearer of such a rod cannot bend his back except at the waist. The man had two large raw ulcerated areas on his lower back where the rod anchors made bumps in the skin that rubbed on his pack. No wonder all he could think of when he got to the creek was how he was going to get out. Strangest of all was that this man's friend didn't know about the rod.

NOTATION

The word *River* refers to the Colorado River

A duck is a small cairn of at least three rocks. Because two rocks can sometimes get piled on top of each other naturally, there is a saying: "Two rocks do not a duck make." Ducks should be dismantled by the last person in a group or on the way out.

The word *Canyon* refers to the Grand Canyon. I follow Harvey Butchart's device, used in his three *Treks* volumes, for locating myself on a map not only by terrain features but also by cartographic ones. These features referred to are on 7.5-minute maps.

BOOKS

Adkison, Ron, *Hiking Grand Canyon National Park,* Falcon Publishing, 1997. A good guide to hiking Grand Canyon trails for newcomers. Does not cover cross-country routes.

Beus, S. S., and M. Morales, editors, *Grand Canyon Geology,* Oxford Univ. Press, 1990. This eminently readable, yet technical, book is remarkably complete. A chapter on side canyons; a chapter on earthquakes and seismicity; a chapter on rock movement and mass wastage; a chapter on the history of the Canyon and River—where did it go before it went where it goes now?; and a fine chapter on hydraulics by Susan Kieffer, whom I reference for my primitive discussion of the same subject. All this besides excellent chapters on the various structures themselves.

Breed, W.J., and E. Roat, editors, *Geology of the Grand Canyon,* Third Edition, Museum of Northern Arizona and Grand Canyon Natural History Association, 1978. This collection of papers by experts in Grand Canyon geology is rewarding for the dedicated reader.

Butchart, Harvey, *Grand Canyon Treks, 12,000 Miles Through the Grand Canyon,* Spotted Dog Press, 1998. This is a reorganized edition of the three classic "Treks" books. This book has information about hiking routes in Canyon backcountry that you won't find anywhere else. The author has made a special study of routes of historical interest.

Carothers, S.W., and B.T. Brown, *The Colorado River Through Grand Canyon,* University of Arizona Press, 1991. I found this a very interesting book. In particular, I learned that the ants may have brought the grubs I fed them back to the surface (see page 28) because my gifts had increased the humidity in their nest to an intolerable level. I also was fascinated by the picture of the damage to the Glen Canyon Dam Spillway after the disaster of late June 1983.

Childs, Craig, *The Secret Knowledge of Water,* Sasquatch Books, 2000. This is a book about water. Water that moves. Water that waits. Fierce water. In a series of stories, Childs describes how he finds water in a desert environment. It is a delicious book, one to be savored. I loaned my copy to a friend and he promptly bought two copies—one to keep and one to give away. It is that kind of book.

Childs, Craig, and Gary Ladd. *Grand Canyon: Time Below the Rim,* Arizona Highways Book Division, 1999. Here in one book, you have the wonderful words of Craig Childs and the wonderful pictures of Gary Ladd. Craig says it best in his introduction: He tries to put into words what cannot be captured in photographs; Gary tries to capture in photographs what cannot be put into words. They complement each other to a remarkable degree.

Crumbo, Kim, *A River Runner's Guide to the History of the Grand Canyon,* Johnson Books, 1981. This book should appeal to hikers as well as River runners—a readable style, and Edward Abbey wrote a controversial foreword.

Darville, Fred T., *Mountaineering Medicine,* Wilderness Press, 1989. A useful book on wilderness medicine. Lightweight and compact.

Ghiglieri, Michael, and Thomas M. Myers, *Over the Edge: Death in Grand Canyon,* Puma Press, Flagstaff, AZ 2001. This book does for hiking deaths what *Fateful Journey* did for boating deaths. It is a must read for all hikers.

Hamblin, W.K., and J.K. Rigby. *Guidebook to the Colorado River, Part 1: Lee's Ferry to Phantom Ranch in Grand Canyon National Park,* BYU, 1968. *Guidebook to the Colorado River, Part 2: Phantom Ranch in Grand Canyon National*

Park to Lake Mead, Arizona-Nevada, BYU, 1969. These two books tell you in great detail what's happening, geologically speaking, along the River. I like the set of aerial photographs, and I like the diagrams showing the rise and fall of the strata as you proceed downstream.

Huntford, Roland, *The Last Place on Earth,* Atheneum, 1984. This book was originally published under the name *Scott and Amundson.* It is an extraordinary volume that compares and contrasts the organizational and leadership abilities of the two explorers. I include it because I find the Antarctic metaphor attractive in thinking about the Grand Canyon.

Mitchell, Roger, *Grand Canyon Jeep Trails, I, North Rim,* La Siesta Press, 1977. This book is a must if you plan to drive to Kelly Point or the Parashant Canyon trailhead.

Myers, Thomas M., Christopher Becker, and Lawrence E. Stevens, *Fateful Journey,* Red Lake Books, 1999. This book analyzes in great detail the circumstances relating to injury and death on Colorado River trips in the Grand Canyon. In general, the risks are less than I would have guessed; however, I overestimated the benefits of life jackets.

Price, L. Greer, *An Introduction to Grand Canyon Geology,* Grand Canyon Natural History Association, 1999. I think this is a wonderful book. There are other geology books on the Canyon with more detail and bigger words, but Greer's book is the place to start. He gives a feeling for what is happening that I haven't found anywhere else.

Redfern, Ron, *Corridors of Time,* Time Books, 1980. I bought seven copies of this book when it came out—four for myself and my children and three for my brother and his. What clinched the sale were the pictures: panoramic photographs that are almost better than the real thing.

Schmidt, Jeremy, *Grand Canyon,* Houghton Mifflin, 1993. I find this book a good one to browse in for general information about the Grand Canyon, though, like its competitor by Stephen Whitney, it does not have very much on insects.

Wallace, Robert, *The Grand Canyon,* Time, Inc., 1973. A good first book with which to get acquainted with the Grand Canyon. It has an interesting and informative text and fine pictures.

Whitney, Stephen, *A Field Guide to the Grand Canyon,* William Morrow, 1982. This book tries to cover everything you may want to know about the Canyon—animal, vegetable, or mineral. For the most part it succeeds. It is good for keying out plants and animals. It is adequate on geology, but sketchy on insects.

The route down to Crystal Creek.

1 Phantom Creek/Crystal Creek Loop

A general statement of condition: "Up schist creek."

AUTHOR UNKNOWN

Length
Six days, plus layover day(s), if any.

Water
Dragon Spring on the first day and Upper Phantom Creek on the last.

Quad Maps
7.5-minute maps
　　Bright Angel Point
　　Little Peak Lake
　　Shiva Temple
　　Grand Canyon
　　Phantom Ranch

Roadhead
On road to Tiyo Point.

ROUTE TO ROADHEAD

Turn west off the highway to the North Rim about 0.5 mile south of the road to Point Imperial. A sign indicates that this side road takes you to the Widforss Point Trailhead.

After 0.9 mile you reach a gate. This gate appears after you pass the parking lot for the Widforss Point Trail and turn left at a Y.

After 3.2 miles you enter a meadow and come to a fork—go left. (The right fork leads to Point Sublime.) A tiny sign a few inches off the ground points the way to Tiyo Point. The road to Tiyo Point has been closed, so you will have to park here.

It takes only forty minutes from the highway to your parking spot at Tiyo Point Road.

HIKING TIMES

Use Areas	Locations	Elapsed Times Between Locations (hours)
▲ NG9	Car	1:00
	Rim takeoff point	2:00
▲ AP9/AQ9 (dry camp)	Shiva Saddle	4:00
▲ AQ9	Dragon Spring	5:30
▲ AQ9	Mouth of Crystal Creek	1:30
	Tonto above Crystal Creek	6:15
	Top of 94 Mile descent	1:30

49

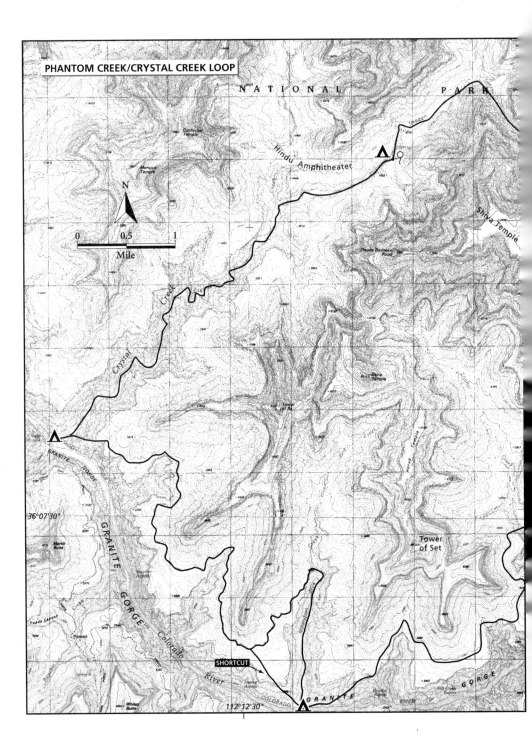

PHANTOM CREEK/CRYSTAL CREEK LOOP

N A T I O N A L   P A R K

Hindu Amphitheater

Confucius Temple

Mencius Temple

N

0   0.5   1
Mile

Crystal Creek

Shiva Temple

Clyde Barrows Point

GRANITE GORGE

36°07'30"

Marsh Butte

Colorado River

Tower of Set

SHORTCUT

Whites Butte

112°12'30"

GRANITE   RIVER   GORGE

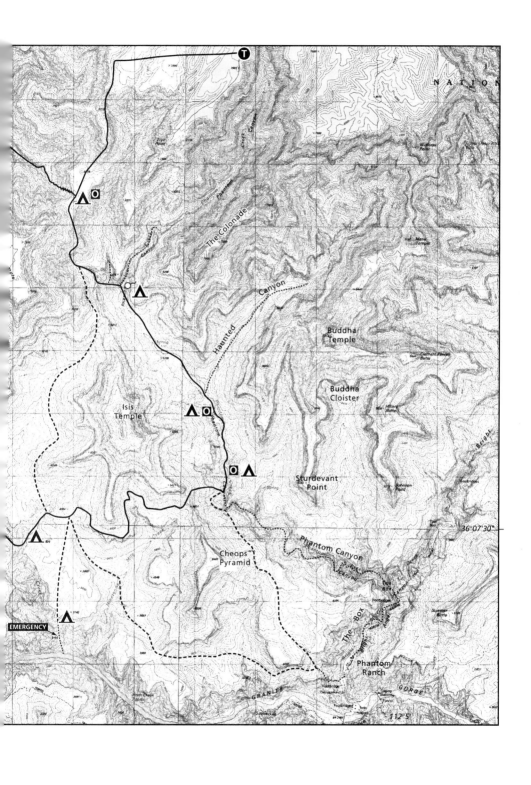

Tiyo Point

The Colonade

Phantom Canyon

Haunted Canyon

Buddha Temple

Buddha Cloister

Isis Temple

Sturdevant Point

Cheops Pyramid

Phantom Canyon

36°07'30"

EMERGENCY

The "Box"

GRANITE

Phantom Ranch

GORGE

112°5'

▲ AQ9	Mouth of 94 Mile Creek	1:30
	Tonto above 94 Mile Creek	3:15
▲ AQ9 (dry camp)	Bed of Trinity Creek	3:15
	Cheops/Isis Saddle	1:00
▲ AP9	Phantom Creek 3,600' contour	2:30
▲ AP9	Phantom Creek Hippie Camp	2:30
	Top of Redwall climb	2:45
▲ AP9/AQ9 (dry camp)	Shiva Saddle	2:00
	Rim	1:00
▲ NG9	Car	

By 1987 I had done all the elements of this loop—and its alternates—separately, except for the Redwall climbing route in Upper Phantom, so it seemed a natural trip on which to take my brother and some of his climbing buddies for their annual Canyon outing. We also had the opportunity to enjoy the company of one of the North Rim backcountry rangers.

This hike was written up by Steve Roper for the November 1988 issue of *Backpacker*.

ROUTE DETAILS

The rim takeoff for this loop is off a point about 0.75 mile west-northwest of Tiyo Point. A V-shaped notch in the 7,600-foot contour marks the descent ravine. To get to this notch, I suggest parking about 0.25 mile north of the bend in the road (about 1.3 miles north of the end of the road) and then heading west to the last ridge before the notch ravine. In getting there you will cross four other major ravines and, depending on where you have parked, possibly a fifth shallower one. You are on the right ridge when you can see canyon beyond the rim on the other side of the notch ravine. Head down this ridge to the rim and then descend westward into the notch ravine.

Another route to the notch point uses the spur road taking off at the 8,122 elevation point and heads down the ridge from the end of this road. It should work but I have not used it for two reasons: I never thought of it, and I would worry about finding my car on the return. If you park at the start of the old Tiyo Point Road, then on reaching the rim on the return all you do is head east to be assured of hitting the road—not necessarily your car but at least hitting the road. Using Amundsen's idea for marking his food caches so he could find them on his return from the South Pole, you can mark the road every 100 yards each side of the car in such a way that when you find a mark, it tells you which way to the car and how far.

A reader of this book's previous edition, Bob Bordasch, used this takeoff point. He writes, "It was very easy and route finding was not a problem. All you have to do is stay on top of the ridge all the way down and you'll end up looking down to your left (east) into the drainage that leads to the notch ravine. The "ridge" is very broad and somewhat indistinct, but not a problem if you pay close attention and stay on the highest level. We had no problem finding the car on our return."

Rim Takeoff
Descend the notch ravine—there is a trail—and contour around to a ridge heading south. Follow this ridge to the end and look for a trail off the east side, close to the point. It takes you through the last Toroweap cliffs and then contours west a bit before descending through the Coconino and Hermit to the saddle northeast of Shiva Temple. This descent is tedious but straight-forward.

Shiva Saddle
Shiva Saddle is broad and dotted with big Supai boulders that can collect water during a rain—but don't count on finding any unless you're there within a few days of the rain. I have been told that there is a small spring in the Supai just below and to the west of the saddle on the north side. Look for some bright telltale greenery as a clue to its location before spending time searching for it. I looked for it once but couldn't find it. I suspect it is seasonal.

The route off the saddle is to the north, where it is narrowest. After you get a little way down, the routes proliferate and you take your pick. Usually I end up taking one that veers off to the east to join the main drainage from the northeast via a fairly large tributary. Only minor obstacles remain before reaching the main Dragon drainage.

Dragon Spring
Dragon Spring is below an impassable chockstone near the start of the Tapeats narrows. Bypass the chockstone to the south by climbing out of the drainage at the S-bend as shown on the map and going down a slope to a ravine that leads to the spring. You will hear the spring long before you see it. The spring has been running well the four times I have been there—once in July, once in September, and twice in October.

It is an easy day from the Dragon Spring to the mouth of Crystal Creek. The water in Crystal Creek is almost too warm for swimming on hot summer afternoons, but there is a big pool beneath a 15-foot waterfall about half an hour from the mouth that feels somewhat cooler.

Crystal Creek
If you keep left as you approach the vegetative tangle at the mouth of the creek, you will find a trail that takes you up to a bluff overlooking the rapids and then down to grassy banks by the River. While you're on the bluff, look along the skyline on the east side of the creek for a ramp leading through the Tapeats Sandstone to the Tonto Platform. This is your exit from Crystal. I usually get to the ramp by going up a ridge a little bit to the south and then contouring over to it.

The rapid at the mouth of Crystal Creek has been a major rapid only since the great flood of December 1, 1966. At certain water levels it is a fearsome rapid; several people have lost their lives in its wild water. Many of the commercial trips and all, I suspect, of the private ones stop at the upstream beach so the boatmen, I should say "boatpersons," can climb this bluff and see what they are up against. The severity of a rapid changes radically with river flow; it pays to check current conditions.

The Great Flood of 1966

A word about the 1966 flood. An estimated 14 inches of rain fell in the area around the North Rim Entrance Station during December 5–7, 1966. Although the area of maximum rainfall was quite small—an estimated 14 square miles—a great deal of this water found its way into Dragon Creek and its tributaries. Extensive measurements were made at a site about 0.5 mile downstream from where the descent ravine from Shiva Saddle meets Dragon Creek. One estimate of the flow at this site was 29,000 cfs—I repeat, twenty-nine thousand cfs. Nowadays, this is considered a high flow for the Colorado River.

The first and last phases of flow were mainly water but the middle phase, the maximum flow, was a mudflow. A mudflow is a mix of everything—rocks, trees, sand, water—and it is estimated that the mudflow was 18 to 20 feet deep in a 60-foot-wide channel at the Dragon Creek site mentioned above. The way the mud stood up in blobs around the edges of the flow indicated it had the consistency of cake dough. The fact that 800- to 900-year-old ruins were either washed away or buried indicates this mudflow was the highest in 800 to 900 years. Perhaps the most noticeable result of the flood was the transforming of Crystal Rapid from a pussycat to a man-eating lion.

The details of the flood given above were taken from the pamphlet *Effects of the Catastrophic Flood of December 1966, North Rim Area, Eastern Grand Canyon, Arizona,* by M.E. Cooley, B.N. Aldridge, and R.C. Euler. It was published in 1977 by the U.S. Government Printing Office as Geological Survey Professional Paper 980.

Route to 94 Mile

Once on the Tonto our next goal was 94 Mile Creek, and all we had to do to get there was "contour around." I hate those words. They are a euphemism for "big trouble." Contouring around sounds so easy, yet it is often so hard.

Route Off Tonto

There are two ways off the Tonto to the mouth of 94 Mile. One is a sporting descent through the Tapeats cliff just west of the point overlooking the mouth. A good system of ledges takes you to a pair of chimneys. I had trouble finding the route down because we were approaching it for the first time from the Crystal side. My brother and I had ducked the route in 1982, but these ducks were almost invisible in 1987. The problem is that the route doesn't look possible from above because the final descent chimney can't be seen very well from there. On our descent in 1987 we put many ducks along the route, so now it should be easier to find.

The top cairn is about 100 yards west of the point. Descend there to a broad ledge about 8 feet down. Contour east to a chimney and descend about 25 feet to another ledge. Contour east again to another chimney and descend to the talus. Once there you have an easy scramble to the mouth of the creek. I don't hesitate to recommend this route. Good handholds and footholds abound, and there is almost no feeling of exposure.

If this Tapeats route is not to your liking or you can't find it, you must contour in to 94 Mile Creek and descend to the bed near the 3,283 elevation marker. You'll reach the bed at the 2,900 foot level. Going down the bed of 94 Mile is easy. Salty water that gets saltier the farther south you find it often flows in the bed in the spring. I have found no water at all there in the fall.

Route to Trinity Creek

The way back to the Tonto on the east side of 94 Mile is up the first major drainage east of the mouth. Once you get on the Tonto, it is about three hours of "contouring around" to get to the bed of Trinity Creek. The descent into Trinity Creek is via the slope on the north side of the small drainage northeast of the elevation point "5,288." You'll reach the bed of Trinity at the 3,320-foot contour.

Reader Bob Bordasch used a more direct route; I quote again: "We got an early start on our fourth day from 94 Mile (it was *hot*) by first heading east over to and then up a steep, shallow drainage. We were planning to cross over to the main diagonal ravine that cuts all the way through the Tapeats, but before we knew it we were almost all the way to the base of the Tapeats. So rather than contouring along the base of the Tapeats over to the diagonal ravine, we looked for and found an easy chimney that ran straight up to the Tonto. The chimney was easy to climb with our packs on (and great fun)."

Exit from Trinity Creek

The exit from Trinity is through a fault crossing the arm of Trinity heading northeast. This fault shows up as a transverse ravine cutting across the exit drainage near the 3,520-foot contour. When you emerge from Trinity, head east up the talus to the top of the quartzite cliffs. The geology of this region between Trinity and Phantom Creeks is a strong brew of the familiar and unfamiliar. Most of it is pretty much like it is everywhere else, but the rest is sometimes very confusing. For example, the Shinumo Quartzite is at least 250 million years older than the Tapeats Sandstone and thus should be lower, yet in this place it is higher. The Fault Map will show you what you are seeing and why.

Route to Saddle

There is a fairly good deer trail on top of the quartzite and you should try to find it. But watch it carefully, because it circles the bay on the south side of Isis Temple. Before the trail crosses the drainage, it goes down steeply. It is lost in the jumble at the bottom of the drainage and reappears on the top of the quartzite on the other side. If the trail continues up to the Cheops/Isis Saddle, I have not found it.

There is a good trail on the Phantom side of the saddle. Follow it north for a few hundred yards until a spur trail takes off to the right and descends quickly in the direction of the red hillside (Hakatai Shale) across the way. Look for a thin broken-up place in the cliffs in front of you where a ridge of talus comes up from Phantom Creek. The trail goes steeply down to the creek just upstream from the narrows.

Phantom Creek

According to the Backcountry Management Plan, Phantom Creek is closed to camping below the 3,600-foot contour. It would appear from the Fault Map that this contour is near the upstream limit of the red hillside of Hakatai Shale. Fortunately, this is where the big pools are.

Layover Day

If you allow a layover day at this beautiful place, you can have more than just the pools to occupy you. One thing to do is make a quick trip to Phantom Ranch and back. At the beginning of the gorge there is a 20-foot waterfall. To get around it you can climb down a rope placed a few feet downstream from the falls on the west or you can go up on the east and contour around for 0.25 mile or more to a ravine where you can get back down to the creek. Without a pack you need about three hours to go from the barrier falls to Phantom Ranch. Unless it is summer you will probably want to bypass the pools with vertical sides.

Exploring Haunted Canyon is something else to do on a layover day, and so is exploring Outlet Canyon (the drainage north of the Colonade) or the narrows at the head of Phantom Canyon, both up near the "Hippie Camp." There is no easy way out of Outlet Canyon, but in the fall of 1975 a young man came over Shiva Saddle from Dragon Creek, took a wrong turn, ran out of water, and tried to find an easy way in. He got partway through the Redwall someplace in Outlet by jumping. He reached water but fractured his skull and broke his legs in the process—one had a compound fracture as I remember. His body was found several days later. This is what can easily happen if you forget the injunction always to explore *from* water and not *to* water.

Hippie Camp

It is about two and a half hours from the 3,600-foot contour camp to the Hippie Camp at the junction of Phantom Creek with Outlet Canyon—the drainage on the north side of the Colonade. The water in Phantom Creek comes and goes once you pass Haunted Canyon, but there is a small flow of water at this junction.

I call it the Hippie Camp because a colony of hippies lived in Upper Phantom at one time, and this camp has several constructions that indicate more than a casual occupancy. One is a good-sized stone bench—we used it as a kitchen table—a small path lined with river-washed stones leading from the main living area to a lower terrace, and a small rock-lined nook.

Redwall Route

The route through the Redwall begins 0.25 mile up Phantom Creek from the Hippie Camp, just past a drainage that goes west. There is a cairn marking the spot where you leave the bed and head up a ridge. Most people, I think, don't go that far before climbing up through small Muav ledges to the same ridge. Eventually, ravines on each side of the ridge meet so that you cross a narrow isthmus to the base of the first of the two 40-foot climbs.

My brother and a fellow climber went up without aid with their packs on, but I and a fellow nonclimber needed a belay. This first climb is at enough of an angle to the vertical that hauling packs is awkward; so, somewhat reluctantly, we also climbed with our packs on.

The second 40-foot pitch is much like the first—just a bit steeper. Both have good rock and good holds. It took us an hour from the bed to the top of the first pitch and another half hour to the top of the second, which is at the same level as the horizontal traverse ledge. We negotiated this ledge without incident. When you enter the exit ravine at the end of the ledge, be sure you go up the small gully that parallels the main ravine to the south. You can climb out of the main ravine, but there are some dry waterfalls to contend with.

All in all, this Redwall route was easier than I expected. Nowhere was there the gut-wrenching feeling of exposure. Yes, I might have fallen 40 feet, but I certainly didn't have the feeling of falling more than that. There was always something fairly close below to stop me. Even on the traverse ledge, which—except in one place—was quite like a highway, I had no feeling of the possibility of a fall—the 400 feet to the bottom was not a concern.

Route to Shiva Saddle

The basic instructions for the route from the top of the Redwall to Shiva Saddle are to go up if you can and to contour right if you can't. Looking north in the direction of the saddle (you can't see it) from the top of the Redwall, you get a foreshortened view of the Supai so that the middle cliffs form the skyline. The "basic instructions" take you north up the talus to the bottom of a set of three cliffs. You work your way up through the bottom two, and then contour right to a point and then up through the last cliff to what was the skyline when viewed from below. The Fault Map shows a fault going through the narrow part of the saddle, and since you can't climb through the remaining cliffs, you should contour right to this fault ravine. It is an easy scramble to Shiva Saddle. The elapsed time from the bottom of the Supai to the saddle was two and a half hours.

We carried enough water to be able to camp on the saddle, but since we were there early enough we dumped most of the water out and continued on up to the car. If we had camped there, we could have used a big overhang just east of the point where we gained the level of the saddle. It could sleep ten easily.

The route back to your car from the saddle is the reverse of your route down, except for the tricky part of reaching the road in the right place. I hate to say this, but we were off by 400 yards.

ALTERNATE ROUTINGS

The Phantom Creek/Crystal Creek Loop can be started at Phantom Ranch. This option means the loop can be done by people traveling without a car and at times when the North Rim roads may be closed because of excess rain, fire hazard, or snow.

There are also two other options: You do not have to do the Redwall climb, and you can use a different routing. All these options are described below.

Loop Begins at Phantom Ranch

There are at least two ways to Upper Phantom Creek from Phantom Ranch. I have already mentioned one: Just go up the creek. This will be difficult during times of high water, but in normal times this is fairly easy even with heavy packs. There is, of course, the problem of the waterfall at the end, but if a trustworthy rope is there even that obstacle is fairly easy. If there is no rope, or if you do not trust the one that is there, then either you must make the climb—I have used a small crack at the lower end of the pool on the west side—or you must backtrack about 500 yards to a fault ravine on the east side. You will have to climb about 500 feet before contouring around and down. I have never done this, though I have seen it from the other side.

Utah Flats

Another route takes you onto the Tonto and across Utah Flats. This bit of Tonto got its name because it reminded someone of the slickrock country of southern Utah. A faint trail up through the schist begins at the northern end of the northernmost campsite—just north of the bridge at the upper end of Bright Angel Campground. It climbs steeply in a northwesterly direction and eventually reaches the northern end of a long ridge that shows clearly in the 3,200-foot contour. A better trail takes you from there through the Tapeats to Utah Flats. Cheops Pyramid is the predominant terrain feature once you are on the "flats," and you want to head to the east of it.

If you make a detour to the east to look over the cliff, don't be misled into thinking you want to be on the trail you see hundreds of feet below you. Stay at the level you're on.

I found no trail through here, but a good one appears as you begin crossing the many drainages on the northeast side of Cheops. Begin your descent to Phantom Creek via faint switchbacks in the ravine just east of the southeast arm of Isis Temple. Contour north around the shoulder and then down to the creek—about at the 3,600-foot contour, a few hundred yards upstream from the waterfall at the end of the gorge. You will find good shelter under big overhangs fifteen minutes upstream on the east and forty-five minutes upstream on the west.

Because it is easier for a nonclimber to climb up than down, both the basic routing and this alternative routing are arranged so the Redwall climb is up instead of down.

Low-Level Route to Phantom Ranch

Your return to Phantom Ranch from 94 Mile Creek need not take you over the Cheops/Isis Saddle. If you started from 94 Mile with enough water for a dry camp, or if you find suitable water in Trinity, you can take a Tonto-level route instead. As you near Phantom Ranch, it is tempting to try to contour around on the red rubble of the Hakatai Shale, but this formation is unyielding and very difficult for the edge of your boot to dig into. To avoid it, I climb up to the base of the quartzite cliff, where there is about a foot of flat ground and the going is much easier. You have to climb up and later back down, but I think it is worth it.

When you reach the fault ravine heading up to Utah Flats, you will notice that the Supergroup has disappeared and the schist is in its familiar place beneath the Tapeats. Cross the fault ravine, head for the long ridge on the rim of Bright Angel Creek due west of Phantom Ranch, and find the rudimentary trail that takes you down to the campground. You will already have used this route if you have gone to Upper Phantom via Utah Flats.

Emergency Route to River

If you don't have enough water for a dry camp en route from 94 Mile to Bright Angel Creek and either need or wish to make one, let me suggest the Tapeats rim due west of the "3742" elevation point. I discovered a route to the River there under what I consider unusual circumstances.

I had planned a loop hike like the one I am describing, except it avoided the Redwall climb in Upper Phantom, and had looked at the copy of Harvey Butchart's map in the Backcountry Office that showed all the places he had been. One of the lines on the map was off the tip of the plateau between Trinity and 91 Mile and down to the River where I have suggested you camp. My plan was to use this route to go to the River and bring water back for a cache to be used on our return.

I expected a "walkdown" kind of break in the Tapeats, but when I got there all I found were Tapeats cliffs everywhere. After considerable searching by all members of the party, I found myself sitting disconsolately on the edge of the Tonto wondering what to do next. Suddenly I realized that I was sitting right by the route.

The "route" turned out to be a 4-foot crack straight down through the Tapeats to the schist below. The far side of the crack was some 10 feet or so higher than the near side, and there were many small ledges on both sides. By leaning across the 4-foot width of the crack—with the schist clearly visible 100 feet below—and using the small ledges alternately, it was possible to "ratchet" down to a broader ledge some 8 to 10 feet below and then walk along it to where the sides of the crack came together in a V. The V was filled with rubble and slanted enough to make the rest of the descent fairly easy. Then it was an easy scramble to the bed of 91 Mile and down it a short distance to the river.

At the end of the trip I asked each of my companions—high school juniors—what they thought was the hardest part of the trip. And I asked them independently so one answer would not influence another. Unanimously and without hesitation they all said, "Climbing down that crack and especially the leaning out across it to get started." One wise guy added, "But I figured that if any old man could do it then I could . . . I mean . . . any fifty-one-year-old man."

The next time I saw the ranger who had showed me the Butchart map, I chided him about what was being offered as a "route." I felt it might be dangerous for some of the less experienced people who might use it. He said, "Show me" and I looked again at the map. The route I had used was gone—

it had been erased. I was the victim of a copying error. The original map is kept in a safe place, and only a copy subjected to everyday use. Apparently I had looked at a new copy that hadn't been checked against the original until after I had used it.

On a repeat of the Phantom/Crystal Loop with the Sierra Club, I had occasion to use this emergency route to get water. About eight started out to go down, but only three actually did. I also had a problem finding the top of the crack. I was looking along the Tapeats rim and I needed to be on a ledge about 15 feet below the rim. It took four hours for the round trip and the three of us brought back eleven gallons. The Tapeats ascent was with a flashlight in our teeth. That is a fine way to do it—you can't see where you'll fall.

I offer this Tapeats route only as an emergency because, although it is safe enough, it will probably be frightening to some. Since it takes so much time to lower and, the next day, to raise packs, I suggest camping on the rim and making a water run to the River.

Loop Avoids Redwall Climb

While it is easy to modify the basic loop to allow for starting it at Phantom Ranch, it is not so easy to modify it to eliminate the Redwall climb. The problem is water. If you do the climb, there is no problem on either the first or last day because both first water and last water are close enough to the rim. Without the climb, however, one or the other of those days will be a rough one.

Start at Tiyo Point
First, let me suppose you are starting the loop at Tiyo Point. The route to Phantom Creek is the same as described in the basic routing, although I strongly recommend you cache at least half a gallon of water per person at Shiva Saddle.

The routing from Phantom Creek to Shiva Saddle is back over the Cheops/Isis Saddle to the Trinity drainage and up the northeast arm of Trinity Creek to the saddle between Shiva Temple and Isis Temple. It is about an hour from this saddle to the top of the Redwall above the climb where the basic routing to Shiva Saddle takes over. I recommend starting from Phantom Creek with at least one and a half gallons of water. Hopefully, you will still have half a gallon left when you reach the Shiva Saddle. When this is combined with the half gallon you left there on the way down, there should be enough for dinner, breakfast the next morning, and the hike back to the car.

Start at Bright Angel Campground
If the loop begins at the Bright Angel Campground, the problem is the same but the solution is different. I suggest a dry camp at the head of the fault ravine into Trinity southwest of Isis Temple. From there it is a four-hour round trip to the River for water via the emergency route described earlier. Bring back enough so you have plenty for dinner and breakfast and can still cache a gallon per person for the return from Shiva Saddle.

Having that much water cached means you have a choice when you get to it on the way back: You can camp there and go over to Phantom Creek or around to the campground the next day, or you can continue on over to Phantom Creek the same day.

The route from the campground to the dry camp at the top of the Trinity fault ravine is the reverse of one described above. Similarly, the routing from Trinity to 94 Mile Creek to Crystal Creek to Dragon Spring and thence to Shiva Saddle is the reverse of the one described at the beginning. The fault ravine on the south side of Shiva Saddle is still the best way for the descent, and I don't think it matters how far down you go before contouring south as long as you get through the top Supai cliffs. When you get to the top of the Redwall, continue south to the thin ridge just north of the "5412" elevation point.

The Redwall is broken up on the southwest side of this ridge by a fault that, unfortunately, doesn't do the same on the other side, and the descent to the Tonto is without incident. I have used the fault ravines to cross the drainage from the southwest side of Isis—one of these figured in the exit from Trinity on the way to the Cheops/Isis Saddle in the basic routing—and you are now close to the water cache left earlier on your way to 94 Mile Creek. You can now retrace your steps to Bright Angel Creek or go over the Cheops/Isis Saddle to Upper Phantom Creek.

Another Option
In April 1991 Don Mattox and I, together with two friends from Wisconsin made a short loop into Upper Phantom. Our routing was this: Down the South Kaibab Trail to Phantom Ranch; over Utah Flats to Upper Phantom; up the Redwall route; back to the top of the northeast arm of Trinity; down Trinity exiting to the east via the drainage mentioned earlier. Then we contoured around as if going directly to Phantom Ranch, but instead of swinging around to take the hazardous "ball-bearing" route, we went up the drainage south of Cheops, exiting it via the drainage 0.7 mile southeast of the summit of Cheops—almost due west of the "4106" elevation point. This put us back on Utah Flats, where we could head for home. This was an easy six-night trip, including one layover day.

HIKING TIMES FOR ALTERNATE ROUTINGS

The following tables of hiking times show how the basic routing is modified to avoid the Redwall climb.

Locations	Elapsed Times Between Locations (hours)
Loop begins at Phantom Ranch to Upper Phantom Creek via Creek	
Bright Angel Campground	5:00
Phantom Creek (3,600' contour)	

To Upper Phantom Creek via Utah Flats

Bright Angel Campground	2:00
Top of Tapeats (Utah Flats)	2:30
Phantom Creek (3,600' contour)	

Loop Avoids Redwall Climb

Loop Begins at Bright Angel Campground

Bright Angel Campground	4:30
Top of Fault Ravine into Trinity	5:45
94 Mile Creek	7:30
Mouth of Crystal Creek	9:30
Shiva Saddle (dry camp)	5:45
Water Cache	3:15
Phantom Creek (3,600' contour)	5:00
Bright Angel Campground	

Loop Begins at Tiyo Point

Car	3:00
Shiva Saddle	4:00
Dragon Spring	5:30
Mouth of Crystal Creek	9:15
94 Mile Creek	9:00
Phantom Creek (3,600' contour)	9:30
Shiva Saddle (dry camp)	3:00
Car	

2 Tuna Creek/
Shinumo Creek Loop

On the value of a small libation (margarita) before fixing dinner:
"It dulls the sharp edge of pain."

AL STECK

Length
Seven days, plus layover day(s), if any.

Water
The first water on the way down is in Tapeats; the next is at the River. There's no water on Tonto traverses except in potholes and after a rain. The last water on the way out is in lower Flint drainage.

Quad Maps
7.5-minute maps
    King Arthur Castle
    Kanabonits Spring
    Havasupai Point
    Shiva Temple

Roadhead
The roadhead is along the road to Point Sublime, about 0.5 mile north of the sharp turn by the narrow neck on the way to the point. Park just up the road (north) from the beginnings of a drainage on the west side of the road.

ROUTES TO ROADHEAD

There are two routes to the roadhead. Neither is routinely maintained; I sometimes find an ax and large pruning saw to be necessary. One route is via the road that also goes to Tiyo Point. Turn off the highway to the North Rim about 0.5 mile north of the road to Point Imperial. A sign at this side road points the way to the Widforss Point Trail.

From the East
After 0.9 mile you reach a gate. This happens after you have left the highway, gone past the parking lot for the Widforss Point Trail, and turned left at a Y.

After 3.2 miles you enter a meadow and come to a fork; go right. The road to the left goes to Tiyo Point (a very small sign a few inches off the ground points left and says TIYO POINT.)

After 7.5 miles over a very bad road, you meet the other road to Point Sublime. At this intersection there is a sign pointing back the way you've come and saying TIYO POINT..

After 5.6 miles you reach the Point Sublime campsites.

This route is not suitable for passenger cars. My VW bus made it—but barely.

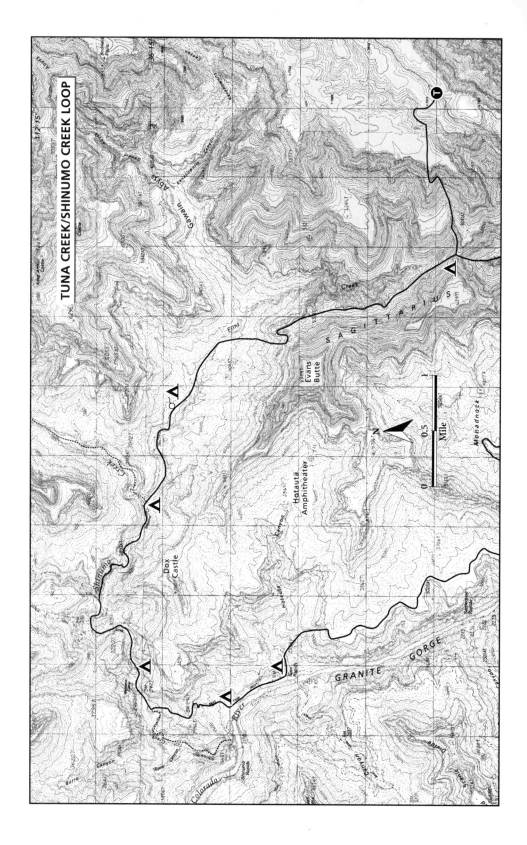

TUNA CREEK/SHINUMO CREEK LOOP

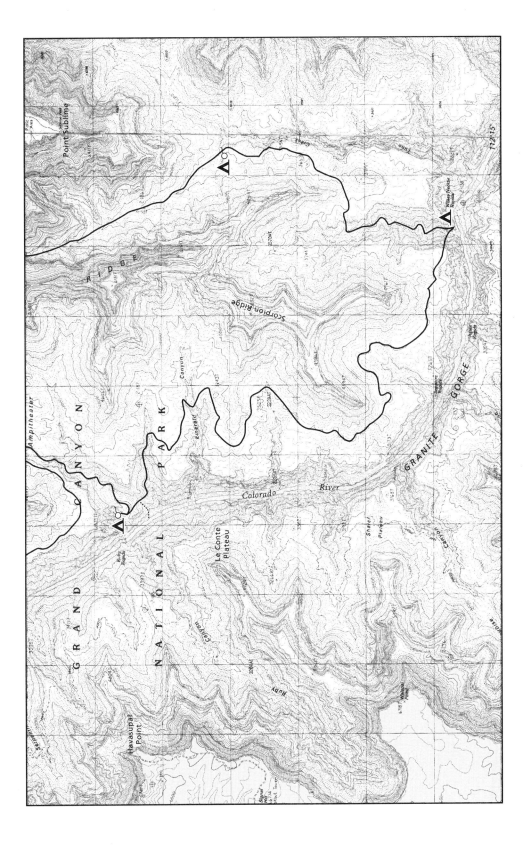

From the West

Mileage

0.0　The other route to Point Sublime starts outside the park where U.S. Highway 67 passes Deer Lake, just south of Kaibab Lodge and 26.7 miles south of Jacob Lake. Turn west onto Forest Service Road (FS) 422.

2.1　After 2.1 miles, at the top of the hill, turn sharply left onto FS 270.

2.9　After 0.8 mile FS 222 goes to the right; you go straight.

4.2　After 1.3 miles turn right onto FS 223.

6.6　After 2.4 miles you meet FS 223A; go straight.

10.1　After 3.5 miles turn left onto FS 268.

11.2　After 1.1 miles veer left onto FS 268B.

11.7　After 0.5 mile you cross the park boundary.

12.0　After 0.3 mile you meet the road to Swamp Point; go left.

13.0　After 1.0 mile you pass a faint road (with sign) to Tipover Spring; go straight.

15.0　After 2.0 miles there is a road to the right; go straight.

17.4　After 2.4 miles a road merges from the left; go straight. This is the Old Point Sublime Road that goes back to the highway near the entrance station. This road should not be used. There is a sign here that I find confusing when I am going the other way. Make a note to go left at this sign on the return.

17.5　After 0.1 mile there is a road off to the right that goes to a cabin; go straight.

17.7　After 0.2 mile go sharply right and down one side of a triangular intersection.

20.3　After 2.6 miles you reach the Tiyo Point Road junction mentioned above; go straight.

25.9　After 5.6 miles you reach Point Sublime. I don't think a passenger car can make this trip, but my VW bus did.

HIKING TIMES

Use Areas	Locations	Elapsed Times Between Locations (hours)
▲ NH9	Car	:45
	Rim	1:45
▲ AR9	Flint/Tuna Saddle	3:15
(dry camp)		
▲ AR9	Tapeats Spring	3:00
▲ AR9	River at Nixon Rock	1:30
	Tapeats Rim	3:00
	Monadnock descent canyon	2:00
▲ AR9	Monadnock Amphitheater camp	4:45
	Tapeats rim overlooking Hotauta	1:30
▲ AS9	North Bass Beach upstream	
	Shinumo Rapids	:45
	Shinumo Creek via high trail	:15
▲ AS9	Bass Camp Historical Site	1:00
▲ AS9	White Creek	1:45
▲ AR9	Flint/Shinumo confluence	2:00
	Base of Redwall	2:15

	Top of Redwall	1:45
▲ AR9	Flint/Tuna Saddle	2:30
(dry camp)		
	Rim	1:00
▲ NH9	Car	

By camping one night at the mouth of Hotauta Canyon (Scorpion Ridge Use Area [AR9]) and the next at the Flint/Shinumo confluence, you can avoid camping in the North Bass Use Area (AS9). This will be necessary when, as it often is, the North Bass Use Area is full.

ROUTE DETAILS

Where you camp the first night depends on when you leave the car. The hiking time to the River for me is just under nine hours, so you may not get there in one day unless you camped the previous night at Point Sublime. Good camping spots for the first night are the Flint/Tuna Saddle (dry camp) and the Tapeats Spring.

After leaving the car and climbing the ridge, keep going west until it begins sloping west into the next drainage. Head north along the ridge until you reach a north-facing slope and can descend to the drainage. This gets you to the bottom without any cliffs, but you will be cursing the thorns of the New Mexican locust. I wear gloves and long pants. After reaching the bottom, go down a few hundred yards until you find a convenient place to climb out. Head west again to the rim as shown on the map. Search along the rim until you have a steep talus slope in front of you that lines up with a drainage heading all the way down through the Supai.

Rim Takeoff

The rim takeoff is down this very steep limestone talus. Eventually you must go south around the small red promontory below you, but there are many small cliffs in between. No lowering of packs should be necessary. A good rule to follow is: If you are in a good place to climb down one of these cliffs, do so; if not, contour left until you can. I find it helpful to leave small ducks for myself for the return trip. If you do, be sure to remove them on the way out.

As you round the promontory, you will find there is still one last Toroweap cliff below you. Contour south on the top of this cliff—I found a small trail (deer?)—until you can get through it to the top of the Coconino, only moderately steep here. I prefer to contour around a little farther and go through the cliff to a ridge that shows clearly on the map as a ripple in the contours immediately north of the Flint drainage marked in blue that flows west toward the Flint/Tuna Saddle before heading north.

This ridge takes you through the Coconino and the Hermit Shale and ends in the Flint drainage near the top of the Supai. Continue down the bed into the Supai until you can contour over to the Flint/Tuna Saddle. The saddle is only 0.25 mile or so away, but the way is slow—brushy and sidehill steep—and it seems much farther.

I heard from two readers about this rim takeoff spot; both had trouble with it. John told me he was sure he was in the right place and had descended some distance only to find that the other members of his party were cliffed out farther south. He went back up, and after some shouted signals they all ended up in the right place. The other reader, Peter, thinks he and his group were in the right place but told me they found the descent too intimidating—the steep talus of unsteady grapefruit-sized rocks together with heavy packs and no walking sticks advised a change of plans. I, too, am intimidated by such talus—even with a walking stick—and I try to work my way to the left as quickly as possible so I can steady myself with one hand on a cliff wall.

Try to leave the rim with enough water so that at least a quart per person can be left at the saddle to be picked up on the return. Some V-8 juice (for electrolytes) and/or a can of fruit (for carbohydrates) will be appreciated then, too. I suggest beginning the loop down the Tuna drainage because it leaves the best part of the trip for last.

Flint/Tuna Saddle

The Flint/Tuna Saddle is about halfway through the Supai, so that not much Supai remains in the descent to the top of the Redwall. The route is south down the talus, but be careful of large (half-ton) rocks that are precariously balanced. A large rockfall covers a good deal of the slope.

Soon after entering the Redwall there is a drop-off that is bypassed up and over a shoulder to the east. If you go down the shoulder, be careful of the "carnivorous" limestone. It is helpful to wear gloves.

Redwall Drop-offs

Once you are back in the bed, there are only two more drop-offs of any consequence—and both have obvious bypasses to the west. One might even have a pothole of water right at the lip. I have never drunk from it, but I have used the water to cool myself off a bit. I have always bypassed the second drop-off by contouring a few hundred yards over to a break in a small cliff above a long talus slope. But in 1984 my brother found a deer trail that led over the rim of the drop-off to a small ledge that takes you to the main bed more directly. His way is a definite improvement over mine.

Tapeats Spring

Below this last drop-off the way is clear to the top of the Tapeats. Someone has been down Tuna through the schist to the River, but I'm not sure how easy it was. In any case, there has been a small flow of water in the bed at the top of the Tapeats, just above the confluence with the east arm of Tuna, each of the three times I have been there—once in July and twice in October. There is a more substantial flow—complete with polliwogs, frogs, small skippers, and the black larvae that you often find in side-canyon fast water— just below the Tapeats/schist contact. This small stream in the schist probably flows year-round in a normal year.

I have no love for these wiggly black buffalo gnat larvae. In trying to send a batch of them to their heavenly reward once, I found that when I tried to dislodge them they remained attached to the rock by a thin thread of something like spider silk. They were able to climb back up it to their original position.

Route to Tuna
There is no particular reason to go to the mouth of Tuna, but if you do, my best route is to contour around on the west rim of Tuna to the notch at the point. A deer trail takes you from there to the bed of Tuna a few hundred yards inside the mouth. It is a hard two hours from the mouth of Tuna upstream to Crystal along the schist because it involves so much climbing up in and around the obstacles. It is also a difficult hour from Tuna down to the next drainage. The low-level route runs into cliffs just upstream from that drainage, and you have to wade about 20 feet to a sandbar along a narrow ledge about 2 feet under water or climb along the face of the cliff. I don't remember whether or not there is a way around above the cliff. We used to try to be here by 9:00 A.M. for early-morning low water or the ledge would have been too far underwater—releases from Glen Canyon Dam are no longer as large.

Tapeats Spring to River
The easiest way to the drainage below Tuna is to cut over the saddle north of the small hill (height 3,919 feet) just west of the Tuna drainage. A well-defined gully leads from the saddle to the Tapeats rim in front of you, and for a while it looks like it will take you through the Tapeats. It won't, but just a few hundred feet farther north along the rim, there is an easy way through to the bed.

As you go down the bed, look closely at the Tapeats rim to the west for the climbing route out of the bed. It is a crack behind a pillar near the point at the mouth of the canyon. Only one bypass (to the west) is needed before you get to the River. There isn't much beach. One reader reported that he found this bypass a serious challenge, requiring a climb of several hundred feet. It could be that heavy rain has altered the landscape.

A big block in the middle of the River, which is very narrow here, creates a small rapid that provides a steady roar through the night. On page 78 of *The Colorado River in Grand Canyon—A Guide,* Larry Stevens calls this block Nixon Rock—named by boatmen in honor of Nixon's departure from office.

Climbing Route Out
There are two ways back up to the Tonto. One is a direct climbing route, although you can keep your packs on. The other is more leisurely: Just go back up the drainage for about 0.5 mile before turning to climb out. Both routes require starting back up the drainage—except instead of returning to the bed at the bypass, the direct route keeps on climbing. If you forgot to look for it coming down, just aim for a buttress that looks like it might be a tower with a chimney behind it.

This is a good route—direct, exciting, and safe. There is good footing on a series of ledges, and getting up 6 feet to the first ledge is about the hardest part of the whole climb—especially now that I broke off one of the footholds. Follow these ledges until you can get under a chockstone that is wedged in near the top of the tower. Go under it, turn back to face it, and continue climbing up the ledges to the top.

You probably won't have noticed any exposure until you get on the other side of the chockstone. Some may find a belay comforting at this point. Transferring yourself from the top of the tower to the mainland is somewhat unnerving; on my last trip eight different people did this in eight different ways. The consensus was that the farther right you go, the easier it is. Even with rests we took only an hour and a half from the River to Tonto rim. We built a medium-sized cairn so others could find the route down from the top.

Route into Monadnock

Once on the Tonto you contour around to the drainage just south of the one that drains the Monadnock Amphitheater; the one you want reaches the River about 0.4 mile upstream from the mouth of Ruby Canyon. If you can't get to the bed of this canyon easily, contour along the rim until you can. Go down it to the Tapeats pour-off; at the lip follow a ledge off to the left until you can get back to the bed. It was on this ledge that a high-level park service official (who shall remain nameless) was crawling on his hands and knees under an overhang when his superheavy pack shifted over his head and forced his nose into sudden and forceful contact with the Tapeats Sandstone. It was an industrial-strength nosebleed.

After negotiating a few obstacles in the bed of this drainage, you should begin looking for the place where you leave it. Look for a shoulder of schist ahead of you on the right with a white band of quartz leading up to it. When you can, leave the bed and climb up to this shoulder. It is about 0.2 mile north of the mouth of the canyon, and you should aim for the 2,820-foot contour. As you round this shoulder, contour over to a saddle to the northwest. From here you can look down to the bed of the Monadnock Amphitheater drainage. In October 1982 there was a nice flow of water visible from the saddle, but in October 1985 there was none. We did find a small flow 100 yards or so down in the schist, but if you're at the saddle and don't see any water in the Monadnock drainage, you may wish to go down the broad slope to the southwest and get water at the Colorado River.

Route Out of Monadnock

I have not found any direct route out of the Monadnock drainage to the north. Although we explored all the likely spots, we couldn't get out until a small ridge led up to some Tapeats ledges almost 2 miles up from the mouth. There are small seeps and springs in the bed for about half that distance. Once on the Tonto you continue contouring—for a while there is a good deer trail— to the point looking down on the Hotauta drainage. This is a great view and a good place for lunch. Imagine, too, what Grand Canyon hiking would be like now if Frank Brown had had his way in the nineteenth century and built a railroad through the canyon. Down below you, in the flats east of the river, there would now be a switching yard—Stanton named it Dutton's Depot Grounds.

The Brown/Stanton Story

The story of Brown and Stanton and the plans for the railroad has at least as much drama, adventure, and irony as the Powell one and should be more widely known. Once you get used to the idea that the immensity of the Canyon does not confer a corresponding immensity to the task—Stanton argued that only the last 200 feet of depth made any difference—you can see that a railroad at the bottom of the Grand Canyon is all too feasible. This is the story.

Railroads were big business in 1869 when the transcontinental railroad was completed. After Powell finished his trip through the Grand Canyon in that same year, it was inevitable that someone would think of the Canyon as a railroad right-of-way. But curiously, the person whose idea for a canyon railroad finally produced results had never heard of Powell's exploits.

All that S.S. Harper, prospector, cowboy, and wanderer of the Southwest, knew of railroads he gleaned from watching a survey being run through the mountains of Arizona and New Mexico. Yet later, spending a day and a half at a place historians think was Lees Ferry, the advantages of a river route to the sea occurred to him—no mountains, no snow, level all the way. Harper must have thought the bottom of the Grand Canyon was everywhere more or less the way it was at Lees Ferry.

Next comes Frank Mason Brown. I don't know how old he was in 1889, but I would guess about forty. Old enough to be a former California state senator and to have made good money in Denver real estate, yet young enough to be looking for adventure and exciting investments. By all accounts he was personable, honest, frank, energetic, courageous, and, above all, of a sanguine disposition.

In January 1889 Harper went to Brown with a mining venture. Brown was not interested and said he'd rather invest in a railroad. You can guess the rest—Brown was off and running. In the next two months he got commitments of fifty million dollars for a Canyon railroad, contingent on a favorable engineer's report.

On March 25, the Denver, Colorado Canyon & Pacific Railroad Company was formed with Brown as president. On March 26 an engineer was hired to run the survey down the Colorado River from Grand Junction to its confluence with the Green River. It began on March 28. A main survey party would later continue the line to the Gulf of California. In April Robert Brewster Stanton was hired to be chief engineer. Stanton's application is dated April 15.

I give all these dates only to show Brown's energy and driving purpose—no flies could land on him.

Stanton and the Georgetown Loop

One of Stanton's early exploits is now a tourist attraction. In 1884, as a division engineer for Union Pacific, he built the Georgetown Loop. The Colorado towns of Georgetown and Silver Plume, now 2 miles apart on Interstate 70, near Loveland Pass and not too far west of Denver, had too steep a gradient between them for a railroad until Stanton designed a series of loops that stretched 2 miles into 4.5. This more than halved the gradient, so a railroad could serve the mines at the upper town. Today, during the tourist season, a narrow-gauge steam locomotive plies its way back and forth between Georgetown and Silver Plume so tourists can ride the loops and appreciate firsthand Stanton's skill as an engineer. There was a two-hour wait when I tried to ride it, so I put off the experience to a later time.

If the Brown/Stanton story has a hero, it is Stanton. He was a capable engineer and a good leader. It's too bad he wasn't on the scene in time to help with the planning. Brown consulted with Powell but apparently didn't listen when Powell described the dangers and impracticability of the venture. Powell's reservations were discounted because he wasn't an engineer. Stanton was later very bitter and criticized Powell for not making Brown aware of the hazards, but I believe that Powell was honest about them and that Brown erred in not hearing what he didn't wish to hear. Besides, I believe Powell wanted to discourage Brown. He saw the Grand Canyon in terms of water storage for the benefit of the arid West, and Brown's railroad there did not fit his vision.

Brown's facility for selective hearing shows in his reaction to what Powell wrote him in reply to a request for advice about boats. Powell described his in detail, but the only message Brown seemed to get was that they were too heavy to portage easily. Consequently, Brown's boats were light—only 15 feet long, 40 inches wide, and 18 inches deep. They were clinker-built of thin, brittle red cedar planking with a round coppered bottom and weighed 150 pounds; Brown was being sure he could portage his boats easily.

No Life Jackets

But having poor boats was not the main problem. There was also inadequate protection for food and for life itself. That's right—no life jackets. I'm not sure why. Some sources say Brown "forgot" them. But most say that, despite pleading to the contrary, he refused to take them on the grounds that they were an unnecessary encumbrance. Stanton, like Powell, had only one useful arm and he was urged to take one for himself, but he refused that advantage over his associates.

The Brown party left Green River, Utah, on May 25, 1889, exactly twenty years and a day from the time Powell had left Green River, Wyoming. The party had sixteen people in six boats. Included in the group were two lawyers, friends of Brown from Denver, taken along as guests—were they investors or were they potential investors?

Getting the survey to the head of Cataract Canyon was easy, but getting through it was not. They soon lost one boat and more than half their food. Not far from the end of Cataract Canyon, the lack of food produced a near mutiny and they split up. Brown and ten others took three boats and hurried to Dandy Crossing (Hite) for supplies, while Stanton and the rest stayed behind to continue the survey. After several days of starvation rations, Stanton's group was resupplied from below.

Five people were left at Hite to run the survey through Glen Canyon to Lees Ferry. Three, including one of the "guests," had had enough and went home. The other eight, including Stanton and Brown, plus an experienced boatman who joined them at Hite, hurried on to continue the survey from Lees Ferry—where the other guest left. The Glen Canyon survey party was to have been resupplied from Lees Ferry but was not and abandoned its task.

So on July 9, eight people with no life jackets left Lees Ferry in three frail boats. The next morning Brown's boat capsized at an "eddy fence" at the foot of Soap Creek Rapid; Brown was caught in the whirling eddy and drowned. On July 15 two others were drowned in a rapid near mile 25. One of these men was Peter Hansbrough. Later in the year his body was found on a pile of driftwood near a place now called Point Hansbrough.

At this point Stanton wrote, "Two more faithful and good men gone! Astonished and crushed by their loss, our force too small to portage our boats, and our outfit and boats unfit for such work, I decided to abandon the trip. . . ." They climbed out South Canyon after caching their gear in what is now called Stanton's Cave. They saw Brown's body go by but could not retrieve it.

Stanton was back in Denver on July 27. The company was reorganized and Stanton put in charge of completing the survey. Profiting from experience, he ordered better boats, this time of oak, 22 feet long, 52 inches wide, and 22 inches deep. He also ordered the best cork life preservers for the passengers and watertight rubber bags for the food.

On December 10 (still 1889) the second party—twelve people in three boats—left from a point near Hite to complete the survey through Glen Canyon. On December 28 they reentered Marble Canyon. Four days later, on January 1, the photographer, Nims, fell while taking a picture and broke his leg. He was evacuated to Lees Ferry via Rider Canyon.

On February 6 one boat was smashed into "toothpicks" while shooting it unmanned through a rapid (à la Powell) after portaging its contents. A few days later, at Crystal Creek, the recruit from Hite left the party and made his way to the rim and through the snow to Kanab. His route to the rim is still a mystery. Because of the added weight of new supplies taken on at Diamond Creek, the three men whose boat had been lost above Crystal Creek were asked to leave the group. On March 17 the party, now numbering seven, reached Grand Wash Cliffs, and on April 26 reached the Gulf.

Survey Records
Stanton's survey through the Grand Canyon was not a detailed one. To save time and money—he was largely financing it himself—he ran what he called an "instrumental reconnaissance." This meant detailed notes on grade and canyon composition but with a detailed survey of only the hard stretches. There was also a detailed photographic record, including about 150 stereopticon views, so that skeptics could be convinced that written claims of feasibility were indeed true.

When Stanton took over the photographic duties after the evacuation of Nims, he did so with some trepidation because he had no knowledge of photography whatsoever. All that anyone knew was that you left the cap off a little longer when it was dark. Through both luck and foresight all the film from both expeditions survived without damage. On the second trip the film was always stored in tins that were soldered shut. More than 2,000 pictures were taken, and only about 10 percent were lost. From the historical point of view, these pictures are probably the most important result of the survey. We can be thankful it wasn't the railroad.

Route off Tonto

Two hundred yards or so east of the Hotauta overlook there is a break in the Tapeats, which shows up nicely on the Fault Map. Go down this break and contour northeast beneath a wall to a broad slope that leads to the bed of Hotauta Canyon. A nice bench by the River has a trail of sorts that leads to the large sandbar just upstream from Shinumo Creek.

Shinumo Creek

There are three ways to get to Shinumo Creek: (1) You can take a climbing route—which will be awkward with packs—over to the mouth of the creek; (2) you can take the trail shown on the map, which perhaps takes you higher than necessary; or (3) you can take a lower trail that goes over a small saddle much closer to the River—about at the 2,560-foot contour.

If, later, you follow the creek through the schist narrows to the River, you will find only one obstacle: a chockstone above a magnificent pool. There are three ways around this chockstone: (1) Climb down a hole nearby that leads to a grotto beneath it; (2) bypass it on ledges and chimneys on the downstream side; or (3) jump off it into the pool. Before you do this make sure the pool is deep enough.

Bass Camp

The Bass Camp Historical Site is an interesting place for a camp. It is only a short distance upstream from the spot where the upper trail joins the creek. Across the creek from this junction, beyond the arrowweed flats near a big catclaw acacia, you may be able to spot where Bass's trail takes off for his asbestos mines in Hakatai Canyon.

William Wallace Bass is an important figure in the history of the Grand Canyon of the nineteenth century. He set up camp near what is now the trailhead of the South Bass Trail in 1884 and lived there or at Bass Camp along Shinumo Creek for almost forty years. He constructed what are now known as the North and South Bass Trails for use by his dudes so he could take them across the Canyon. For a while he took them across the River by boat, but eventually he put in a cable, which wasn't cut until 1968.

Asbestos Mine

Bass also developed copper and asbestos mines and got a particularly good long staple asbestos from a mine in Hakatai Canyon. The fibers that are still seen littering the ground at the Shinumo Camp are up to 2 inches long; I have read that the mine produced even 4-inchers. Some of these fibers found their way into European theater curtains.

Orchard

Across the creek from his camp, where the artifacts now are, is a broad flat alluvial plain where Bass had his orchard and garden. Nothing is left except remnants of some irrigation ditches and a storage pond. If you follow the main ditch upstream along the cliff, you will see where Bass drew his water from the creek. There is an iron rod on top of a small buttress at the creek's edge with wire trailing from it, which I take to be a support for a flume that dipped into the creek near here.

A flat rock about 3 feet square and 2 feet high between Bass Camp and the creek has a hole in it that mystifies me. I used to speculate that Bass had a small suspension bridge across the creek or a waterwheel to assist in irrigation, but if that were the case there should be other holes on other rocks. There are likely candidates but no holes.

If you stay on the Bass Camp side of the creek en route to the Flint/Shinumo confluence, you will nearly get cliffed out by the Shinumo Quartzite. You can get by, though, and just beyond where the sand broadens out again there are a variety of Indian ruins along the cliff—some granaries and a shelter. You will already have passed the "eye" granary, but I'll leave that for you to find.

White Creek
About an hour beyond the granaries you pass White Creek, which is the easiest way to Muav Saddle. I used the lower part of the North Bass Trail precisely once. The next dozen times I have used White Creek because it is so much easier and so much more pleasant.

Flint/Shinumo Confluence
Going up on Shinumo Creek beyond White Creek is a struggle. It isn't really very difficult, but it is a struggle, though nice pools make pleasant swimming in hot weather. It is about two hours from White Creek to the Flint/Shinumo junction; on the west wall above it there is an Indian ruin. A quarter mile or so down the creek from this junction on the south side I saw a nautiloid fossil on a faint trail where I was walking.

Layover Day in Upper Shinumo
A layover day spent in Upper Shinumo is a day well spent. If you continue on up the creek, you will get pooled out. There is a large over-your-head circular pool about 100 yards from the Flint junction. It is great for swimming but a bit cold unless you are there at midday. To get past it, you must climb the schist at the mouth of Flint and pick up a trail near the bottom of the Tapeats. It will contour around and down to the creek several hundred yards above the pool. There are lots of cottonwoods and other pleasing greenery in happy contrast to the mainly thorny stuff elsewhere.

Without packs, you should, in a day's time, be able to get at least as far as the Merlin/Modred junction. There are some large and inviting pools where the Tapeats comes out, so be sure to go at least that far.

Rainbow Plateau Loop
Both arms of Shinumo are fun to explore. My wife saw a good-sized waterfall in the Modred arm. About an hour beyond the Modred junction, the creek turns sharply east and in another hour turns north again. This fault ravine leads to the rim if you are of an adventurous frame of mind. Together with

the North Bass Trail, this route makes a nice loop that takes you around Rainbow Plateau. It will be described in chapter 10.

Wasps

It was in these parts that I once saw ten rattlesnakes in one week's time, never to see any there again. Another time I was sitting by a big cottonwood near the creek and heard a great whooping and yelling punctuated by a loud splash—more yelling and another splash—and then laughter. Four younger members of the party had disturbed some ground wasps, which had chased the wildly vocalizing youngsters until they had jumped into a pool big enough to hide almost every square inch of all four of them until it was safe to emerge. I, too, was attacked by a swarm when I stepped on a rock that slid out from under me. I was stung fourteen times. This was in August. Other times of year have not produced such annoyances.

Close Encounter

My usual equanimity was sorely tested here at the Flint/Shinumo junction one summer night years ago. I always tell people with whom I'm camping in the Grand Canyon never to swat something crawling on you without first looking to see what it is. You certainly don't want to swat a scorpion. So the injunction is "Brush—don't swat." That's fine in theory, but can you imagine the frustration of wanting to brush something off and not knowing exactly where or how hard to brush? The night in question was so warm that I was sleeping in my bathing suit on top of my sleeping bag. I was also lying on my back.

I awoke instantly with the first touch and could feel a tug at my skin as a foot tried to get a purchase on it. Something was lifting itself off the ground to begin climbing up onto my leg. Successive steps were slow and deliberate—like tiptoeing. What could it be? The night before, a frog had jumped onto my face and almost startled me into the next world. But a frog arrives suddenly and sits on you like a wet lump until, just as suddenly, it is gone. This was no frog. They don't tiptoe along your leg. Neither do chipmunks or squirrels.

What else could it be? I could feel each foot as it was carefully placed and couldn't help noticing that the feet were very widely spaced. Whatever the "something" was, it was about the size of my hand. I wasn't about to swat, but neither was I sure where to brush—that would obviously depend on how big the thing was. It slowly crossed my trunks and began its methodical way up my bare stomach. By this time I had a pretty good idea how many legs it had—certainly more than four. I was also sure that nothing this big would have only six. I didn't have to open my eyes to be sure it had eight—I knew it had eight.

But that was both good news and bad news. The good news was that I couldn't imagine a scorpion that big. If the thing working its way across my chest toward my neck were a scorpion, it would have to be as big as a small lobster. The bad news was that if it weren't a scorpion, it had to be a tarantula—and a big one at that. But the good part of the bad news was that tarantulas are not supposed to be very poisonous.

It was now stepping up off my chest and onto my chin, and brushing it off was out of the question. I didn't want to make it angry. All I wanted was to appear absolutely and totally inedible. I wondered if it could sense my muscular tension and increasing pulse rate, which, unfortunately, would signal just the opposite. The spider stepped on my lips, paused briefly at my nose—I was holding my breath—and stepped on an eyelid. I had been unable to open my eyes earlier, and now it was obviously too late. I was still holding my breath as the tarantula proceeded slowly across my forehead, into my hair, back down to the ground, and into the night.

Up and Out
Now it is time to talk about "up and out." It is a long way to the car from the Flint/Shinumo confluence; my hiking times estimate nine and a half hours. If the days are short you may wish to camp on the saddle—not a bad idea in any case. If you do, you will be glad you left water for yourself.

Redwall Routes
Go up Flint about to a point 0.2 mile downstream of Gawain Abyss. This will take an hour. There is sometimes enough water to make it possible to camp up Flint a way if you are in a hurry or if it is hot and you need an early start. The Redwall route is in a bay about 0.6 mile south. This bay is also 0.5 mile northeast of Evans Butte. It is tempting to try to continue up Flint to the saddle, and I have done so, but getting out involves so much brush and so many complicated bypasses that I will describe an easier way. After you leave the Flint drainage, climb up along a ridge and through some small Muav cliffs to the base of the Redwall. The upper wall meets the lower at the far right-hand side of the bay, where a scary 30-foot climb takes you to the bottom of the bay. There is a slightly less scary 20-foot climb on the far left-hand side of the bay.

The rest is easy. Contour around and up to the base of a chimney high up on the far left-hand side of the bay. After you climb it, you will be on a sharp ridge leading to the mainland. It is so sharp and so steep on each side that I prefer to be on all fours for the worst parts.

Back in the Saddle
It is about two hours from the top of the Redwall to the saddle, and my recommendation is not to climb the Supai cliffs until you are almost under the saddle.

The first time I went up to the rim from the saddle, I went up the gully under the cliff that is to the south of the ridge I like to go down. Somewhere in there, below the Coconino, was a large Coconino boulder with a dinosaur track on it. I didn't see it, and the person who did could not give an accurate description of where it was. So lots of luck if you look for it.

I will leave you on the saddle to retrace your steps to the car. As I said before, there will be less route-finding if you left small cairns for yourself on the way down. If you did, don't forget to remove them as you climb back out.

Entrance to the Redwall Narrows in Saddle Canyon.

3 Shinumo Creek/ Tapeats Creek Loop
Circumambulation of Powell Plateau

A futile effort to explain why off-trail hiking on the Tonto is easy:
"All you have to do is contour around."

DON MATTOX

Length
Nine days, plus layover day(s), if any.

Water
There may be stagnant pools at the top of the Redwall in Saddle Canyon, and there's often some flow in the middle of the Redwall, but don't count on it. There has almost always been a good flow of water at the Saddle/Stina junction. Occasional water surfaces in the bed between this junction and the stream from Tapeats Cave, and there is usually water flowing out of Crazy Jug. There is no water between Tapeats Creek and Stone Creek. You will have frequent access to the River between Stone and Blacktail Canyons, and may even find some flow in the side canyons. Blacktail has a small flow at or just inside the mouth. Jim Haggart and Art Christiansen discovered a route to the river 0.3 mile north of the "2113T" elevation point in Stephen Aisle. Look for a broad, squarish ledge in the Tapeats that is well below you. The route descends via small ledges at the down-river edge of the large ledge. There is access to the River 0.4 mile southwest of Explorers Monument and 0.2 mile downstream at the "2532T" elevation point and there is a good flow in the drainage 0.4 mile northeast of the "4850T" elevation point.

Jim Haggart and Bruce Grubbs found an easy route to the River down the nameless canyon 0.8 mile downstream from Walthenberg Rapids. Hakatai Canyon has water near the entry point, and Burro Canyon has a modest seep in the bed where the trail crosses it. Shinumo Creek and lower White Creek have plenty of water. You will find good springs in the Tapeats Narrows near the top of the Tapeats, in the bed near where the trail starts up the Redwall and near the top of the Supai. Finally, a reliable spring is located at the base of the Coconino, at the southern end of the trail that contours into Muav saddle from the south; it has served both horse and human for a long time.

Quad Maps
7.5-minute maps
  Tapeats Amphitheater
  Powell Plateau
  Fossil Bay
  Topocopa Hilltop
  Explorers Monument
  Havasupai Point
  King Arthur Castle

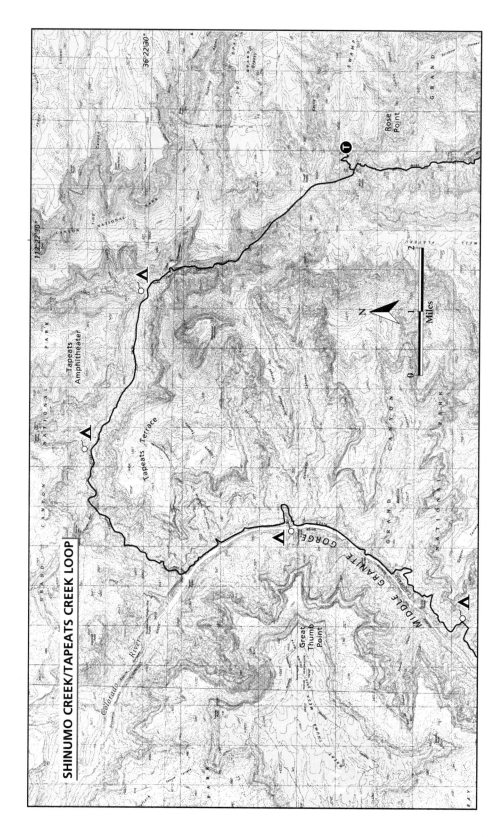

SHINUMO CREEK/TAPEATS CREEK LOOP

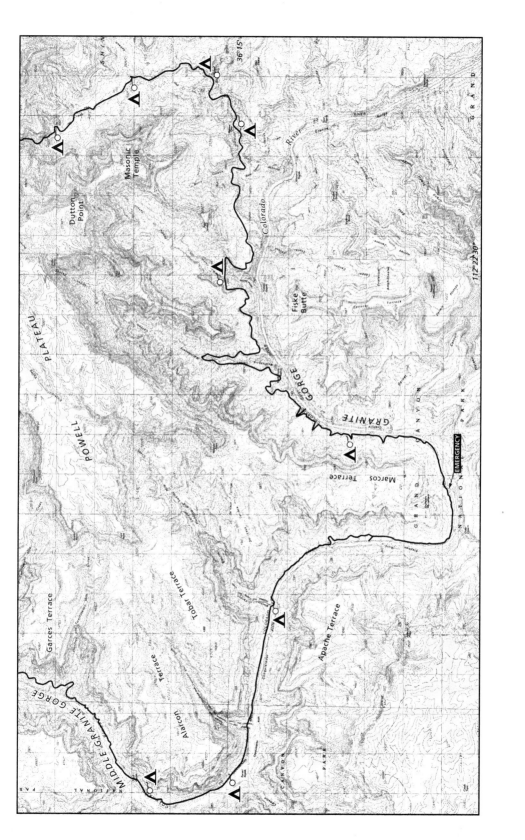

Taking a portion of the park map is more useful and less expensive than taking the seven individual quad maps. But remember that the cartographic descriptions may be different.

Roadhead
Swamp Point.

ROUTE TO ROADHEAD

Mileage

0.0	Go south from Jacob Lake 26.7 miles (just down the hill past Deer Lake) and turn right onto Forest Service Road (FS) 422.
2.1	After 2.1 miles, at the top of the hill, turn sharply left onto FS 270.
2.9	After 0.8 mile FS 222 goes off to the right—go straight.
4.2	After 1.3 miles turn right onto FS 223.
6.6	After 2.4 miles you pass FS 223A—go straight.
10.1	After 3.5 miles turn left onto FS 268.
11.2	After 1.1 miles veer left onto FS 268B.
11.7	After 0.5 mile you cross the park boundary.
12.0	After 0.3 mile you reach a delta intersection. Turn right onto the road to Swamp Point.
19.6	After 7.6 miles you reach the end of the road at Swamp Point. These last miles are difficult for a passenger car, but it can be done. It is easy going with a VW bus.

HIKING TIMES

Use Areas	Locations	Elapsed Times Between Locations (hours)	
		1981	1988
▲ NJ9	Swamp Point (car)	:30	:45
▲ AT9	Muav Saddle	5:00	8:00
▲ AU9	Stina/Saddle Canyon Junction	2:00	3:15
▲ AV9	Junction with Tapeats Cave Canyon	2:30	2:30
▲ AW7	Thunder River		
	(Designated Site camping only)	2:00	2:00
	Point above mouth of Tapeats Creek	2:30	2:30
▲ AU9	Stone Creek	1:15	1:30
	Bedrock Canyon	2:15	5:00
▲ AU9	128 Mile Canyon	2:30	2:45
	127 Mile Canyon	2:00	4:00
▲ AU9	Fossil Rapids	2:30	3:30
▲ AU9	Forster Rapids	2:00	2:45
▲ AU9	Mouth of Blacktail Canyon	3:15	4:15
	Explorers Monument (opposite Elves Chasm)	2:30	3:45
▲ AU9	Good water opposite R in GRANITE	4:00	5:00
	Bed of Walthenburg Canyon	2:15	3:15
▲ AU9	Bed of Hakatai Canyon	4:15	5:00

▲ AS9	Bass Camp Historic Site		1:00	1:15
▲ AS9	White Creek/Shinumo Creek Junction		1:30	1:45
▲ AS9	Tapeats Chockstone and Spring		2:00	3:15
▲ AS9	Bottom of Redwall		2:00	2:15
	Top of Redwall (bed of Muav Canyon)		1:45	2:15
	Muav Saddle		:45	1:15
▲ NJ9	Swamp Point (car)			

* The 1988 times are longer because the author was seven years older (age sixty-three) and because daytime temperatures were up to 114 degrees in the shade.

_____

ROUTE DETAILS

Powell Plateau is a large wooded island separated from the Kaibab Plateau mainland of the North Rim by Muav Saddle. It thrusts southwest from the saddle some 6 miles, causing the Colorado River to make a detour and take 20 miles to do what it could otherwise have done in 10.

The hike around Powell Plateau from car back to car—about 50 miles— is the quintessential loop hike, and the Muav Fault, which joins the Shinumo and Tapeats drainages, makes it possible.

The Muav Fault

The Muav Fault was not exploited as a highway right-of-way as was the Bright Angel Fault, which provides the routing for the Bright Angel and North Kaibab Trails, but the Muav Canyon branch of the fault was used commercially by W.W. Bass to bring his dudes up to the North Rim. His route exists today as the North Bass Trail. My friend Don Mattox and I found out in the late 1960s that the Saddle Canyon branch was also passable. Later we found Bass's old trail over to his asbestos mine in Hakatai Canyon and made our way over into Walthenburg Canyon. By this time I had also been from Tapeats Creek over to Stone Creek, but despite all this exploration I was surprised when in 1980 Don suggested we try a hike around Powell Plateau. This was an inspired idea.

First Try 1980

Even though I wasn't sure I was up to such an expedition, Don and I started down the North Bass Trail in early October. It was his first trip of the year and despite his strength and endurance, he was woefully out of shape. Usually I like hiking with Don because I figure that if I get into trouble he can carry me out on top of his pack. He is also the only person I know who puts his sixty-plus-pound pack on by first laying it on the ground, reaching down with his arms crossed, and grabbing and swinging the pack over his head so it slides down his arms and lands snugly on his back.

But this time Don was having a bad time of it and was really beat by the time we reached the White/Shinumo confluence. The wine and fondue dinner revived both of us somewhat. And I learned that the wee beasties that roam at night do not eat fondue. They may eat my pack and my bootlaces, but they don't eat my fondue. Maybe real mice don't eat quiche, either.

Route to Hakatai Canyon

It took a while the next day to rediscover the route to Hakatai. Standing dripping with sweat on the lip of our descent route into Hakatai and looking down the shimmering expanse of Tonto between us and Explorers Monument, I had a strong "what am I doing here?" feeling. Study from the south side of the River had led us to believe we might find a way down to it from Explorers Monument, but we couldn't be sure. Besides, that looked days away, and we wished we knew how many hours it was to the next water after Hakatai. All we knew for sure was that there was none in Walthenberg.

First Try a Failure

It was our second day, so we had many pounds of food; at eight pounds per gallon, the water was a burden, too. I was discouraged and ready to turn back. But it was Don's trip and I couldn't very well ask him to go back. So I used psychology. "Don," I said, "don't feel you have to make this trip on my account. It sure looks hot out there and I just enjoy being in the Canyon. I don't have to go around Powell Plateau." I made my plea short so the impact would be more subtle and we rested and downed a little more of my Gatorade/iced tea/Tang drink mix.

After a few minutes of enjoying the view of the sweltering chasm, I set the hook that I had so carefully presented. "Besides," I said, "I think we can do something else that hasn't been done before." I didn't know whether I was right or not, but it sounded good at the time. "A few years ago I found a Redwall route out of a branch of Upper Merlin. We could use that—and as Harvey says, 'There are many ways through the Supai.' We could get back to the rim to the north, go across to the Swamp Point road, and hike back to the car. If we can't go around Powell Plateau, we can at least go around Rainbow Plateau."

Don didn't say a thing. He just got up, slung on his pack, and started back toward Shinumo Creek.

This ended our first try at going around Powell Plateau. We decided to be cleverer next time and start from the Tapeats side at a cooler time of year. That way we would be along water much longer at the beginning and would be in better shape and have lighter packs when we reached the waterless(?) stretch that defeated us the first time.

Second Try 1981

A year later, in the middle of October 1981, Mattox and I and a young friend and fellow Grand Canyon explorer, Robert Benson Eschka (aka Robert Benson), were once again at Swamp Point ready to start down—this time down Saddle Canyon. I had been down Saddle several times since first going down it with Don in 1969, and I was taking a tape recorder so I could make notes while I was hiking instead of while I was resting. This first try at high-tech note taking was not too successful. I got ON and OFF mixed up so the machine was off when I was talking and on when I wasn't. I ended up with no data at all—just long stretches of heavy breathing, snatches of comments yelled back and forth, and the incessant "click . . . click . . . click . . ." of my walking stick. It was just as well. I found I couldn't hike and dictate at the same time—like the man who couldn't walk and chew gum at the same time.

Route Down Saddle Canyon
The route is straight down the drainage through the brush to the big drop-off in the Supai. It was here, years ago, that one of the youngsters in our party decided he had carried his watermelon far enough. We all had a most refreshing break, and he hid the rind behind a rock to be carried out on our return. At that time, a week later, we found that all traces of rind had disappeared—eaten, I guess, by mice that found in those scraps an abundant supply of an otherwise rare commodity, water.

At this Supai dryfall we contoured left and up to a ridge, then down it a bit until we could descend westward to a minor drainage that quickly joined the main one. The ridge is marked with the "5459T" elevation point. Once back in the main drainage, we were at the top of Redwall, and after 100 yards or so, the bed—actually the line of the Muav Fault—being blocked by an ancient rockfall, turned sharply into a deep cleft that is wonderfully cool in summer.

Redwall
We traveled down this drainage to the big falls at the Redwall pour-off near the junction with Stina. Although in 1981 we found no serious obstacles in between, we were forced to lower packs at a few places. In 1988 we found that one of these obstacles was more serious than it had been before. This is a chockstone that comes just after a 10-foot fall, which can be downclimbed fairly easily. We didn't consider this chockstone a problem in 1981 because the bed was probably only 5 or 6 feet below it, but in 1988, with more efficient scouring, the bed was more like 10 feet below it. We had to improvise something to lower ourselves. There is a bypass high on the right along the steeply sloping wall that I usually use going up Saddle Canyon; this time it seemed awkward for going down. On a later trip, however, I found a small ledge over my head that I could reach by stretching. It provided excellent handholds and support for my anxious psyche.

Note that although this falls is indeed easily downclimbed, there is a jump to the bed at the end. When I returned here in 1990, this last jump was into a pool of indeterminate depth. This is a spooky thing to do with a pack on, so I tried it first without one. I bent my knees in case there were any sharp rocks down there. There weren't any, but the end result was I went in over my head. Standing up, I found it was about shoulder-deep and the bottom was slippery mud. This meant that an ordinary obstacle became a time-consuming one. If the pool had been over our heads, this obstacle would have become *very* time consuming as well as taxing. Let me describe again what I have found to be the easiest way of dealing with such an over-your-head-pool problem.

1) Establish a reasonably tight line across the pool. Both ends will have to be held or tied off on a rock or tree limb. The bigger the line the easier it can be held.

2) Tie a light line that will stretch across the pool to a carabiner and clip the carabiner to both the pack and the original tight line.

3) Holding the light line, let the pack slide down the tight line. The people holding the first line tight will only have to apply enough tension to keep the pack above water.

Other, riskier, ideas I have seen tried include using a pack as a pendulum, and tying two lines to a pack and pulling on one while the other is payed out. The first idea requires a suitable vantage point for the pivot, and the second requires great strength and coordination by the person(s) pulling in the line and those paying it out.

The first time we went down Saddle Canyon, several of the obstacles seemed just bad enough that one of us jumped or climbed down each one and then climbed back up, to make sure we could get back up if the way was blocked below—thus avoiding the predicament that Abbey describes in *Desert Solitaire* when he jumps into a pool and just barely gets back up after further descent proves impossible.

Slicky Slide

One obstacle provides a welcome diversion. It is the "Slicky Slide," a long 45-degree chute of polished limestone, sometimes with the added lubrication of water, algae, and slimy moss. It is difficult to get down with a pack on your back because everything is so slippery. Two other possibilities are to lower the packs or to wear them in front. And I forgot to mention that the slide ends in a frigid chocolate pool of indeterminate depth until the first to descend checks it out.

If the packs are lowered and carried through the pool by one kind soul, then the rest can bypass it dry shod by very careful cliff hanging. I call this route Dale's High-Water Low-Level Traverse in honor of its discoverer, who was just an ordinary Joe who didn't want to get his feet wet. I am amazed at how strong that motivation can sometimes be. This bypass is roughly 2 or 3 feet above the water on stream left and consists mainly of small bumps for your feet and tiny fissures for your fingers on an otherwise fairly steep—but not vertical—smooth limestone wall.

Good Camping at Stina

The final big drop into Stina at the Redwall pour-off comes fifteen minutes after the Slicky Slide and is bypassed along a narrow, steeply sloping bench leading to a talus slope. Once, our descent of this precarious tumble was greatly complicated by the angry attention of a swarm of wasps intent on stinging us to death. I have often camped at Stina, and (except for 1988) there has been plenty of water and good camping on smooth, level, friendly Muav ledges.

This lovely, friendly campsite that I have used so often and of which I have such pleasant memories was, on a later trip, almost the death of me.

It was the second night of the 1990 Sierra Club trip around Powell Plateau, the first having been spent on Swamp Point in intermittent heavy rain. The descent of Saddle Canyon was uneventful except for two almost-over-your-head pools, one of which wasn't expected. We arrived at the Stina campsite in late afternoon, under an overcast sky, that produced a few sprinkles from time to time. We had plenty of time for the usual nesting procedures.

Some of us camped on the high ground between the Stina and Saddle drainages, some camped lower down between the drainages, and some went on down around the corner to flat ground there. I chose my usual spot in the Stina drainage under an overhang. After dinner, as the cleanup was being finished, it was obvious the weather was deteriorating. I was thinking about moving my camping spot to the big flat rock that had served as our dinner table when it was chosen as the place on which to put all the food bags. I stayed where I was.

As darkness approached, we were able to watch an especially violent display of lightning up near Muav Saddle. The sky up there was black. I counted the seconds after each flash to try to tell whether the storm was moving our way, or not. Gradually, the flashes occurred close enough together that the second flash would come before the first boom, and the third flash before the second boom. I tried juggling the numbers for a while and then gave up.

I was under my overhang by the time it was dark, and as quiet descended I could hear a faint roar—like a strong wind blowing through the trees. It was soon clear that this noise was not being produced by wind. It was being created by a large amount of water seeking lower ground. A flash flood was on its way down Saddle Canyon. Even knowing that, I felt no apprehension—secure in my belief I was in a different drainage. Rather, the thought of watching a flash flood safely from close by created a sense of exhilaration.

False Security
The insistence of the roar—slowly growing steadily louder—chased away all thoughts except those relating to what was soon to happen. But there were several reasons why I knew I must be safe. (1) I was in a different drainage. (If I had looked at a map, I would have seen that the Stina Canyon drainage itself was substantial, and not knowing exactly where the storm was centered should have stirred a faint alarm within me.) (2) The Saddle Canyon drainage was small. After all, it was only about 3 miles to Muav Saddle. (If I had looked at a map, I would have seen a sizable tributary canyon to Saddle Canyon.) (3) Besides, the bulk of the rain had probably fallen on the other side of Muav Saddle, anyway.

I feel stupid writing down those reasons, but my brain created them, saying essentially, "Stop worrying, get to sleep." I was stupid then, too, for allowing myself to believe them, but I did—wholeheartedly. Soon the character of the roar changed markedly. I could hear a splashing sound. The water was going over the 90-foot falls just upcanyon from us. Then someone was yelling, "Here comes the water." This got my attention. I thought, "This is great, I've got to watch this."

I hurriedly shed my sleeping bag, put on my tennis shoes, stood up, retrieved my flashlight from the top of my pack, and started toward the sound of approaching water. After two steps, I was suddenly knee-deep in surging water. With a feeling of being betrayed by events, I quickly moved to the cliff on my left. It provided support and the water was moving less swiftly there. The water rose a few more inches as I struggled up Stina, but then subsided as I moved across the flow to dry land on the other side. Fortunately for me, there was no water coming down Stina. Unfortunately, where I had camped was in an overflow floodplain for the Saddle Canyon drainage.

Out of Danger

Now that I was out of danger, I moved up the hill to where the four smartest ones had put their tents and two of the less smart had also sought refuge. These six, plus el stupido, made seven. Three others were still unaccounted for. The water was still roaring so yelling was only marginally successful as a means of communication. It was better to count flashlight beams. Soon we could count two, and that meant only one person was missing. After maybe ten minutes—it seemed like an hour—that person was found, too. There was joy in Mudville that night. Now we only had to worry about what was lost—not who. At that point I curled up in a donated sleeping bag under a donated plastic tarp and went to sleep. We could take inventory in the morning.

Morning Light

Water was still running in the morning and as I moved down toward the center of the previous night's action, I saw that the food was safe. Then I saw a "something" over where all my stuff had been. Something covered with debris. It was my pack—just where I had left it. There had been a foot-high ledge above my sleeping spot, and a foot-high flat rock at the edge of that ledge. I had put my pack on that rock, and the bottom foot of the pack frame, where I usually put my stuff sack, was bare—only tubing and webbing. Thus, the bottom of my pack was about 3 feet above where I had been sleeping. The waterborne debris came 8 inches up on my pack. Water got inside and stuff was soggy, but the main victims were the zippers. Zippers hate silt.

All that I lost was the stuff I have around me when I sleep. Ground cloth, pad, sleeping bag, boots—to hold down two corners of my ground cloth—plastic tarp, socks, shirt, stuff bag—with spare clothes, including my Patagonia jacket—cup and spoon ready for breakfast, and my walking stick.

The other victims fared better. Stan had yanked his tent out of the path of rushing water at the last minute and didn't even lose a tent peg. In the night Bob thought he had lost his pack, boots, and camera, but the light of day produced all three. The pack had washed only a short distance before jamming in the rocks, and his boots and plastic-wrapped camera were inside. From the evidence left behind, it appeared the water had been about 4 feet deep where it went by our camp.

Search and Regroup

While I was eating breakfast, I began a search for my lost items. I went up and down the stretch of creek below where I had been sleeping at least ten times and each time I found something. Socks, shirt, stuff bag—empty, spoon, ground cloth. I found everything beginning with *s* except my sleeping bag. Except for having no boots, I was in good shape—and I did have a pair of old sneakers.

But what about the trip? The previous night had been the first of twelve. Should we go on? Retreating might well be more difficult than going on—those almost-over-your-head pools could be scoured out and be very difficult with their steep upstream sides. The only sensible thing to do seemed to be to go on until it was apparent we couldn't. If my sneakers began to give out, there were other pairs in the group I could wear. So, under a bright sun our battered group continued.

The first thing found was a fragment of my sleeping bag sticking out of the rocks and mud. I regret to say I left it. But it really wasn't mine any more. The legal theorists have said that trash belongs to the last person who touches it, and Mother Nature clearly had her hands on it after I did. My Patagonia jacket was next. It looked like a dead purple retriever—and weighed about as much. When Jarold handed it to me, it felt like it weighed 25 pounds. Washing it in the still running chocolaty creek reduced that somewhat—to 20, perhaps. Jarold offered to carry it for me. That was a double gift for I had already borrowed one of his walking sticks.

One Boot Returns

After about 2 miles the creek finally spit out one of my boots. That raised my morale greatly. With one boot I was ready for anything, and, besides, we might find the other one. We never did, but if someone else does, it is a left hightop Red Wing Voyager. The final treasure returned to me was my ski-pole walking stick—about 2.5 miles down. Gary saw it first, stuck in among the rocks at a 45-degree angle about 4 feet above the current level of the creek. He gave it a tug to pull it out, but it wouldn't budge. Add to that the fact that we had camped last night within the domain of the 7.5-minute King Arthur Castle quad map and you have the beginning of a good story. However, Gary was eventually able to release the walking stick by removing some cobbles and wiggling it around—it was well wedged. Sadness. I like a good story.

This ends my account of our encounter with the Flashing of Saddle Canyon. Our trip ended happily and my jacket finally returned to its proper weight, though for a week after it was dry, I could still pound it against a rock and release a shower of silt. I still wear it. By the time my wife mended thirty of the pound holes she gave up and told me to throw it away. My shirt, socks and ground cloth also have pound holes. For those of you who don't know what a "pound hole" is, let me say that when a cloth item is roiling down a flashing stream it is also rolling with fist-sized—maybe football-sized—rocks that beat the cloth against the streambed. The result, when viewed against the sun, is a constellation of small pound holes.

Tapeats Creek

Back to 1981. Water came and went the next day as we proceeded down the canyon. For a while a substantial flow came above ground among cottonwoods near a 15-foot waterfall. But the main flow in Tapeats Creek doesn't come down Tapeats Creek; it comes down the canyon from Tapeats Cave. That's not to say flash floods don't come down Tapeats Creek. They do and I've seen one, but the source of all the creek water is near the cave.

Travel was not as easy when we reached the stream. There is enough water and a steep-enough gradient that you don't cross with impunity. Sometimes in late spring and early summer, I don't dare cross it—period. A hundred yards or so of narrows is another place to be cautious. In the fall you can wade the narrows, and we did—except for Benson, who preferred to pioneer a high-level traverse of the cliffs on the west side. It took him quite a while but it is nice to know such a bypass exists.

Designated Camp Sites

The first of two sets of Tapeats Creek Designated Camp Sites is just below the junction of Tapeats Creek and Thunder River. The second set is on the beach at the mouth of the creek. The thousands of rafters who visit Thunder River every summer have turned a good trail from the River into a highway. But now in the fall there were very few boat visitors. The only people we saw were National Park Service workers trying to reduce "multiple trailing" by planting chollas to block unwanted pathways. It seems to work.

About the same time a year later in about the same place, I ran into another NPS crew milling around in the brush with clipboards. When I asked one young lady what was going on, she said, "It's a sociological experiment to see how long it takes before one ranger flips out and kills another in the course of such tedious work." They were running a transect and counting all plants and plant types 0.5 meter on each side of their line.

Scorpion Terrace

We wanted to get over to Stone Creek for camp so we didn't dawdle much on the way down. Except for lunch at Scorpion Terrace, where there is sort of a mini Niagara—a trio of falls in a U pouring into a narrow slot forming a cauldron of foaming white water. I call it Scorpion Terrace because it was there on one stormy night, complete with flash flood, that a friend was stung by a scorpion and had a very bad time of it—we had to shake her to get her to breathe.

Jumping Fish Falls

While resting there, Mattox said he saw a huge fish trying to jump the falls. This is a typical Mattox trick—a subtle form of one-upmanship—so we humored him by saying "yeah," "wow," "how big was it?" until finally there really was a big fish trying to jump the falls—2 feet long, at least. After much more fish watching than we had time for, we were rewarded by seeing the "try, try again" philosophy eventually succeed.

From this falls it is only two creek crossings—or none if you contour around instead of crossing—to the place where the Stone Creek trail leaves Tapeats Creek and follows an emerging shelf of Bass Limestone. At this same place, the trail to the mouth of Tapeats Creek goes up the corresponding shelf on the other side of the creek.

Stone Creek Trail

Upstream from the point above the Tapeats delta, the trail to Stone Creek comes and goes, but following the bench is easy. There are at least two ways off the nose at Stone Creek, but they are more easily found from below. We eventually gave up trying to find one from above and followed the now distinct trail around into and down Stone Creek. The sun had gone from the falls so we took only the briefest of showers before going down to camp by the Colorado River.

From now on—except for the 0.25 mile to the mouth of Galloway—it would be new territory for all of us. That is always exciting. We didn't expect to be turned back by anything insurmountable, but the unknown always adds a special flavor to an activity. I wondered, though, about how difficult it was going to be. Don didn't seem to care much one way or the other—he just takes what comes—and Robert, I expect, was hoping for "almost" impossible barriers to overcome. He liked his physical medicine strong.

Route to Bedrock Canyon

It was easy going along the River for the first hour or so, although it would certainly be more difficult when the water is higher. Getting to Bedrock Canyon is a process of avoiding being cliffed out by following a rising diabase sill, then climbing down to the River through some rather crumbly stuff (Hotauta Conglomerate?), and then taking another ramp into Bedrock. We crossed the canyon at the mouth, entering a little upcanyon on the north side and leaving by climbing the nose on the south side to the same ramp we entered on. The water in Bedrock didn't taste very good, so we went to the River to pick up extra in case we had to make a dry camp farther on. The next drainage, about 0.5 mile farther, had a fine flow of good water with dunking pools, so we had lunch there. I call this canyon Switch Level Canyon because we entered it on the Bass and left it on the Tonto.

128 Mile Canyon

So far we had stayed below the Tapeats, but now we had to climb up on top of it. We found a burro trail that made it easy to contour around the gullies and into 128 Mile Canyon—our goal for the day. The way into 128 Mile is via the first side canyon on the north about 0.5 mile in from the point. It is opposite a steep exit chute. The top half of the descent is over talus, and there is one pour-off that looks formidable until you get to the edge and can look over. Bensen hiked down to the River to look for good campsites but there were none—not even on the delta. We ended up camping where we had entered the canyon. It was a fine place—a good flow of tasty water and an easy route back up to the Tonto.

The following year I was making the same trip in the reverse direction as part of a lengthwise traverse of the Grand Canyon, and found an easy way off the upstream nose to the mouth of 128 Mile where a deep, warm, grungy pool was backed up behind the sandbar at the mouth.

Route to Forster Rapids

The next morning around 8:30 we climbed back up onto the Tonto and followed the slowly descending Tapeats. We had lunch, still on the Tonto, just downstream from Fossil Canyon. A little farther on, the Tonto disappears and we could hike along the River. An obnoxious travertine obstacle gave us a headache for a while but mostly it involved a lot of boulder hopping. We were rewarded, though, by finding a few beers and sodas. Around 4:00 P.M. we reached the sand- and rock bar at Forster Rapids and made camp. It is possible to get from 128 Mile to Blacktail in one day, but we didn't want to move that fast.

The night we spent at Forster Rapids is memorable for two reasons. It was the night we discovered a revolutionary new way for the National Park Service to make money, and it was the night I won my engineering battle with the ringtails but lost the war.

There was a wintry feel to the air and we were in our sleeping bags even before it was dark. That's one of the problems with late-fall hiking—you may spend twelve to fourteen hours in the sack. That is too long, and as we were lying there wide awake, we considered what we could do about it. One good idea was to get a coupon book from the Backcountry Office entitling you to shorter winter nights. But we decided that if and when the park service got around to issuing them, they would be too expensive—and after all, the long nights would not be so tiresome if you could have a campfire.

"Cheery Little Fire" Coupons

Then the light bulb went on over our heads. All we had to do was get the park service to sell a book of coupons, each entitling the bearer to a "cheery little fire"—CLF for short. After lengthy discussion we decided that, to prevent hoarding and scalping, these coupons would have to be dated and non-transferable. There would be one coupon for each night of inner Canyon camping; a book of five would cost $5.00. A notation on the Backcountry Office copy of the permit would show these coupons had been purchased, so the park service would not necessarily have to react to every fire it saw.

A year later I described this CLF coupon idea to a park superintendent friend of my brother's as if it were fact. He got more and more agitated the farther I got in my story. Finally, he interrupted and explained such an idea was impossible—there was no way monies collected in that fashion could get into the general coffers, and the fellows at the Backcountry Office who sold me the coupons had a scam going. He remained agitated long after I told him I had made up the whole story.

Outwitting the Ringtail

Fantasizing about CLF coupons is a right-brain activity. Dealing with cacomistles is strictly left brain. We knew we were in for trouble from the very beginning. The campsite we had chosen was covered with "wee beastie" tracks. I was sure they were cacomistle tracks—too big for mice and too small for other worse things. For the uninitiated, a cacomistle is a relative of the raccoon. It is half tail, looks like a weasel, and is commonly called a ringtailed cat. A Time/Life book on the Grand Canyon calls it "beautiful, intelligent, playful, and sometimes even affectionate." That may be, but the book forgot to use the additional word *omnivorous*. But I knew that from previous encounters. Over the years I have unintentionally fed them enough to have bought all available affection. But I have none for them; they are pests that rob you blind.

Knowing ringtails were about, I cantilevered my ski-pole walking stick out from a chest-high boulder as far as I could get it by putting a large rock on the thick end and wedging smaller ones in under the pole to bring the thin end farther off the ground. Unfortunately, the rocks were well rounded and my construction was barely stable—yet it seemed serviceable. I hung my food from the end of the pole. Both Mattox and Benson had seen the trouble I had with the construction and bet it wouldn't last the night. During the night I had several opportunities to check on my ski pole; all was well. My main problem came in protecting my fruit cocktail.

Usually I put the dehydrated fragments in my cup, add water, and cover with a flat rock. Tonight, anticipating trouble, I inverted our cook pot over the cup and put the flat rock on top of the pot. Around midnight there was a rustling and rattling around the pot, and eventually I was wrenched from my sleep to check it out. I was afraid that whatever was about would push the pot around enough so the rock would fall off, or the cup would upset under the pot, or perhaps both pot and cup would fall off the big rock they were on.

Ringtail Face-off

Checking things out with my flashlight, I found myself face-to-face with a ringtail. Without my glasses I have to get quite close to whatever I'm looking at to see it, so our heads were no more than 20 inches apart—the ringtail was pushing on one side of the pot and me holding the other. I tried to scare it with something mild like "scat," but it wasn't the least bit intimidated. It made its chittering chipmunk noise and looked angry. Finally I let loose with a multidecibel "shoo" that woke both Don and Robert, and with a final snarl this affectionate beast left me alone for the rest of the night.

The next morning everything was exactly as it should be. My fruit cocktail was untouched; my food bags still hung from the end of the walking stick. Everything was intact, that is, except my food. It was hanging some distance from my sleeping bag, and since I had taken my breakfast out the night before, I didn't check it carefully until we were packing up. Then I discovered that these "beautiful, intelligent, affectionate" creatures had foiled me again.

They had jumped up from below—about 3 feet—hung on by their front claws, and chinned themselves up to where they could chew through the lowest food bag. This simple act rewarded them with a shower of powdered milk, cereal, noodles, and jerky. The frenzy of footprints in what remained of the stuff that had fallen on them outlined the drama through which I had slept.

A thought occurred to me—perhaps the ringtail that attacked my fruit cocktail was only a diversion to distract me from what the rest of the troops were doing. Of course, they didn't get *all* my food, so I still had much better than starvation rations ahead of me. But I had lost something more precious than food—my pride.

Long Tapeats Sidewalks

Our sleeping bags were so wet with dew the next morning that we waited for the sun—which, luckily, hit us early. The going was easy. We climbed up on a Tapeats ledge for a while and then dropped back down just before 122 Mile Canyon. Both Fossil and Forster Rapids had long Tapeats ledges at water level that were like sidewalks with watery mouths snapping at us from the gutter.

Blacktail Canyon

In Conquistador Aisle we climbed with the rising Tapeats and again picked up a burro trail that made travel easy and fast. We had lunch on the beach at the Blacktail Canyon then climbed down the nose on the downstream side. Water was flowing at the mouth but not up in the drainage above the chockstone. The same was true in 1982 and 1988. We explored a little and then had an early dinner before pushing on a mile or so.

In 1989, a boatman showed me a nautiloid fossil in the lower part of the canyon. It is on the stream-side face of a boulder—4 or 5 feet in diameter—on the west side of the drainage (stream right), about 100 yards or so up from the mouth. The fossil is about five or six inches long.

Although we thought we could get down to the River at Explorers Monument, we weren't sure, and since the time to our next water was uncertain, we wanted to shorten tomorrow's run. The route back to the Tonto is up a series of ledges about 100 yards upriver from the mouth of Blacktail.

On the 1990 Sierra Club trip, we went upstream from Blacktail along the River for almost 1.5 miles to a fine beach just north of a big mushroom rock—possibly 40 feet high—which even shows up on the 7.5-minute Explorers Monument Quad map as a tiny circle of 2200-foot contour about 0.25 mile south of the second R in RIVER. The route to the Tonto is up the drainage behind this rock.

The Tonto rises in two steps as you go south from Blacktail. Two faults cross the river here—the Monument Fold. At the southernmost of these faults we got a dramatic view of folded Tapeats on the other side. The going got much more difficult as we climbed and remained so until we were opposite Elves Chasm. In 1988, however, we discovered a burro trail close to the edge of the lowest cliff. We found no water until we came to a small, sad, grungy pool in the drainage at Explorers Monument.

Route to River

We did, indeed, find a way off the Tonto to the River in a notch just 0.2 mile west of the main drainage. There is a little Tapeats to go through, but the talus rises a long way to meet it. Still, having watched chocolate syrup flowing by for the last two days, we decided that the sad grungy water we had was no worse than the sad grungy water we could get. So we strained out the dead bugs and made do.

While Don and I rested in the heat of the afternoon, Robert tried to climb the Redwall via the Monument fault ravine. The crumbly cliffs stopped him, though, and he returned disappointed. Later in the afternoon, as the shadows lengthened, we hiked on around the bend for about 0.5 mile.

Here we made a dry camp, used the rest of our good water, and boiled the smelly stuff we had brought with us from Explorers Monument.

While I was on a River trip in 1989, I found a route through the Tapeats from the River to the Tonto in the drainage by the lower camp just before Elves Chasm. Annerino mentions such a route on page 289 of his book *Hiking the Grand Canyon*. To find this route from on top, you must look for a rectangular white marking on the Redwall. It looks like a window—roughly 3 feet wide by 4 feet tall—and is approximately halfway up the wall in a small bay. The route begins in about the middle of the upstream side of the bay. I put in many ducks, so look for them alongside the burro trails as well as at the edge. The Tonto takeoff is down a 3-foot-wide chimney for about 20 feet to a shelf. From there you descend to a ledge and then work your way along a sequence of ledges to a talus slope on the downstream side of the bay. The talus gets you to the bed of the drainage that leads to the beach. We were going to use this route in 1990, but we found ample water in pot-holes in the drainage on top.

Good Flowing Water

We started early the next day. Don promised us a hot, dry day, and he wanted to hike as much as possible in the cool of early morning. In about fifteen minutes we crossed a flowing stream. We dumped the bad stuff and filled up with the good stuff, trying not to think of how much nicer a camp we would have had if we had just hiked a few more minutes the evening before. Oh well, that's life.

This water was also flowing the next October as well as in June 1988; there was burro scat around, so it is probably dependable. The existence of this spring makes this loop doable in hot weather and is so crucial I call it Key Spring. However, the last two times I camped there I remember a subsequent daylong bout with diarrhea. Since we had treated our water with iodine and Clorox in one case and filtered it in another, I am sure the problem is chemical. I do not remember what happened in 1981. Because of the possibility of having to retrace your steps to the River access point near Explorers Monument if Key Spring is dry, I recommend trying to find this access point as you pass it.

Good Burro Trail

The rest of the day was as Don promised: in and out and up and down. But a burro trail helped enormously. The biggest pain was Walthenberg Canyon. It seemed to go on forever. We spent three hours getting from the downstream point to the upstream one—a distance of less than 0.5 river mile. The ramp into Hakatai Canyon from northwest of the mouth was a little hard to find from the top, but within half an hour we had found it and were heading down to water. We found it by going down the east side of a small cleft. We had planned to camp at Shinumo Creek, but since there was flowing water in Hakatai we decided to stay there. I went down to the River, Robert went upcanyon to try to find the end of Bass's trail, and Don took a nap.

Hakatai Bass Camp

Even in 1982 there was quite a bit of memorabilia still left in Hakatai—tent platforms, cooking stuff, and of course, mining stuff. By 1988 the tent platforms were gone. The mines near our camp were very small, though it is conceivable that gravel has filled them up to some extent. Near the mouth of the creek, you can climb up to a saddle overlooking the River where the old cable was anchored. Robert found the Hakatai end of the Bass Trail almost at the upper end of the drainage. At first he thought it was a burro trail, but as he followed it he found evidence of trail construction.

Route to Burro Canyon

The next day we declined to use the trail Robert had found and instead took the familiar ravine more or less in line with the ramp we used to enter Hakatai. It's the first ravine on the east, upstream of the river. There is only one obstacle: a large chockstone. Coming on it from below, we felt sure we could climb it with our packs on—that is, until we tried. But it is easier to climb up than down. After this it was smooth sailing over to Burro Canyon. The route into Burro is down a small ramp under a cliff and along a wide place between the 3,360- and 3,440-foot contours about 0.7 mile southeast of Fan Island. As you turn the corner to head north before descending to the bed of Burro, you may intersect the east end of Bass's Hakatai trail. Our trail continued on across Burro Canyon, up a ramp, and around and down into Shinumo Creek.

Bass Camp Historical Site

After we crossed the creek to the east side, it was only fifteen minutes or so to Bass Camp Historical Site. For information about Bass and Bass Camp, see chapter 2, Tuna Creek/Shinumo Creek Loop. We had lunch on the Shinumo Quartzite slabs just upstream from Bass Camp. There's plenty of water for a cooling dip if you don't mind minnows nibbling your toes.

Route to Tapeats Spring

It is an easy and beautiful three hours from these quartzite slabs up Shinumo Creek to White Creek and up White to the Tapeats narrows and a lovely spring. I often camp on the Tapeats slickrock above the chockstone at the spring, and Don and I and Robert did this time, too. Muav Canyon (White Creek flows in Muav Canyon) was dry above the chockstone, but water reappeared near the top of the Tapeats. It also reappeared in the Muav at the top of an extensive, though unnecessary, bypass where an overhanging rock and smooth Muav ledges can provide good camping. By this time our route had joined the North Bass Trail, and two hours after we left the Tapeats spring, we reached the bottom of the Redwall climb—well used and marked. Harvey Butchart calls this a "surprising" Redwall route, and indeed it is. Fortunately, in this case "surprising" doesn't mean "difficult." On top, the route crosses three drainages from the west before dropping back into Muav Canyon. A well-marked, though brushy, trail leads across these drainages now.

Route to Muav Saddle

For the next mile or so we followed the creek to the 5,692-foot benchmark. The North Bass Trail, now a well-beaten path, leaves the drainage at a spot where a log has been placed across the drainage. You will have passed other logs similarly placed, so be observant. The trail climbs steeply up the Hermit Shale to the base of the Coconino. Eventually we reached the main route, which contours along the top of the shale to Muav Saddle. A little to the south on this trail there is a mapped spring that can be useful if you are hurting for water.

Back to Swamp Point

A few hundred yards more and we were once again on Muav Saddle, having successfully concluded our circumambulation of Powell Plateau. All in all it was easier than I expected—quite easy, I would say. Another forty-five-minute climb up the trail and we were at the car—a seven-hour trip from the Tapeats chockstone. I remember hoping the car would start.

Deer Creek Falls.

4 Tapeats Creek/ Kanab Creek Loop

An expression of the feeling of gratitude at seeing
the approaching end of a difficult hike:
"All's well that ends."

JIM HICKERSON

Length
Six days, plus layover day(s), if any.

Water
Fairly reliable spring at Redwall/Supai contact for trip down.

Quad Maps
7.5-minute maps
Tapeats Amphitheater
Fishtail Mesa
Jumpup Point
Kanab Point

Roadhead
Indian Hollow Campground.

ROUTE TO ROADHEAD

Via Jacob Lake
Mileage
0.0   Go south from Jacob Lake on Highway 67 toward North Rim.
0.2   After 0.2 mile turn right onto Forest Service (FS) Road 461. There is a blue-and-white sign here with an arrow saying CAMPING. After the turn you will see a sign saying BIG SPRINGS 16. Be careful, though, to avoid the service road that turns off about 100 yards before the one you want. In what follows it is assumed that you have just turned off Highway 67 onto FS 461.
4.5   After 4.3 miles turn left at a fork and down a steep hill.
5.4   After 0.9 mile you meet FS 462 and turn right. It is now 10 miles to Big Springs.
8.4   After 3.0 miles you meet FS 422 from Fredonia and turn left.
14.8   After 6.4 miles you pass Big Springs Ranger Station.
19.6   After 4.8 miles turn right onto FS 425. You will now see a sign saying THUNDER RIVER TRAILHEAD 10.
27.7   After 8.1 miles turn right onto FS 232. A sign reads INDIAN HOLLOW CAMPGROUND 5.
32.7   After 5.0 miles you reach the end of the road about 0.25 mile beyond the campground.

The total time from Jacob Lake is an hour to an hour and a quarter.

Via Fredonia, Arizona
Turn right onto FS 422 just outside Fredonia on the way to Jacob Lake. After

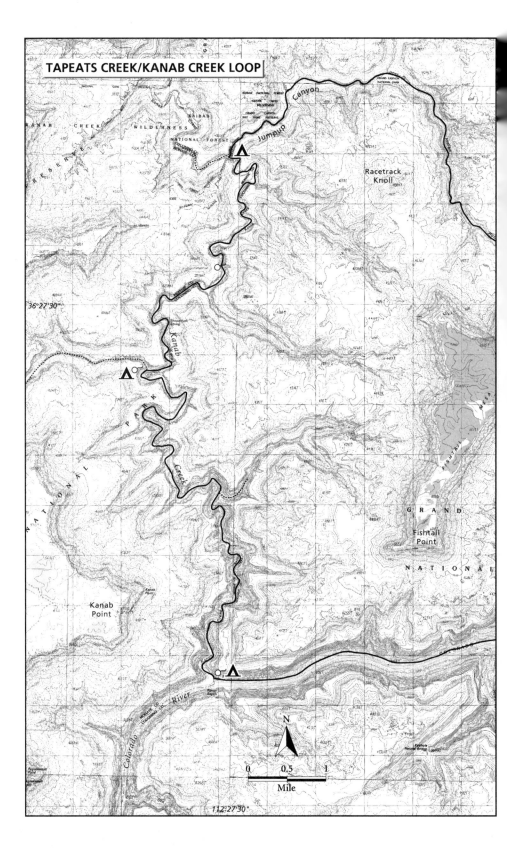

TAPEATS CREEK/KANAB CREEK LOOP

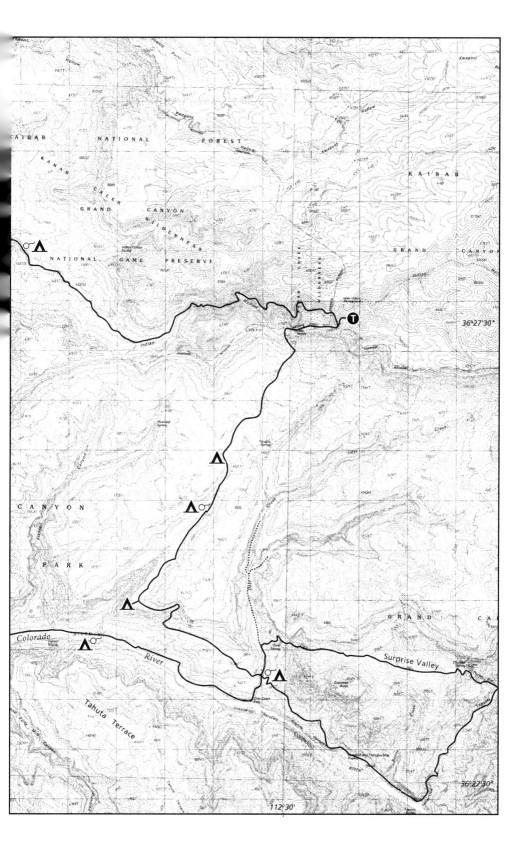

about 22 miles you meet FS 462. Go straight on FS 422. After passing this intersection, proceed as described above.

TWO SETS OF HIKING TIMES

I hiked this loop in each direction one fall and collected the two sets of times shown in the following table. You can see that sometimes they are quite different. This difference is due principally to the fact that one trip was made in hot weather and one in cool weather. The hot-weather hike went to Kanab Creek first and the cool-weather hike went to Deer Creek first. Rest stops are self-perpetuating when it is hot and self-limiting when it is cold. Also, hiking times are lengthened considerably in hot weather because of time spent dunking in cooling pools found along the way.

HIKING TIMES

Use Areas	Location	Elapsed Times Between Locations (hours)	
		Cool	Hot
▲	Car	1:45	2:15
▲ AZ9	Ghost Rock	:45	1:30
▲ AZ9	Cranberry Spring	1:00	1:15
▲ AZ9	Point overlooking river	1:30	1:30
	Base of Talus	1:00	1:15
▲ AX9	Deer Creek Campsite	:15	:30
	Deer Creek Falls	1:45	1:45
	Siesta Spring	1:15	1:00
▲ LA9	Fishtail Canyon	3:45	5:00
▲ LA9	Mouth of Kanab Canyon	3:00	3:30
	Slide of Susurrus	3:00	4:15
▲ LA9	Scotty's Hollow	:45	1:00
▲ LA9	Overhanging Spring	3:00	3:15
▲ LA9	Jumpup/Kanab confluence	1:15	1:45
	Indian Hollow/Jumpup confluence	:15	:15
	Obstacle Pool*	:45	4:00
▲ LA9	Big Pool Camp	3:30	4:00
	Base of Coconino	:30	:45
	Top of Coconino	2:00	2:00
▲	Car		

*Time of Obstacle Pool does not include time to pass it, which will be from thirty minutes to an hour depending on size of pool and size of party.

ROUTE DETAILS

This loop takes you to three of the "must-see" areas of Grand Canyon National Park: Tapeats Creek, with the fascinating waterworks at Thunder River; Deer Creek, with the deep narrow gorge and beautiful falls; and Kanab Canyon, with the 1,200-foot walls and scenic delights like Scotty's Hollow.

I think of this loop as taking seven days, but it could be done by fast hikers in six or even blitzed in five. To maximize pleasure I recommend the seven days or even eight or nine. The extra day(s) can be spent camping at Tapeats Creek or exploring the upper reaches of Deer Creek or Scotty's Hollow.

I will describe this loop as going to Deer Creek first because I think this is the easier way. Even though it means a long day, I recommend the extra effort required to get to Deer Creek the first day because that is where the assured water is. But three good places are shown on the map if you decide to camp en route. Usually the hike to Deer Creek requires about six hours, including rest stops but not lunch, and in that time you will travel about 7 miles and descend about 3,000 feet.

It is about a five-minute walk along the trail from car to rim, and I am never quite prepared for the suddenness of the view. If you have camped at your car, this will be the first verification of the fact that: (1) you are in the right place and (2) the canyon is still there. A great deal of your route can be seen from the rim, so try to identify the 40-foot-high east-facing, overhang called Ghost Rock and the drainage you will take to get down to the top of the Redwall.

Rim Takeoff

The trail, which is the original horse trail to Thunder River, angles down through the limestone and contours west along the top the Toroweap Limestone for about 0.5 mile to a break. Follow the zigzags of the trail down through the Coconino until you can angle down and west to a small red knoll of Hermit Shale. Keep angling down and west until you can find a convenient gully to take you down to the top of the Supai Formation. This broad expanse is called the Esplanade.

Ghost Rock

I can't place Ghost Rock on the map exactly, but I think it is either at or near the small sock-shaped bit of 4,800-foot contour, with a benchmark of 4,811 feet. You won't find any water at Ghost Rock unless rainfall has collected in pools on the Supai, but it is still a good place to camp.

Cowboys and Indians

Ghost Rock provides a small terrace protected by the overhang where people seeking shelter have camped over the years. Except for the large "ghostly" figures painted on the east-facing wall and a small metate, I have seen no evidence of Indian occupancy. There is, however, a great deal of evidence of cowboy occupancy—storage cans, a horseshoe, and fragments of leather tack. Possibly the pockmarks left by bullets fired at the ghost figures can be attributed to them as well.

From the late 1800s until only recently, ranchers brought their cattle down to the Esplanade on one of the several trails connecting it with the rim and left them there to graze during the summer. The remnants of these constructed trails can still be seen. They built other trails so they could take their horses down from the Esplanade to graze on the top of the Redwall. Good examples of both can be found in 150 Mile Canyon.

There are other cowboy camps on the Esplanade besides the one at Ghost Rock—one between Kanab Canyon and 150 Mile Canyon and one between 150 Mile Canyon and Tuckup Canyon. The latter camp is under a large overhang covered on its underside with elaborate pictographs.

To continue on to Deer Creek you go south, working your way down through the upper Supai layers, to the head of a drainage leading down to the canyon between Fishtail Canyon and Deer Creek. It is unnamed on the map, but Harvey Butchart credits David Mortenson with giving it the name Cranberry Canyon when, on Thanksgiving Day, Mortenson first used this route to get to Deer Creek.

Cranberry Canyon

Cranberry Canyon is an expression of the Sinyala fault, which extends southwest across the Colorado River even beyond Havasu Creek. The fault also continues northeast across Deer Creek. There are two fault ravines leading down to Cranberry Canyon. I use the western one because it is closer. You will find a small, dripping spring behind a big boulder just below the spot where the two fault ravines meet at the Redwall/Supai contact. This spring has provided me with water every time I have been there—once in summer and four times in fall—and gives a quart of water in about ten minutes. In 1988 we also found water by a redbud on the Redwall in some heavy greenery on the west side of Cranberry.

Continue on down the drainage from the spring until it is convenient to climb up to the east onto the broad terrace lying on top of the Redwall. It is easy going out to the point overlooking the Colorado River. This point is also a good place to camp. There is no water, but there is a great view.

The Redwall Limestone forms an imposing cliff, and despite the thousands of miles of Redwall in the Canyon, there are very few breaks in it where a hiker can get through. Like the descent to Deer Creek, the great majority of these breaks are along faults. Continue east from the overlook at the mouth of Cranberry along the top of the Redwall for about 0.5 mile to the sharp bend in the Supai wall about 0.2 mile south of the "4635T" elevation point. The chute you want goes down steeply in a series of steps that unfortunately blocks the view of where you want to go, so you may think you are off route. Once this happened to me and I went on to the next chute—which looked even worse. The second time around, the correct chute look much better. (I think the correct chute is the one below the "3" in the 3,400-foot contour designation up against the Supai cliff.)

Redwall Break

The chute is narrow and steep, but no rope is needed unless you want one for lowering packs. Be very careful to avoid knocking rocks loose. If you do, yell *"rock"* as loudly as you can so those below you have some time to get out of the way. A series of steep pitches, amounting to 100 feet or so, leads to a drop-off; here you must contour around to the right (west) for 50 yards or so to the top of a big talus slope. Go down it carefully because the whole slope seems above the angle of repose. Still, if you think the talus slope is

104

steep, try looking over the eastern edge. There the rubble forms an almost vertical cliff. It looks scary.

Descend until you can cross the drainage safely near the 3,700-foot contour a little above the dry lake bed to the east. A word about crossing drainages cut deeply into rubble. *Do not* attempt to climb up or down them. Instead, contour in and out, stepping very carefully on the smaller boulders.

Contour around and down to the dry lake bed and go over a saddle to the south. It is tempting to go over a lower saddle to the east, but it leads to steep terrain that is tedious to climb through. After crossing the higher saddle, pick your way down the other side to the flats 300 feet below and then turn east and work your way down the hillside to Deer Creek. When you get to the creek, you will be near the spot where it cuts through the Tapeats Sandstone to enter the narrows. According to the Grand Canyon National Park Backcountry Management Plan, you are permitted to camp anywhere here as long as it is upstream from the "upper end of the narrows."

Purify Water
Unfortunately, I must caution you to purify the Deer Creek water, as several people I know, including me, have become sick after drinking it. In the summer inconsiderate hikers and visitors from boat parties bathe and wash their hair in the creek. As a result there is considerable soapy pollution and fecal contamination of the stream. There is less bathing in Tapeats Creek because it is colder, but I would purify that water, too.

Deer Creek
The water for Deer Creek comes from two springs. One is in the main bed about 0.5 mile from the upper end of the narrows; the other, called Deer Spring on the quad map, forms a falls in the cliff on the western edge of Surprise Valley. Coming from Surprise Valley by trail, you can hear this falls long before you get a chance to see it. The trail has now been rerouted to pass near the falls, and there is a short spur trail to them.

Round Trip to Tapeats Creek
If you have the time for it, I certainly recommend the nine-hour hike to Thunder River and Tapeats Creek and back. But should you wish to camp over there and spend more time exploring, be advised that Tapeats Creek is a Designated Site Use Area. This means camping is restricted to specific sites: namely, to the Upper and Lower Designated Sites (AW7 and AW8). You should request permission for use of one of these campsites when you apply for your permit. The Upper Sites are distributed along the west side of Tapeats Creek downstream from its confluence with the Thunder River, and the Lower Sites are on the beaches by the Colorado River. In addition, the whole Thunder River drainage, from Tapeats Creek to the lip of Surprise Valley, is closed to camping.

Route to Tapeats Creek
The route to Tapeats Creek through Surprise Valley begins with the trail up the west side of Deer Creek, which crosses the creek under some huge cottonwoods by an inviting pool. After crossing, you follow the trail up through

the rocks to the lip of Surprise Valley. You pass the spur trail to the falls at Deer Spring, which is the last water until you get to the Thunder River in about two hours.

Surprise Valley

The trip through Surprise Valley is mainly uphill and, unless you get an early start, *hot* in the summer months—May through September. Once, on a summer's afternoon, I urgently needed something with which to dig a cat hole and unwisely picked up a dark piece of rock. I blistered all the fingers that touched that rock. My thermometer read 135 degrees at ground level but, fortunately, only 95 degrees waist-high. But it isn't always hot in Surprise Valley. Once we hiked through with our boots going squish, squish, squish. An extensive thunderstorm had dumped an inch of water over the whole valley in just a few minutes.

Slump

Surprise Valley, and the smaller valley and dry lake bed that you crossed earlier in getting to Deer Creek, represent a spectacular geological event. According to Ford, Huntoon, Billingsley, and Breed (see the article "Rock Movement and Mass Wastage in the Grand Canyon" from the book *Geology of the Grand Canyon*), they are the result of a huge rotational landslide or slump. Visualize a segment of Canyon wall, from the Bright Angel Shale on the bottom to the Esplanade on the top, that is 0.5 to 1.5 miles wide and 2,000 feet thick, extending from the Thunder River on the east to Cranberry Canyon on the west. Suddenly this hunk of wall slips on the shale, breaks loose from its moorings, and rotates, with the bottom portion moving out and away as the top portion falls. It is possible that the shale was lubricated by water backed up behind the lava dams farther downstream. In any case this huge landslide dammed the Colorado River at a point just below Deer Creek, which you can see on your way to Kanab Canyon.

The results of the slump are very visible in Surprise Valley. For example, you may have sought shade behind great Supai boulders that are about 1,500 feet below their former neighbors on the Esplanade. And off to the north, near where the Thunder River Trail heads up to the Supai rimrock, you can see segments of Redwall with their Esplanade caps below and tilted toward the cliff from which they slumped.

Thunder River

Coming from the oven of Surprise Valley, you find a startling contrast at the Thunder River. Besides being the shortest river in the world—it is 0.5 mile long—it also has the dubious distinction of being the only river in the world that flows into a creek. But whatever it is, it is cold. Standing in the shade where the downdraft of the falls blows a strong wind of evaporatively cooled spray on you, you can feel *freezing*.

Such a luxuriance of water seems out of place—a most wonderful contradiction—and it is easy to shoot a whole roll of film of just water. Water in many forms—running water, falling water, spraying water, dripping water, white foaming water, dark calm water; they are all there. It is possible to

106

climb up to the opening from which the majority of the water flows, and, indeed, spelunkers have mapped thousands of feet of cave, but it is a dangerous climb and I do not recommend it. There is considerable exposure; it is certainly not for the acrophobic. For those who are so inclined, a special permit, obtained from the resource management people, is required for any cave exploration in the park.

It is less than a mile on a good trail from Thunder Springs to Tapeats Creek and the upper campsites.

Tapeats Creek

In the early 1980s, the park service installed a solar-powered privy at the Upper Tapeats Creek campsites, so don't be surprised when you see the solar cells. The idea is to power a small fan to dehydrate the contents of the holding tank so a helicopter won't have to come in as often to replace the tank.

Just below the southernmost campsite, the main trail crosses the creek. It crosses back about 2 miles on down. However, if your trip is during high water in spring or early summer, when the flow is so deep and fast you might lose your footing and never recover it, there is another route, less used and more up and down, that stays entirely on the west side. To minimize multiple trailing, it should be used only when it is dangerous to cross the creek.

Not far above the place where the trail crosses the creek the second time, the water pours into a narrow slot in the red shale. This creates a U-shaped falls that makes a real cauldron of frothy water. If you sit on the edge and watch the falls carefully, you, like Mattox, may be rewarded by seeing a very large trout trying to jump it.

It was also near here that I saw my first hyperthermia victim. I am going to describe the incident because the condition, though not common, is so very possible and at the same time so dangerous.

Heatstroke Victim

The young man in question, about eighteen or nineteen, well built and athletic, was a member of a small group of nudists whom I first saw dunking themselves in Deer Creek on a hot afternoon in August. They had just come from Monument Point through the oven of Surprise Valley, so their nudity in the water was most natural, and I thought nothing of it. But later, when they came through camp, I could see it was no ordinary group. The leader asked about the route along the Colorado River upstream to Tapeats Creek. I described it as best I could and told him we would also be going that way the next morning and they could follow us. He went off and they camped above us on a knoll.

The next morning we passed them as they were having breakfast. In midmorning, as we were resting before taking the ramp down to the River, I saw them high up above us contouring around among the cliffs. This must have been very hot and slow and they were wearing nothing but their boots—not even a hat. The next evening we were camped near the Thunder River and the leader appeared and said one of his party was sick with an upset stomach and asked whether I had any appropriate medication. He suspected bad water. I said I didn't and he left.

The next noon when we were playing in the cauldron by the U-shaped falls, the leader appeared again saying the young man was worse, still couldn't keep any food down and had chills; would I take a look at him? They were all in clothes by this time. I did look at him but couldn't offer a diagnosis. He was shivering, though, and wanted a blanket. But he seemed to be hot, and his friends were trying to cool him off. They finally used a signal mirror to call for help, and within an hour a helicopter was there. The paramedic checked the pulse (a little fast, but not much) and checked the armpits for sweat (there was none). Not sweating is a critical part of the diagnosis of hyperthermia, and the helicopter took the young man to the clinic on the South Rim. That was the last I saw of him.

A year or so later, when I was in their part of the country, I called the man who had been their leader to find out what had happened to the young man. He told me it had been hyperthermia. When the doctor couldn't stabilize him at the clinic, he had been transferred to intensive care in the hospital at Flagstaff. The doctors there worked on him for a week before his core temperature returned to normal and stayed that way. He had nearly died and would have to be very careful about heat for the rest of his life.

What I didn't know then about hyperthermia—and the reason I have described an occurrence of it at such length—is that it is so easy to misread the symptoms.

How can the victim's sensation be one of cold when he is overdosing on heat? The answer is that usually the blood is in the capillaries near the surface trying to give up heat to the sweating exterior, but if the body can't get rid of the heat fast enough, it gives up and says "why bother." The capillaries are shut down, the blood is withdrawn to the core, and the patient's sensation is one of cold.

That ends the digression. But remember, if you see someone in the heat of summer who feels cold and is not sweating, get help immediately because that person may be near death.

Route to Stone Creek

Many inviting pools lurk in the lower part of Tapeats Creek. Some have SWIM IN ME signs, so allow time to oblige. When the diabase sill with its Bass Formation cap emerges, the trail follows the ramp up and around to a break where there is a quick drop to the beach below. A trail going up the corresponding ramp on the east side ends up at Stone Creek.

The route back to Deer Creek continues downstream at River level to Bonita Creek. At high water you will get cliffed out and must go up and over a basalt shoulder that extends out into the water. At low water you can go around near the water, but be careful. The handholds are good, but the polished wet rock can be very slippery. Again, it is a good idea to undo your waistband while making this traverse.

You have a choice of routes when you reach the drainage about 1.2 miles past Bonita Creek. One is to follow the ramp in the Bass Formation capping the emerging schist. The River is very narrow here—one book says it narrows to 35 feet. I like this ramp. The going is easy, and overhangs provide shelter or shade as needed. The other choice is to take the steep route straight up to the top of the Tapeats and contour around and up to the small saddle mentioned below.

Grand Canyon Supergroup

The ramp and the strata above it are members of a formation called the Grand Canyon Supergroup. These Precambrian rocks are the oldest sedimentary rocks in the Canyon. Between them and the bottom of the Tapeats there is about 800 million years of geology missing. The Supergroup is visible only occasionally in the Canyon, so its appearance is always interesting.

After you have topped out the ramp, you will soon cross a small wash and begin climbing up to a small saddle just east of the hill marked with the "2677T" elevation point. From there it is an easy drop back to camp.

If you happen to be going the other way through here on your way upstream to Tapeats Creek, you have your choice of routes as soon as you start down from the small saddle. What appears to be the better trail takes you over to the steep descent to the beach. This is probably the way the nudists were going when I saw them high above me. If you want to find the ramp, you have to cross the good trail and continue on down to another trail you will find below you.

I have been to Deer Creek more often than I have been to any other place in the Canyon, not because it is my favorite, though it is one of them, but because it is so easy to get to—only a long half day off Monument Point. It is also a friendly place. I especially like lying on the smooth warm rock like a lizard—after the shade has come—and listening to the different sounds the water is making. Sometimes you also hear the water ouzel and the canyon wren making their distinctive calls.

Jacuzzi

And don't forget the Jacuzzi. Just before Deer Creek drops into the gorge, there is a place where its swirling action has excavated a bathtub-sized hole about 3 feet deep. This is the Jacuzzi, and to prepare it for use you may wish to spend some time removing the cobbles from the otherwise smooth bottom of the tub. Then you can brace your feet against the downstream lip and submerge yourself for some pounding in the rushing turbulence.

Upper Deer Creek Canyon

There are many things to do besides stretching out on the warm rocks like a lizard. Going up Deer Creek Canyon makes an interesting day. But take enough water; I have learned from experience that a quart is not enough. It is pretty easy going until you get past the spring a way. After that you encounter gigantic rocks piled in the canyon wall to wall that are a challenge to climb through. Eventually this jumble, which probably resulted from the same slumping action that filled Surprise Valley, is behind you, and the canyon forks.

If you go straight ahead, the Redwall narrows until only a slot remains; you have to swim in yucky water if you want to go any farther. I always give up at this point, so I don't know if the route goes or not. If you go east at the fork, you will eventually dead-end at a 100-foot dryfalls in a big amphitheater. There is a way to climb up on the north to the top of the dryfalls, and my brother and I were going up easily (his word, not mine) until I strongly suggested (*demanded* is a better word) we go back. He is a good climber, but I needed either a belay or a net.

Exploring this canyon is very rewarding, and the climb through the jumble very strenuous—all in all a typical activity for a rest day.

For the more sedentary I recommend the waterfall at Deer Spring for the morning, the big falls by the Colorado River for midday, and the gorge for the afternoon. The gorge comes last because only the midafternoon sun shines down there, which makes better pictures. Also save some time in the late afternoon for enjoying the Jacuzzi.

Deer Creek Gorge
The entry to the gorge is off a shoulder just below the first chockstone on the opposite side of the gorge from the trail. It is easy to get down the ledges to a small rounded buttress, but getting down that buttress is harder. It can be done free if you trust your friction, but it is psychologically helpful to have a rope to hold on to even if you don't need it.

As you go down the stream, you will pass an alcove. For years this alcove harbored a small redbud tree that often struggled to hang on to life through flash floods. It must have been the most photographed tree in the park below the rim. (I am stold that a flash flood in the late 1990s finally removed the tree.) A little farther and you come to a chockstone with about a 20-foot pour-off. I have anchored a rope here and climbed down beside the falls, but another chockstone, this one with a 90-foot pour-off, comes so soon after the first as to make the first descent a waste of time. There are, however, pitons at the pour-off, so someone has gone on a bit farther, at least.

If you value your life, it is best not to be in the gorge when there is the threat of a thunderstorm. Flash floods do happen here. Sometime in the 1980s a large segment of the west wall fell onto the Tapeats slickrock, completely burying the rocky beauty of the place—including my lizarding rocks and the Jacuzzi—under tons of rubble. I visited Deer Creek twice while it looked like that and heaved great quantities of debris into the gorge trying to tidy up. I shouldn't have wasted my time, for a year or so later a flash flood came through and did the job for me—everything was shoved into the gorge. The bigger rocks didn't get beyond the first falls, so they form a pile of debris there while waiting for a bigger flood.

It is such a long day of boulder-hopping from Deer Creek to Kanab Creek that, after the first time, I have always split it into two half days. The first of the leftover half days can easily be spent at Deer Creek Falls.

Indian Handprints
The way from camp to the bottom of Deer Creek Falls follows a well-defined trail along the west rim of the gorge. In some places the gorge is only about 6 feet wide at the top; I have been told that some River runners have jumped across despite the 50-foot penalty. As you go along this trail, note the many

whitish handprints, like spray-painted outlines of hands, that are relics of the Indian occupancy. I hate to admit how many times I had been to Deer Creek before I saw them, and even then it was only because a ranger told me they were there. They are obvious in an odd way—when I didn't know they were there I never saw them, yet when I did know, I saw them in almost every likely spot. There are big ones, small ones, right-hand ones, left-hand ones, and even a few of leaves.

After you get out to the point where you can look down on the boats below, if there are any, the trail goes down steeply to the River. The point is also a good place to go for an after-dinner stroll to watch the sunset or just to admire the view up past Tapeats Creek to Powell Plateau.

Deer Creek Falls

Like those at the Thunder River, the falls here also create a strong down-draft that turns horizontal when it hits the pool, blasting you with icy air while you are trying to get up courage for a plunge into the cold water. Once, on a dare, I swam under the falls and came up behind them. I had a ledge to stand on and enough air to breathe but I was still frightened. This stunt was stupid because rocks go over the falls, too.

It is an easy three hours down to Fishtail Canyon. As you proceed along the River, you almost get cliffed out by the Tapeats Sandstone about 0.8 mile downstream from the falls. Fortunately, there are ledges that make it possible to get by. The interesting thing (Ford, Huntoon, Billingsley, and Breed, loc. cit.) about this bit of Tapeats is that it was once on the south side of the River. Before the slump that I described earlier created a dam, the River flowed somewhere farther north, perhaps under the dry lake you crossed. The dam forced it to seek the new path it follows today.

Beyond the bend with these Tapeats ledges you come to a broad beach, and downstream beyond it you will see cliffs that stop you from continuing on down. A trail, which goes up and over the cliffs, leaves the beach to follow a draw going northeast about a mile downstream from the falls. Soon the trail leaves the draw and begins contouring around to Cranberry Canyon. Actually there are several paths contouring around at different levels, so don't be disturbed if you see one below you. Eventually they all converge.

Siesta Spring

A beautiful flow of water comes down one of the drainages you cross. It is such a delightful place for a siesta that I call it Siesta Spring. Not far beyond the spring, the path descends to the Colorado River. Note the wall of cobblestones as you go down. The stones look river polished and may date from the time when the River was flowing farther north. After you reach the River, it is less than half an hour to the many possible campsites at Fishtail Canyon.

It is a straightforward half day of boulder-hopping to get from Fishtail Canyon to Kanab Canyon; I would guess it is 90 percent boulders and 10 percent soft sand. It is surprising how much concentration is required to hike on a boulder field like this, and when it is hot you will find that there is not much shade. Still, all things pass and after a while you will find yourself at

Kanab Canyon. If the water is high, a sizable estuary is formed where the water of the creek is "dammed" up by the River. If the River is not too high, you can wade to the other side where the good camping places are, but if you do, try it first without a pack to test the mud.

If you can't wade, take the high road. Begin by going north through the trees next to the cliff until you can scramble up to a path that goes along a ledge. Contour along above the creek until you can drop down to the cobbles below. Then cross and go back to the campsites on the other side.

Route to Scotty's Hollow

Actually, no route finding is required; just head up the creek. It's an easy six-hour hike if you don't rest too much. But if it is summer, a few swims can add an hour or so, and detouring to see the Slide of Susurrus can add another hour or so. Still, they are hours well spent. Two of the sights to see along the way are the long walkways on Muav ledges. One is long and the other is very long, and they are both on the east side of the creek. These smooth ledges help make the Muav Limestone a "friendly" formation.

Slide of Susurrus

But the Slide of Susurrus is the main attraction for today. It is a short distance up the major drainage that comes into this creek a little more than 3 miles up from the mouth—about 0.4 mile north of the "3395T" elevation point on the quad map. The name, Slide of Susurrus, is offered by my nephew. The slide is known by many names: Whispering Falls, Mystic Falls, Ponce's Pond, the Trogolyte Grotto. It is mystical; it is whispering; it is a grotto; it even has a pond of crystal clarity. But it is *not* a waterfall; it is definitely a slide. Well, maybe there is a little falls a foot high at the end of the slide, and there are drips into the pool from high up, but I still maintain that it is not a falls. So *slide* is the right word. The term susurrus is an onomatopoetic word describing a rustling or whispering sound and suggests a much more mystical quality than whispering. So the Slide of Susurrus it is, right? O well, I tried.

The slide is much photographed—a challenge in itself—and I always sample the restorative powers of the pool through complete immersion. It is a place for reflection and the music of a recorder. A word of caution, though, for every beautiful apple can have its worm. This worm is the fact that this water, too, must be purified.

You can climb up to the ledge above the slide about 0.25 mile upstream from the mouth of Slide Canyon and contour back and in. If you do, I'm told you will find a game trail, and where it crosses the water that forms the slide there is a mucky wallow and bushels of droppings. Well, so much for the crystal clarity of Ponce's Pond.

Scotty's Castle

It is about three hours from the mouth of Slide Canyon to Scotty's Hollow. This name is suggested by the name Scotty's Castle, already given to the tower that stands at the point where Kanab Creek does a 180-degree turn by the mouth of the side canyon. You can see from the quad map that there is a similar tower more than a mile downstream, so don't confuse the two. There is a fine cave to camp in during a storm, located on the south side of this false Scotty's Castle, a little downstream from the drainage that comes in from the west. The dryfalls at the mouth of this side canyon sometimes provide a small dripping spring. Sometimes a deer trail goes up and over a neck of land formed by a sharp turn, although you have to look carefully to find it.

A good flow of water comes down Scotty's Hollow, but again I have to warn that it needs purification.

Scotty's Hollow

There are two things to do here on a layover day—explore the side canyon or climb the castle. I have never wanted to do the climb, though my brother and a friend did, so I spend my time exploring the hollow. After the climb to get above the first falls, you find a series of pools strung in a cascade. Farther on you find a polished limestone pavement connecting small bathtubs.

About 1.5 miles up the drainage, a side canyon comes in from the southwest that will take you through the Redwall and on up to the Esplanade if you so desire. This Redwall route is one of the few that is not on a fault, and a group I was with used it once to go from Kanab Canyon to 150 Mile Canyon.

Going up it is one thing and going down it is another. I was told by my friend Robert Benson, an experienced Canyon explorer, that it can be very difficult for a solo hiker to come down this arm when all its pools are full of water. On his first try Robert gave up trying to enter the steeply sloping upper ends of these deep pools with his heavy pack. Later he came back with a one-man inflatable vinyl raft and made a successful descent. This route through the Redwall is a lot of fun without a pack, requiring, as it does, chimneying and layout traverses to avoid getting your feet wet.

Continuing from Scotty's Hollow to Indian Hollow is another fun day with few challenges. Just remember to turn right at Jumpup Canyon and right again at Indian Hollow.

Dripping Spring

Showerbath Spring is less than an hour from Scotty's and certainly drinkable without treatment, at least I hope so. The creek has sharply undercut the bank that supports the spring, and the spring in turn supports a luxuriant growth from which a sizable flow of water rains down on the opposite shore. There are stretches of creek downstream from the overhanging spring, between Slide Canyon and Scotty's Hollow, filled with Supai blocks. The going is tiresome and tricky.

On one trip here, some hikers from a Phoenix psychiatric hospital—they never did say, but I assumed they worked there—passed us while we were preparing to camp near the overhanging spring. Since it had rained on us on our hike from Scotty's Hollow and was still threatening, their leader pointed out that there was good shelter directly behind us against the cliff. It takes a few minutes to climb up there and the floor under the overhang slopes some, but it does keep you dry. However, none of us went up there until the middle of the night when it started raining. I should point out that if Kanab Creek flashes, you should already be there.

Pencil Spring

Another place, much closer to Jumpup Canyon, has a small pencil-sized stream of water squirting out near the bottom of a wall like a leak in a dike, and a few feet farther there is a good spring from which to refill your water bottles. There is no more good water until you are in Indian Hollow for a while. On occasion, Kanab Creek may be flowing past Jumpup, but it flows through cattle country so treat the water before drinking it.

Kanab Spring Upstream Jumpup

If you ever get to the Kanab/Jumpup junction badly in need of water, perhaps wanting to camp there, I have always found some about twenty minutes up Kanab Creek. Pass the first cleft on the left and enter the second. You will find water behind the chockstone; it is best to have two people in case one has to help the other over the chockstone. Sadly, graffiti now graces this quiet alcove. You may also be surprised, as I once was, to see jeep tracks here at Jumpup.

Obstacle Pool

As I said earlier, turn right onto Jumpup Canyon and in a little more than an hour turn right again into Indian Hollow. About fifteen minutes after that, you encounter the fun part of the day. The first time I came through here, the obstacle was only a chockstone, and an easy one at that. Now it is a chockstone with a big pool, and until it changes back you have the choice of swimming or climbing. In September I found the swims to be refreshing—I think I swam the pool at least ten times to bring all my stuff across. In November swimming was out of the question, so climbing was the only way. Fortunately, we had eager climbers with us. But things change, and in another October the pool was small enough to wade. At another time it was even dry.

There is a route up the south wall by a small tree. One of us climbed up and belayed the rest. If there is no one in your party who wants to climb the wall without a belay, the only alternative is for a belayer to swim through the ice water and contour back above the rest. Even in summer this is not a bad idea. One person swims and hauls up all the packs, then the rest swim, but only once.

On my most recent return to this place, one companion—an accomplished climber—was climbing the right-hand wall as you face the chockstone with his pack on when a handhold pulled loose near the top and he fell about 20 feet. He landed in the sand on his side with his head just inches from a rock that would probably have given him a depressed skull fracture. All he suffered was some severe bruising. After that bit of discouragement, he, too, climbed the chockstone.

One correspondent, who was there just about the same time we were, wrote that all her party climbed this right-hand wall. One climbed free without a pack, one climbed on belay without a pack, and the rest climbed on belay with a pack. There was "some damage to one pack from the sharp rock." Carnivorous limestone eats again. Another correspondent, who considers himself "an experienced rock climber" tried the right-hand wall and abandoned it in favor of a route on the opposite wall. He wrote, "The route I found goes up the opposite wall—as you are looking at the pool, it is directly behind you. The climb is easy and can even be done with a pack—which might be better than hauling, since the rock there is carnivorous. Then you can follow a ledge around the back of the bay and past the pool. Just past the pool, the ledge narrows and there is an awkward and exposed, but easy, step around. At this point I lowered my pack into the creek bed—then it was easy. The ledge ends after another 100 feet and you can walk back and pick up your pack."

Redwall Knife

Not far above Obstacle Pool the canyon narrows ominously, and sure enough there is another set of chockstones with a big pool. This time, though, there is a bypass on the left. You go up a draw about 100 yards back and contour around until you can climb back down by the chockstones. Near the top of the draw there is a piece of Redwall that justifies my claim that the Redwall is "unfriendly." This chunk of limestone has a sharp knifelike crystal blade embedded in it. The blade is about 2 inches long, 1 inch high, and ⅛ inch thick. If I had fallen on it, I would have been sliced open as neatly as with a razor blade.

I should note that during an October 1991 trip, there were no pools here. Our party was able—with some gymnastics—to continue up the bed, thus avoiding the bypass with the crystal knife blade.

Over-Your-Head Pool

There is a big over-your-head pool about an hour beyond Obstacle Pool; it is a good place for a camp. It is also the only pool you will see beyond the chockstones in Indian Hollow that is deep enough in which to swim, and I did so even on that cold November day.

One of my correspondents told me that she could find no such pool. When my brother and I and friends went through a few weeks later, my brother spotted it after I had given up. At first I didn't believe him because the pool looked too small. But I saw where we had camped, prodded the pool with my walking stick, and found it was at least 4 feet deep—we didn't give it the ultimate test of submersion. This pool will be on your right as you pass it going upcanyon and will be 2 to 3 feet wide and 8 to 10 feet long. As I remember, it has a slight dogleg in the middle. The water was slightly murky when we passed it and the pool appeared of indeterminate depth. This could account for its being missed.

Ojojojo

My notes from a 1991 trip indicate that this over-your-head pool is fifteen minutes upcanyon from the major junction with a canyon coming in from the east almost exactly 0.5 mile south of the northern edge of the Fishtail Quadrangle. Because our bruised climber was beginning to stiffen up, we decided to camp at this junction. The only problem was we had seen no water since leaving Jumpup. My son Mike went upstream looking for water; Joe Brennan was getting ready to explore the canyon to the east. Suddenly Joe said, "Shhh, I think I hear a waterfall." My first instinct was to laugh—a waterfall in this place? But then I shhhed and, by golly, I heard the marvelous sound of falling water. Actually, we could see the water as a streak of dark at the top of a Supai wall. In a flash we were all heading for this miracle—all except poor Mike, who was still trudging upcanyon. It turned out he turned around just minutes from the over-your-head pool.

The waterfall must have a certain permanence to it because there was a mound of travertine at the base and general roughness elsewhere. The "waterfall" was more of a "mistfall." Approximately a cup per second came over the edge of the cliff, but it was buffeted by the wind into a shower of drops of varying sizes. The wind also made sure the drops did not pour steadily in one place. It was like a shower with a moving showerhead. But there was a definite statistical regularity, so as the water swept back and forth certain places got more than others. Careful placement of a pot netted about a teaspoon out of every cup coming over the edge. Three teaspoons to the tablespoon, and sixteen tablespoons to the cup meant our pot harvested about one teaspoon per second or about one cup per minute. That was fine, except we overlooked one minor detail in our excitement at finding this totally unexpected water source. We were very close to having another unexpected water source. The sky was black and rapidly getting blacker.

Since Ojo—pronounced "oho"—is used in Spanish to mean "spring" and since Jo Jo is an affectionate nickname for Joseph with the Spanish pronunciation "Ho Ho," I suggest the name Ojo de Jo Jo—or, more briefly, Ojojojo—for this spring, provided it is permanent, of course, in honor of its discoverer, Joe (Jo Jo) Brennan.

Our stuff had been left completely without protection, so we hurried back with our pots and water bottles held clumsily in one hand while the other helped balance us through the logs and big boulders—we were a herd of incompetent Gunga Dins. We reached camp just in time to begin putting up our shelters. We finished in a downpour and had more water than we needed just pouring off our tarps. Although the main drainage did not flash, the tributary one did and the roar of the approaching water made us very happy we were not just then at the Obstacle Pool.

I hope very much that others traveling in Indian Hollow will write me of their experience with this water source. I would like very much to know whether it is permanent or seasonal.

Beautiful Supai Gorge

The big pool is about at the top of the Redwall, and the next few miles take you through the Supai. I am fond of Supai gorges, especially if they have flowing water. Then they provide a peaceful mix of reds, blues, and greens and reflections of all three. Small life-forms are in abundance, cottonwoods flourish, and, for the most part, the way is flat.

As you near the top of the Supai Formation it is important to keep track of where you are. Southeast of Racetrack Knoll you will have four choices to make at a series of intersections, so be prepared. Eventually you leave the comfortable surroundings of the Supai and work up through rubble to the top of the Hermit Shale. Here the going gets rough as you climb up and around the huge boulders that block the way until you reach the maple glade that marks the bottom of the Coconino Sandstone. There will possibly be a small trickle of water here, and it is certainly a cool place for a rest.

Coconino Clefts

The route through the Coconino is in three steps. The first step takes you up a cleft directly on your left as you face up the drainage. It is an easy climb, but the cleft is so narrow that your packs have to be hauled up. From here you contour around and up to a second cleft that is almost too narrow for packs. It is jammed with logs fitted into cracks, so it would be very easy without a pack. This is the second step.

From the top of this cleft you work your way back into the drainage, fight some brush, and finally reach the final chockstone and the last step—a short ramp by a tree. If you don't like fighting with the tree, you can crawl up under the chockstone—part of a tree branch is placed there to help you.

Tedious Brush

The brush is 3 to 4 feet high, so it is helpful to have brought long pants: Two hours of brush like this can remove some skin. This final part of the trip is tedious, and I often found myself thinking we were almost at the car long before we actually were.

When I get back to the car at the end of a trip it is time for refreshment, wine and cheese and crackers or beer or whatever, and it is also time for another important ritual. The shower. I always bring enough water for this treat and try to leave it in the car in such a position that it gets afternoon sun and is warm, hopefully hot, when I need it. I'm sure my companions on the ride home appreciate my showers as much as I do.

Final descent to the bed of Tuckup Canyon.

5 Tuckup Canyon/ Stairway Canyon Loop

A possible title for a book extolling the
beauty of the Grand Canyon outback
(with apology to the Reverend Dodgson):
"Talus in Wonderland."

ANONYMOUS

Length
Five and a half days, plus layover day(s), if any.

Water
Water can be expected, though not guaranteed, in the Redwall narrows of lower Tuckup beginning with a small surface flow about fifteen minutes up from the Cottonwood junction. Sometimes there is flowing water out of Cottonwood and sometimes there is none. Farther down there are usually pools. In Tuckup Canyon, more than in most drainages, availability of water depends on how long it has been since the last rain as well as on how much rain there has been that year. Colorado River water is available from Tuckup to Stairway and there are pools in the lower part of Stairway. There is a small marshy place at the top of the Redwall in Stairway with cattails and other reeds and some surface water, but it, too, must be considered seasonal. The named springs—Willow (called June Spring on the Monument map) and Cottonwood—have been there a long time and can be considered reliable. I have been told the same is true of Schmutz Spring.

Quad Maps
7.5-minute maps
 Fern Glen Canyon
 Gateway Rapids
 S B Point (western edge only)
 Mt. Trumbull NE (for Graham Ranch road)

There is also the Grand Canyon National Monument map with a scale of 1:48000—half the scale of the 7.5-minute map. This map does not show June Tank—you need the Heaton Knolls quad map for that—but it does show the Graham Ranch road.

Roadhead
The end of the road 1.6 miles south and a little west of the location of Schmutz Spring on the Fern Glen Canyon quadrangle map.

ROUTE TO ROADHEAD

There are two ways to the Tuckup Trailhead: south from June Tank or east from near Graham Ranch.

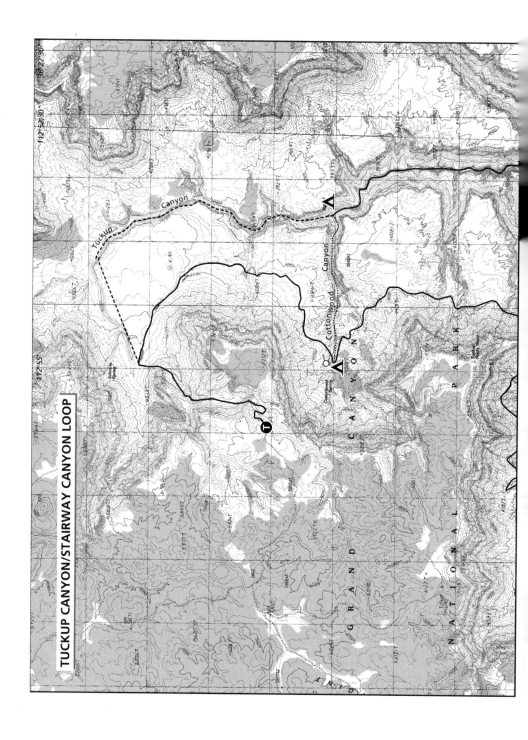

TUCKUP CANYON/STAIRWAY CANYON LOOP

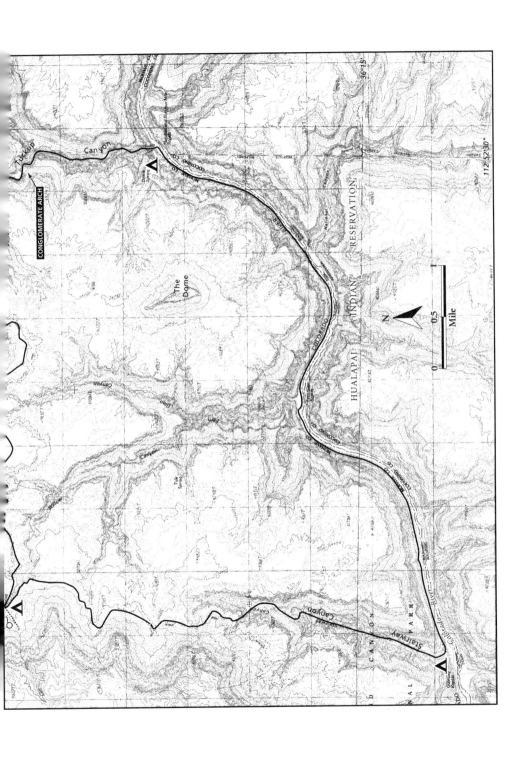

CONGLOMERATE ARCH

N

0 0.5 Mile

Via June Tank

Mileage

0.0	Take Arizona Highway 389 west from Fredonia.
8.3	After 8.3 miles turn south onto Mt. Trumbull Road.
31.6	After 23.3 miles you pass Hack Reservoir on your left.
40.2	After 8.6 miles you reach the northernmost road in to June Tank. Turn left.
41.4	After 1.2 miles, during which you pass a corral and a round storage shed, you reach a cattle guard. Go through it.
41.5	After 0.1 mile you reach a threeway fork. Take either the middle or righthand fork. The left fork takes you to the 150 Mile Canyon Trailhead. The middle fork has been bulldozed into creation and parallels the right fork. I expect them both to be a problem after rain or snow.
48.6	After 7.1 miles on this new road you reach an intersection. Go straight. The road is now much better.
49.1	After 0.5 mile you reach the park boundary.
50.8	After 1.7 miles you reach a fork. Go right.
51.5	After 0.7 mile you may see a road merging from the left. It is on another map I have, but I missed it.
51.7	After 0.2 mile you reach an intersection. Go left.
55.1	After 3.4 miles you reach a fork. Go left.
57.0	After 1.9 miles you reach the trailhead.

Via Graham Ranch

Mileage

0.0	Take Arizona Highway 389 west from Fredonia.
8.3	After 8.3 miles turn south onto Mt. Trumbull Road.
31.6	After 23.3 miles you pass Hack Reservoir on your left.
40.2	After 8.6 miles you reach the northernmost road in to June Tank. Go straight.
49.8	After 9.6 miles you reach the road that goes east up the hill about a mile south of Graham Ranch. The ranch is on the map, but I have never seen it. Turn left up the hill. This road is shown correctly on the Mt. Trumbull NE Quad map but incorrectly on the Monument map.
51.4	After 1.6 miles you reach a fork. Go left.
52.9	After 1.5 miles you pass a road T-ing in from the left. Go straight.
53.1	After 0.2 mile you pass a road T-ing in from the right. Go straight.
53.5	After 0.4 mile you reach a fork. Go left.
55.0	After 1.5 miles you reach the park boundary.
55.6	After 0.6 mile you pass a tank on your left.
57.5	After 1.9 miles you reach an intersection. Go straight.
60.9	After 3.4 miles you reach a fork. Go left.
62.8	After 1.9 miles you reach the trailhead.

HIKING TIMES

Use Areas	Locations	Elapsed Times Between Locations (hours)
▲ NL9	Car	1:30
▲ LB9	Tuckup drainage near 4,000-foot contour	2:15
▲ LB9	Junction with Cottonwood Canyon	2:30

	Conglomerate Arch	:45
▲ LB9	Junction with NE arm of Tuckup	1:45
	Start of final bypass	1:30
▲ LB9	Tuckup Canyon delta	1:45
▲ LC9	Opposite National Canyon	1:45
▲ LC9	Mouth of Fern Glen Canyon	3:00
▲ LC9	Mouth of Stairway Canyon	:45
▲ LC9	Start bypass of 50-foot falls	1:00
▲ LC9	Top of 50-foot falls	2:00
▲ LC9	Top of Redwall	2:30
▲ LC9	Top of Supai	2:00
▲ LC9	Willow Spring	4:00
	Junction with Dome Trail	2:15
▲ LB9	Cottonwood Spring	2:15
	Cubical rock	1:15
▲ NL9	Car	

ROUTE DETAILS

I first did this loop in October 1988 with the Sierra Club. It took us eight days and, except for the top part of the Redwall in Stairway Canyon, it was mainly a piece of cake.

Trail to Schmutz Spring

We left the cars at 8:00 A.M. and followed the old road down through the basaltic rubble to the sharp rim of the canyon draining north toward Schmutz Spring. This road is shown as a trail on the Fern Glen Canyon quad map and I have followed it down to the sagebrush at the bottom of the bay above the headwall but have found no lead in to the trail—even when coming up when it should be most obvious. I prefer to leave this road when it begins its sharp turn to the south along the 5,600 foot contour and, instead, head down more directly toward the edge of the drainage where the trail is.

We had no difficulty following the trail for it has been maintained by horses and cattle. We saw about ten Herefords browsing in the shade on the east side of the drainage under the basalt cliffs. (Today the fence has been repaired and there shouldn't be any cattle.) As we rounded the bend and approached the flats, we could see a roughly cubical room-sized boulder all by itself out among the sage. It is a useful landmark and we would use it again on our return from Cottonwood Spring. Schmutz Spring should be visible from this rock, but I have not seen it. (At press time, the spring is being rehabilitated from its years of use by cattle.)

There are several ways to the bed of Tuckup Canyon. One of them is to continue along what is shown as the Tuckup Trail on the quad map. Another is to proceed directly down the bed of the west arm of Tuckup. Our route was to head for the prominent knoll in the northeast arm of Tuckup, shown as the "4323T" elevation point. This route lead us to a break in the basalt rim that allowed access to the bed. The elapsed time from the cars to the bed of Tuckup was ninety minutes.

Cottonwood Canyon

There is usually water at the junction of Cottonwood and Tuckup. But not always. We found some pothole water there in the fall of '88, but in the fall of '89 there was not even damp sand. In the fall of '90 there was a small amount—enough for three people for the night. Fortunately, there is a more reliable source in Tuckup Canyon at the top of the Redwall about twenty minutes up Tuckup from the Cottonwood junction. Besides the water we found at the junction in 1988, we found two other prerequisites for a perfect lunch spot—shade and smooth flat rocks. It had taken us more than two hours to get there from where we first reached the bed of Tuckup, and we were ready for a restful lunch.

Redwall Break

One-and-two-tenths miles below Cottonwood, at approximately the 3,000-foot contour, there is a break in what is left of the Redwall on the east side. It is possible to get up to the Esplanade that way. The route through the Supai takes you diagonally up to the base of the final cliff toward the "3967T" elevation point. I describe this route to the Esplanade in greater detail in section 2 of the next chapter.

Conglomerate Arch

The next major feature of the Tuckup descent is the Conglomerate Arch—about 0.25 mile up from the junction with the lower northeast arm of Tuckup. The chockstone just up from the bridge can be downclimbed or bypassed on stream left on a route that takes you to the top of the bridge, where you can descend to the bed. This bridge is a remarkable geological feature. Conglomerates are river gravels cemented with travertine and are stronger than sandstone, but to find such an arch spanning a major drainage like Tuckup is rare.

One of Us Is Missing

We had spent considerable time in our Tuckup descent just enjoying ourselves. Besides it was our first day and we were tired and it didn't look as if we would make it to the River by dark; so just beyond the bridge, on some relatively flat and polished limestone slabs, we made camp. That is, most of us did. One of our party had been so energized by the day's activities that he had surged ahead of the group. When we found we were one person short, we made do as best we could with the extra dinner we had. It was unlikely anything had happened to our errant member, and it had already been stated that no searches would be made under such circumstances.

The next morning we still had not found him by the time we reached the side canyon coming in from the northeast, but we explored it, anyway. Not very far up this canyon we came upon a large whitish lumpy boulder—maybe 6 feet across—that I take to be stromatolites. These are large fossil algae colonies that occur principally in Devonian rocks according to my dictionary. Live stromatolites still exist in the shallow seas off the coast of western Australia. It is possible to get almost to the top of the Redwall in this side canyon and I think if I could get past the 40 foot falls that finally stopped us, I could make it through the Redwall. It would be interesting to come down this canyon and see if you get stopped by the same falls.

Final Muav Descent

It was after lunch before we started on down Tuckup again and very soon met our missing companion—a little hungry, perhaps, but none the worse for his time alone. A few bypasses still remained before the final descent to the beach through the Muav and it was two hours before we reached it. If you have stayed in the bed, you will know you are almost there when you find a chockstone at the top of a 40-50 foot pour-off. If you reach the pour-off, back up a way and take the trail contouring around on stream right. This trail is soon quite high above the drainage—100 feet or so—and if you are looking for an easy way down you will be disappointed. Instead, look for a very steep chute in the bedrock with a small ledge almost at the bottom. Once I missed it and went all the way out to the point above the beach. If that happens to you, retrace your steps with your expectations set a little lower.

The descent of the chute is fairly easy even though it is very steep and there is only one place—almost at the ledge—where I wish to pass my pack. Beyond the ledge there is an almost vertical 20 foot drop to the bed. At the beach side of the ledge, a small ramp provides access to the hand- and footholds that take you diagonally down across the face to the point where you can scramble to the bottom. This climb down the wall requires some climbing skills—it helps not to be acrophobic—and I recommend that you lower your packs and use a belay. This all takes time and the ten of us spent ninety minutes making this descent. Camp was on the beach along the River at the mouth of Tuckup.

Tuckup Beach

My nest for the night was under a small overhang and I shared this sandy bed with ant lions and spiders. This spot is big enough for two and is at the base of the cliff just downstream from the mouth of the canyon. A flurry of excitement erupted during the night when a few raindrops fell and a wind came up, but I was oblivious to it all.

En Route to Stairway Canyon

We were on our way to Stairway Canyon along the River talus by 8:15 the next morning. It is about 6.5 miles and took us all day. We were opposite National Canyon by 10:00 and at Fern Glen by 11:45. We spent two hours at Fern Glen and went up to the travertine falls (dry), which has steps cut into it. My son Stan and nephew Lee have climbed these steps but were cliffed out very soon after the two of them disappeared around the corner. I remember the three hours to Fern Glen passing very quickly. The next three, fighting the tamarisk down to Stairway, went very slowly, and I was tired by the time I got there.

The canyon opposite Stairway is Mohawk; both are formed along a single fault. One year we carried an inflatable raft down Tuckup—I should say my son, Mike, carried it—and we crossed and explored both National and

Mohawk Canyons before crossing back and going out the Lava Falls Trail. Since we are in the neighborhood—Lava Falls is only 8 miles away—I will describe a most remarkable event that took place at our camp at the head of Lava Falls. Long after I have forgotten what the word Alzheimer means, I will still remember this.

The Flying Cervezas

We reached the bottom of the Lava Falls Trail early in the afternoon and hoped to watch some boats go through the rapids. We waited and waited, but no boats. Finally, toward the end of the afternoon, we saw two motor rigs approaching. "Aha," we thought, "now there'll be some action." But no. They pulled in to the beach on the other side. We hoped this was just to scout the rapids. But there was no action. People just sat around doing nothing.

To pass the time, son Mike and nephew Lee, both amateur percussionists, began using my pots as bongos to beat out a complicated rhythm. To add to the general gaiety, I got my recorder and blew out an assortment of shrieks and whistles as an accompaniment. Then we got tired and stopped. Whereupon some men sitting on the sand across the way clapped. Lee looked this gift horse squarely in the mouth and yelled back, "Don't clap, bring us some beer." One of the men got up and started walking down to the boat. We were incredulous. Was this guy really going to get in his boat and come across at the head of Lava Falls to bring us a beer—perhaps, even beers? We watched his every move with the keenest interest, and our disappointment was almost overwhelming as we watched him walk back up the hill to his companions.

But he didn't sit down again, and there was another flurry of activity we couldn't understand. Six people were milling around without much apparent purpose. Finally, two groups of two men each stood still while the other two went around behind them. We were very confused. What kind of a game were they playing? Then one of them yelled out, "Heads up, we'll try an apple." What the devil did that mean—an apple? Then it all suddenly became clear. Each pair of the standing men was holding on to something that the third pair was pulling back. They had arranged themselves into a giant slingshot.

An apple. By God, they were going to shoot an apple across the River. My guess is the distance was 200 yards—others say less. (There is a pool at the head of a rapid and an especially big one at the head of Lava Falls.) I saw the elastic snap and could track the apple briefly. It was in a very flat trajectory and traveling very fast. Then I lost it and threw myself facedown in the sand with my arms over my head. I wasn't about to play Goliath to their David. I could imagine it: "Poor George, how did he die?" "Oh, Steck? He was killed by a flying apple." Then there was a splat in the rocks behind us as the flying apple disintegrated into a cidery foam.

Now the full significance of the first shout became clear. First they'll try an apple and then . . . the beer was next. I saw the elastic snap again and followed the can of beer for a moment and then lost it, too. I quickly hid behind a rock because I wasn't sure that arms over my head would protect

126

me against a flying cerveza. It, too, smashed into foam in the rocks behind us. The next beer was sent in an arching trajectory and landed in the water about 25 feet offshore. In the attending surprise, it was swept away and lost to the Lava Falls River God. Then they found the range, and the cans began landing 10 to 20 feet offshore. They were retrieved in an instant despite the cold water. Many beers were launched. In total, counting the one that was smashed and the one that was lost, perhaps three sixpacks were sent flying, one by one, across the River by that human slingshot. An extraordinary achievement in both conception and execution and I don't think any beer ever had a better taste. Here's a toast to the wonderful people who sent it. I hope they read this and write me so I can thank them.

We speculated at some length about what the propulsive material could have been. Surgical tubing seemed the only answer. I found out some years later that warring boaters often use a similar slingshot made with surgical tubing to bombard their enemies with water balloons so I guess our conclusion was correct.

Exploring for the Stairway Canyon Exit

Ordinarily, I don't take a group of people to places I have not already been—I don't like surprises when I am responsible for others' safety. Once, years ago, I had climbed the Redwall out of Stairway, but that route was unsuitable for me let alone a group. However, I had read someone's trip report about coming down Stairway off the Tuckup Trail so I knew it had been done. It was just a question of finding the route. I made the next day a "rest day" so I could explore and find it.

Four of us set off on the exploration. I like the lower part of Stairway—the limestone narrows. There are smooth "marble" walls and there is smooth "marble" to walk on—usually with a small trickle of water to reflect the blue sky. This lower part rises steep and straight and you can look down canyon and across the River to see the corresponding steep and straight part of Mohawk along the fault.

There are basically only four Redwall obstacles and you encounter them in their order of difficulty—the easiest coming first. This is a small pool in a sharp turn. You have two choices here. One is to skirt the pool and climb the left side of the falls. The other is to climb the right wall. Your choice will probably depend on how much water there is. The next small obstacle comes shortly after going through a chockstone tunnel where the canyon widens some and there is a 10 foot wall diagonally across the drainage. This is a pretty place, with water and greenery, and I once saw a dragonfly powering along trailing about 6 feet of spiderweb. You reach the third obstacle shortly after climbing this wall: a 50-foot pour-off. My son Stan has climbed this—because it was there, I guess—but he said he felt stupid afterward for having taken the risk. The final obstacle is a 200-foot pour-off from the top of the Redwall.

The 50-foot pour-off can be bypassed in two ways. Our "rest day" exploration team climbed a chute to a saddle on the left side of the 10-foot wall (as you face it from below—this is stream right), but Stan also explored a small cleft farther downcanyon on stream left—my notes say "about 100 yards upcanyon from the chockstone tunnel."

To find our way past the final pour-off, we first went to the base of it and climbed up the talus to the left (west), staying near the base of the cliff. After rounding the corner and climbing a small cliff with plenty of ledges, we found ourselves at the apex of the talus—probably the fault goes through here—with about 40 more feet of Redwall cliff above us. Fortunately, there is a crack—more evidence of the fault?—and the only difficulty is getting up the first 6 feet. If you are alone, you might have to stand on your pack and then haul it up after yourself.

This ended the "rest day" exploration. We now knew how to get through the Redwall in Stairway Canyon. Our return to camp took two hours.

A Successful Exit

We were off and running by 8:00 the next day and were at the site of the first major bypass forty-five minutes later. Stan thought the route we had used the day before was a bit risky for a large group—too much loose rock in the chute—so he opted for the cleft he had previously explored. As I said, it is about 100 yards upcanyon from the chockstone tunnel on stream left.

We left the drainage and climbed the cleft, diagonally up to the right (east), until we were above a pair of buttresses. Then we contoured upcanyon on top of them—in and out—until the deer trail we were following went diagonally down to the top of the 50-foot fall. The cleft is steep, and in one mostly vertical place I needed to pass my pack up. Getting all of us over the bypass to the top of the falls took an hour.

We also took a slightly different route up the talus to the final crack. Rather than slap the base of the final pour-off, we left the drainage somewhat earlier when it appeared to make sense to do so. We were on top of the final falls by 11:45—just in time for lunch. Close to the pour-off there are some reeds and some standing water in a marshy setting. This could be a spring, but more likely it is just a large collection pool for rainwater; however, we managed to get plenty of water from it.

Willow/June Spring

After an hour's break for lunch, we started up the drainage. We exited by the first draw to the west and in an hour and a half were on top of the Supai on the Tuckup Trail. After two more hours we reached Willow Spring—on the Monument map this is called June Spring. It was a nice setting with a small flow of water over the slickrock. Fortunately, it had not been trashed by cattle.

Route to Rim from Willow Spring

The next day was also a "rest day" and some went off to follow the Dome Trail. Others went to explore Willow Canyon. Stan and I went to look for the trail that connects Willow Spring with the rim. We found it and have shown it on the map as a possible exit route. It took us an hour and forty-five minutes to get from camp to rim and an hour and fifteen minutes to get back. It is not much of a trail, but there were some mining implements along it. We found a cairn at the top; the beginning of the trail was marked by an arc of stones. When you get to the rim, you will be about 5 miles from your car.

Results of Robert's Earlier Explorations
Those who went on other explorations also had a good day. No one circumnavigated the Dome, but some got part way down Willow Canyon. My friend Robert had explored this area quite thoroughly. His map shows he went down Fern Glen Canyon via a drainage just west of the 4,286-foot benchmark north of the Dome and camped on top of the Redwall at the junction of Willow and Fern Glen on the broad flat promontory there. Then he went up Willow as far as the 3,400-foot contour. His map shows a pour-off as impeding further progress. He also got down the bed of Fern Glen to the Willow confluence. His map shows Dome Spring to be dry on December 13, 1980 and he notes a constructed trail from the Esplanade to the top of the Redwall down the drainage below the spring.

Route to Cottonwood Spring
After the "rest day," our routing was from Willow Spring to Cottonwood Spring. Despite the trail, it took us four hours to the junction with the trail down to the Dome. After lunch at a nearby viewpoint, it was still more than two hours to Cottonwood Spring. Coming upon it was the low point of the trip for me. It was thoroughly spoiled by cattle. I had camped there almost twenty years earlier and didn't remember any such devastation. The thought of having to drink that fecally contaminated sludge was almost enough to make you sick. But we went as far up as there was sufficient water and began the extraction and filtering process. Trying to take as few chances with my health as possible, I also doused my filtered water with iodine.

The condition of this spring so angered us that many of us wrote letters of protest to congressmen, the park service and Interior Department officials. Perhaps this collective action is responsible for the enforcement of existing law and the withdrawal of the cattle before my next visit.

Up and Out
The next day—our final one—was short: just over two hours to the cubical rock and another hour to the top and our ice chest of beer. My notes end at this point with a final remark. Someone expressed the thought that a book on the beauty of the Grand Canyon outback might be called Talus in Wonderland. So far, no one has admitted authorship so I have listed it at the head of this chapter as "anonymous."

A view of 150 Mile Canyon.

6 150 Mile Canyon Loops

Section 1: Descent of 150 Mile Canyon

> An emergency room physician's view of
> Grand Canyon hiking trauma:
> "All bleeding eventually stops."
>
> GIL ROBERTS, M.D.

Length

The descent of 150 Mile Canyon will take two days. Closing the loop in either direction will take an additional six days, plus rest days, if any.

Water

The first water is at Buckhorn Spring—it has never failed me. Intermittent water can be found through the Supai and spring water is available at Hotel Spring in a side canyon by a cowboy camp. Water is also available at top of Redwall—under the worst-case scenario, you might have to get it from the plunge pool below the chockstone. Easiest way to do that is to set up a fixed line on stream left at the end of the sheltered ledge and descend to the bed via a small series of cracks—75 feet of webbing should be enough. Frequent water sources in Redwall narrows—some close to chin-deep. Water can be expected at the chockstone at end of the narrows, but if there is none, you will have to climb down to the River. A hundred feet of webbing for a hand-line will be helpful during the descent on the 150 Mile side of the upstream point.

Quad Maps

7.5-minute maps
  Hancock Knolls
  Heaton Knolls
  Robinson Canyon
  Surprise Ridge
  Havasu Falls
  Hitson Tank
  S B Point

The first four 7.5-minute maps are only for showing roads.

Roadhead

At end of road by the corral 0.35 mile south-southwest of Buckhorn Spring on the Hitson Tank quad map.

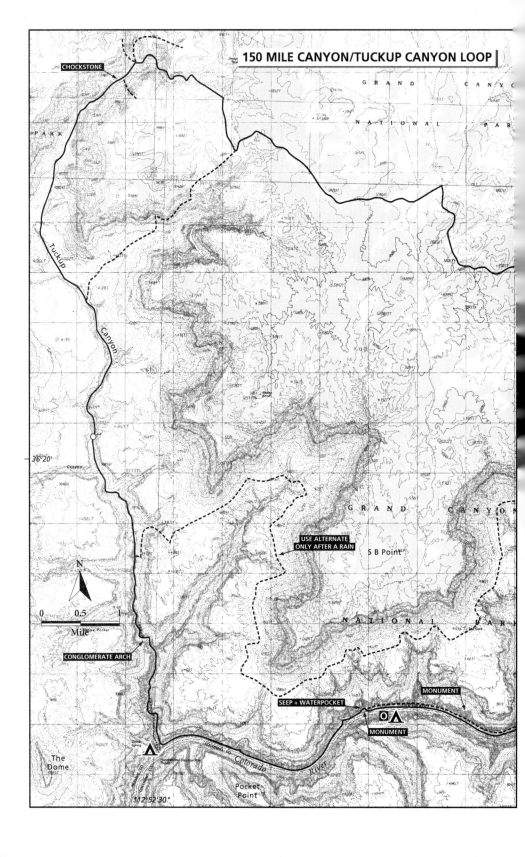

150 MILE CANYON/TUCKUP CANYON LOOP

CHOCKSTONE

GRAND CANYON

NATIONAL PARK

PARK

Tuckup

Canyon

36°20'

N

0   0.5   1

Mile

USE ALTERNATE
ONLY AFTER A RAIN

S B Point

GRAND CANYON

CONGLOMERATE ARCH

NATIONAL PARK

MONUMENT

SEEP + WATERPOCKET

MONUMENT

The
Dome

Colorado River

Pocket
Point

112°52'30"

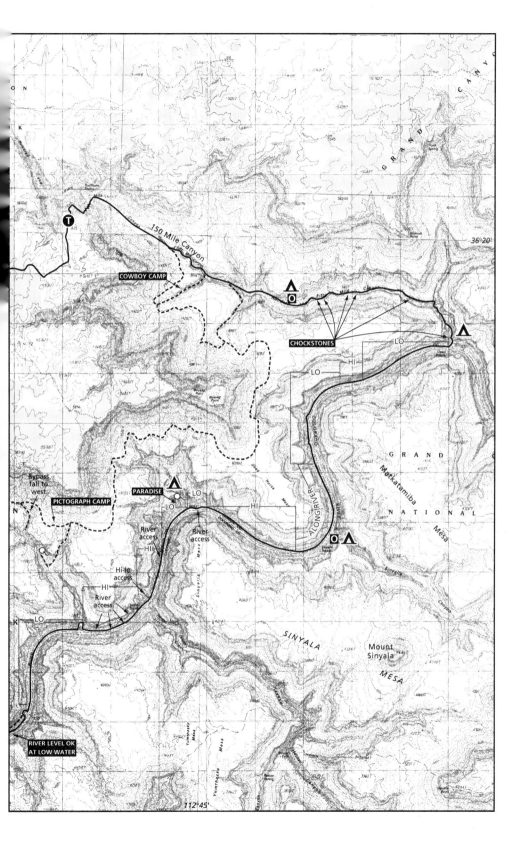

GRAND CANYON

36°20'

150 Mile Canyon

COWBOY CAMP

CHOCKSTONES

LO

HI

LO

PARADISE

LO

LO

HI

Bypass
fall to
west

PICTOGRAPH CAMP

N

River
access

River
access

Hi-lo
access

HI

HI

LO

River
access

K

GRAND

Matkatamiba

NATIONAL

ALONG RIVER

SINYALA

Mount
Sinyala

MESA

**RIVER LEVEL OK
AT LOW WATER**

112°45'

ROUTES TO ROADHEAD

Via June Tank
Mileage

0.0　Routing starts in Fredonia, Arizona, at the junction of U.S. Highway 89 and Arizona Highway 389. The gas you get here will be the last gas you get until you return to Fredonia. Leave Fredonia going west on AZ 389.

8.3　After 8.3 miles leave the blacktop and turn south onto the well-graded Mt. Trumbull Road to the Tuweep Ranger Station.

31.6　After 23.3 miles you pass Hack Reservoir on your left. The best road goes left to Hack Canyon. Go straight.

34.6　After 3.0 miles you reach the junction with the road to Jensen Twin Tanks—there is a sign. Go straight.

40.2　After 5.6 miles you reach the junction with the third road in to June Tank. Turn left.

41.4　After 1.2 miles you reach June Tank and cross a cattle guard.

42.3　After 0.9 mile you cross another cattle guard.

42.9　After 0.6 mile you pass a corral and loading chute on the left.

45.0　After 2.1 miles you reach a fork. Go left.

46.6　After 1.6 miles the road from Jensen Twin Tanks Ts in from the left. Go straight.

46.8　After 0.2 mile you reach roads going off to the left and right at Niniger Tanks. Go straight. The road to the left doesn't go anywhere useful, but the road to the right can be used to bypass the ditch you will have to cross after a few more yards. It may be a difficult crossing. Past the ditch, head left out across the flats—possibly tracks, but no road—to a road on the other (east) side. If the ground is wet, you may wish to explore on foot. There is a good road continuing southwest on the west side, but do not take it—it rapidly deteriorates.

47.0　After 0.2 mile you should be on the road on the east side of Niniger Tank.

50.3　After 3.3 miles the road from Hitson Tank comes in from the left. Go straight.

52.2　After 1.9 miles a road comes in from the left. Go straight.

53.3　After 1.1 miles you cross a pretty good road. If you turn to the right here, you will eventually have access to the Tuckup Canyon drainage. You will turn left here when you go to Kanab Point. There is a signpost but no sign. A 5,757-foot benchmark is close by. To get to the 150 Mile Trailhead, go straight.

56.8　After 3.5 miles you reach the trailhead. There is a corral and a large loop-type turnaround. En route you will cross a pair of deep ruts spaced about a yard apart. My old VW bus had enough clearance to make it, but it makes sense to throw in a few segments of 6-by-8-inch planks to lay in the bottom of the ruts. Also, about a mile in from the signpost with no sign, you will pass a faint road going off to the right to a magnificent view off Boysag Point. This road is on the map.

Via Jensen Twin Tanks
I used this routing for several years after I almost got stuck in a quagmire at June Tank.

Mileage

0.0 At the intersection of Mt. Trumbull Road and the road to Jensen Twin Tanks—there is a sign—turn left. This intersection is about 3 miles beyond the Hack Canyon turnoff, where the best road goes off left to the mine and you go straight.

1.9 After 1.9 miles you reach a fork with a sign. Bear right to Jensen Twin Tanks.

2.1 After 0.2 miles you reach a fork with a sign. Go straight to Jensen Twin Tanks.

3.3 After 1.2 miles you are at Jensen Twin Tanks. There is a fork. The left road goes to the tanks. Go right up an incline.

3.6 After 0.3 mile turn left through a gate. Leave the gate as you found it and cross a field.

3.7 After 0.1 mile you reach a second gate. Go through it and head south.

6.7 After 3.0 miles you pass a tank on your right; there is a short wiggle to the east to get around the tank. Continue south.

8.6 After 1.9 miles you intersect the road from June Tank. Turn left and around the knoll to Niniger Tank. Now you are on the routing from June Tank.

HIKING TIMES

Use Areas	Locations	Elapsed Times Between Locations (hours)		
		1986	1989	1990
▲ NK9	Car	:30	:35	:45
	Buckhorn Spring	3:15	3:30	2:30
	Hotel Spring Canyon	1:15	1:15	1:15
▲ LB9	Start of Redwall narrows	:10	:10	:10
	Entry to Redwall narrows	:40	:50	:30
	Top of first chockstone	:45	:30	:20
	All down	:01	:01	:01
	Top of second chockstone	:25	:20	:25
	All down	:45	:30	:45
	Wide safe place	:15	:15	:15
	Top of third chockstone	:30	:35	1:15
	All down	:10	:10	:10
	Top of fourth chockstone	1:00	:25	:30
	All down	2:15	1:15	2:00
	In drainage after long bypass	:45	:30	:45
▲ LB9	SOB Chockstone Camp			

ROUTE DETAILS

This route description for the descent of 150 Mile Canyon is written as Don Mattox, Gary Ladd, and I experienced it on our attempt to close the loop via Kanab Creek in the fall of 1990.

Route to Buckhorn Spring

An old stock trail leaves the rim down a small arroyo a few yards west of the corral at the end of the road above Buckhorn Spring. With care I could follow this trail all the way to the spring. From remnants of constructed trails still showing in the lower Supai, I conclude that stock must have been brought down this canyon to the top of the Redwall. The difficulty of doing this led to the canyon's being called a real "son of a bitch," which degenerated ultimately to the more affectionate appellation, SOB Canyon. Bureaucratic cartographers, being the staid, meticulous people they are, found SOB unacceptable and shortened it to S B. Hence the name S B Point for the promontory that overlooks the mouth of Tuckup Canyon between it and 150 Mile Canyon. This historical tidbit is offered by the late John Riffey, the notorious leg puller who occupied the little stone house at Tuweep for more than forty years under three federal jurisdictions—BLM, forest service, and park service. John's job kept changing, but not his home. So John's story of the origin of the name SOB Canyon may not be true, but if it isn't, it should be. In Riffey's memory I will refer to 150 Mile Canyon as SOB Canyon for the rest of this description.

There has been water at Buckhorn Spring all eight times I have been there and I consider it very reliable. Be aware, however, that in dry years there will be less water than in wet years. There is often intermittent water flowing in the Lower Supai all the way down to the beginning of the Redwall gorge.

The trail passed the spring and crossed the drainage. A little later it appeared to lead us back into the drainage at a small cairn. But instead of going down it, the trail continued on across to the flats on the west side. Eventually, it descended to the drainage near the top of the Supai.

Lizard versus Snake

It was along in here that Don and I came upon an epic, if miniature, struggle. Unfortunately, neither of us had a camera and Gary was too far ahead to get his attention without the possibility of spoiling the drama that was unfolding before us. A fat 8-inch lizard was locked in a fierce embrace with a thin 14-inch snake. What kind each of them was I never knew. All I can say for sure is that the snake was not a rattler. The lizard had a firm hold on the snake's body with its teeth and the snake had a firm hold with its teeth on a lizard foot and a tight set of coils around the lizard's midsection.

For the most part, this reptilian knot was quite static with no gain being made by either side, but every so often a violent, short-lived thrashing would take place that left the standoff exactly where it was before. It seemed clear to me that neither was appropriate prey for the other, but it was not clear what was going to happen next. At the moment the animals were in the shade, but soon the sun would hit them. It was Don's view that as they got hot, they would disengage and casually go their separate ways as if nothing had happened.

Don and I watched this struggle for about ten minutes and the longer I watched, the closer I came to laughing. What was happening probably seemed like life or death to them but what did it really matter? Would God be laughing, too?

Cowboy Camp

There are a variety of pictographs in the lower Supai on both sides of the canyon bed near the 2,400-foot contour. The box of old dynamite that also used to be there has thoughtfully been disposed of by the National Park Service. I suppose it is for historical reasons that part of the box yet remains. There is a fascinating cowboy camp on a ledge above the spring almost all the way to the top of the Esplanade in the side canyon containing Hotel Spring. A large storage box there contains a *Reader's Digest* from 1950.

Redwall Gorge

I estimate the beginning of the Redwall gorge to be at about the 2,960-foot contour. From here it is still about 2.5 miles to the Colorado River. This is a difficult 2.5 miles, with four or five chockstones blocking the way. Getting through the gorge will take most of the day if the party is large and the water high.

I say "four or five" chockstones because, although there are usually only four, once there were five. When my brother and I first went down SOB Canyon in July 1982, we found four, but three months later, in October, when we were going up, we found an extra one—the messiest of all. So it appears that chockstones can come and go—as can pools. Sometimes there will be a big plunge pool below a particular chockstone, sometimes not. What happens depends, I think, on the volume of water going through during the last storm, as well as whether the flow tapered off suddenly or slowly.

A small party with climbing skills, traveling light and fast and starting early, could probably get from rim to river in one day. I generally choose to camp on the Redwall bench where the gorge begins. There is shelter under overhangs for at least eight, and there is often flowing water. Even if there is no water either flowing or in potholes, there has always been a big plunge pool below the chockstone at the top of the gorge. To exploit it, you can either use the pot-on-a-string trick or place a fixed rope and climb down a crack on the north side to the floor just below the lower end of the pool. It will help to have 75 feet of webbing to set up as a handline.

Gorge Entry

The entry to the gorge is on the north side about 100 yards from camp. The way down is very steep; you may look at it for some time before you realize it is the way you have to go. I have been up or down six times and, although I will climb up with a pack, I will not climb down with one. So you probably will pass or lower your packs down over the carnivorous limestone. A handline will be useful if you have as much concern for your physical well-being as I have for mine.

First Try

The first chockstone comes in about 40 yards and the second in about 40 more. But all the drops are only about 15 feet. In fact, the longest is less than 25 feet. Even then, you rappel onto a rock 6 feet off the water. On my first try of 150 Mile in 1981 with Robert, these first two obstacles came so quickly that I was totally demoralized, intimidated, and discouraged. My statistical mind took two chockstones in 80 yards and created more of them between me and the River than I cared to think about—and what about the two we had already passed that were up by camp?

If half the height of the Redwall—say 300 feet—consisted of drops, there could be as many as twenty small ones of 15 feet or, horrors, four of 50 feet and one of 100. Just one big one would be one too many. On my own I can handle 15 foot rappels—maybe even 20 foot ones—and with a gun to my head I could do a 25. But 50 or 100 feet? Shoot me. The result of all this calculation was that Robert and I abandoned our descent of SOB and instead took the Redwall down to Cork Spring, looping back on the Esplanade.

Second Try Succeeds
Later, in July 1982, when my brother and I persevered and found only four chockstones and two bypasses, we were elated. Since we were on an exploratory day hike to the River and back, we put in a bolt with hanger, carabiner, and fixed rope at each chockstone for our return. On our way back we left a long loop of light nylon cord through the carabiner fastened to the wall below each chockstone so we could pull a rope through the carabiner from below when we came up SOB in October. At that time, however, we found every nylon cord had vanished—worn through and washed away by flash floods. Fortunately, my brother was able to upclimb all the obstacles.

October 26, 1982
That last simple declarative statement sums up the most extraordinarily intense day of my canyon life—our journey up the Redwall narrows of SOB Canyon on October 26, 1982. We were en route to a food cache on day fifty-two of our eighty-day journey from Lees Ferry to Pearce Ferry. After stoically suffering through drizzle and light rain and anxiously enduring the inchworming of the chockstone climbs, we eventually emerged triumphant in a heavier rain. The day ended in exultation. This feeling of elation was later tempered with fear and thoughts of mortality when a flash flood roared by.

The following few pages tell the story of that dramatic day as I wrote it soon after the end of our odyssey. It begins at our camp at the chockstone at the end of the SOB narrows above Upset Rapids. The participants were brother Al, son Stan, friend Robert, and myself. I quote:

"Well, we needn't have worried about being washed away during the night by a flash flood. There were even times when we were favored with stars. It is always a comfort to see them, like the twinklng of the eyes of some benevolent watcher-over-us. Robert came down from his upper camp and joined us for coffee after breakfast and then we were off to whatever awaited us. Today was a key day. Success or failure didn't hang on the outcome, but failure to get up this canyon would cause great hardship because we would then either take the Muav ledges down to Tuckup—which might not go—or go back up to Kanab Creek and take the long way back to SOB.

"The stars of last night had retreated and left low clouds that threatened rain in their place—and rain we did not need. There was no thought of not going on, so on we went. The first part of the drainage was fairly steep, and we climbed up the boulders that blocked our way. The canyon was narrow—about 30 feet wide—and deep. All we saw above us were the Redwall cliffs, and they seemed to close in. Gray skies and shiny gray walls gave a wintry feeling to the air. Soon we came to the first major bypass and Al went right on past, even though he had been here twice before. We yelled at him and soon we were all climbing up on the right-hand side. This bypass was just past the first major eastern drainage; we climbed up some 250 feet before contouring back into the main drainage. Sometimes the ledge was pretty narrow, but it was easy enough. Soon there was another bypass on the left, but this was much shorter and nowhere near as high.

Flash Drizzle?
"By now it had started to drizzle, and the possibility of a "flash drizzle" occurred to each of us. I suppose there was a chance we could have been washed away, but the skies were so uniformly gray and the drizzle so light I felt we were safe enough. There were occasional wide places in the drainage that offered sanctuary if we could get to them. Furthermore, if the rain were light over the entire area, my feeling was that even if the water came down on us, it would not be a sudden wall but would rise more slowly, giving us time to seek safety. About this time we had lunch, and it was a great comfort to have some hot coffee to warm the core. It was raining hard enough that we sought shelter for our packs but not so hard that we sought shelter for ourselves. Still, the wet limestone was slippery when we started up again.

"In good weather these narrows can be gloomy. Bright sky and an occasional sunlit cliff contrast unhappily with the uniform gray of the walls to give a feeling of gloom and confinement. But now the skies were gray and our surroundings a glistening and gleaming white and the feeling was one of brightness and subterranean openness.

Hint of Trouble
"The others saw it—Al at first thought it was a pale dried root stretched across his path. I was glad I missed it; it would have depressed me. Al was more pragmatic—he picked up a catclaw log. He knew right away that one of the light nylon lines he and I had rigged earlier to get the climbing rope up through the carabiners was washed away. When we reached the first chockstone, we thought the carabiner was gone, too. There was so much debris on the bolt and hanger that the carabiner was partially obscured. Fortunately, it was still there. Without it our task would have been even more difficult than it was.

Climbing Skills Needed
"I had always known Al had the reputation of being a good climber, but the next few hours were to show that his abilities were all real and not some inflation of an admiring journalist. As it turned out, *all* the light nylon lines we had put in were washed away. But all the carabiners were still in place. The upclimbing of each of the four bolted chockstones was accomplished in the same fashion. Al would climb it, rig the climbing rope in the carabiner, and the rest of us would prusik up. While all this was going on, we would raise the packs. All that Al had to work with, besides his skill, was

one Friend and one Crack-N-Up—and, at the end, one catclaw log. He used these climbing aids for direct aid as well as for protection by belay. To the uninitiated, a Friend is an engineering marvel with cams that collapse against a spring when they are inserted in a crack and that expand and wedge in when you try to pull it out.

Pool

"The second chockstone was an exception to the protocol. The pool below it was 30 feet or so long and part of it was over my head. The first idea for getting our packs across to the rock at the base of the chockstone was to pendulum them across using the bolt. After Al had climbed up, he fed a rope through the carabiner and Robert prepared to pull quickly on the rope when I had the pack in position. This was necessary because the point of support was across the pool. Even with no slack, my pack—I was forced to volunteer mine because it was my idea—would dip into the pool as it swung to the other side unless the rope were pulled quickly and strongly during the swing to lift the pack somewhat. I waded out into the frigid pool slithering and slipping on the bottom with the pack over my head, trying to maintain my footing. I was more or less successful but had to keep fighting for my balance. Finally I began slipping under and shouted, "Hurry, Robert, pull. It's all yours!" He pulled vigorously. The pack swung out just skimming the water. I swam the pool and climbed out on the other side and lifted my pack so Al could grab it. It was wet, but not very, and nothing of importance was damaged.

Pool Requires Plan B

"But it was clear we needed Plan B. It called for Al to climb as high as he could conveniently and move to a point more directly over the center of the pool. That way we could pendulum packs across without getting our feet wet. At least that was the theory. And that was the way it worked out in practice, too. The only weak link was having Al perched on a tiny 60-degree ledge holding our packs with the barest of friction on the wet, slippery limestone. As long as he didn't have to do any lifting things were okay. Fortunately, he was high enough so that was all he had to do. We got all the packs across with no dunking.

A New Climbing Outfit—None

"By this time it was drizzling harder and we were wet and cold with our shirts on. We had already shed our shorts because we had been wading a good deal of the time in waist-deep water. We found it more comfortable to strip and wear a poncho to trap the warm air the body produced. Unfortunately, I didn't have a poncho, but I used Stan's some of the time.

Unexpected Chockstone

"After the second chockstone, there comes a long middle section—maybe a mile—of slot pools and bathtub pools, only one of which is deep enough to cause problems. It was in here we encountered an unexpected chockstone—an unbolted one. Was it new? Or was the bed more filled in the last time we were here? Anyway, there was a big pit—10 feet in diameter and about 5 feet deep—lined with thick, stinking, gooey red mud. We all climbed up on the left, using the Crack-N-Up—moving it from a low position to a higher one as we climbed. Each person left a slathering of slippery goo in his wake so the climb became increasingly more difficult. The last person—me—needed a hand at the top.

Catclaw to the Rescue

"The third chockstone was easy but still tiring. By the time we came to the fourth, we were tired and our hands cold. Al's, especially, began to cramp up. His fingers refused to obey his instructions and curled up into an arthritic fist. The secret to this climb was a well-thrown catclaw log. Since all the ropes were wet, the prusik knots tightened up and were hard to loosen when it was time to slide them up the rope. This required use of the fingers and ours, too, began to refuse to do their assigned tasks. Eventually, though, we finished all our climbing.

Finally Out

"I was the first one to go on up to where we climb out of the narrows, and I found myself some shelter under a bulge in the wall and waited for the others. In the last hour or so the drizzle became a steady rain, and as the others came up we all felt it was time to get the hell out. I had been vaguely terrified when I descended that part of the Redwall the first time, but subsequent encounters bred a small bit of contempt. Now, even with my pack on, I scampered up as though the demons of the pit were after me. Fortunately, carnivorous limestone is no slipperier wet than dry. I thought I tasted blood, but it was only the rain washing salty sweat into my mouth. There are some smooth ledges under overhangs where the narrows begin, and this is where we camped. It was now 4:00 P.M.—it had taken us eight hours to go 2.5 miles.

"Since we had been in the rain for most of the day, we had a lot of wet clothes which we now strung up to dry as best we could under the overhang. There was some wind, however, so whatever we hung up on the sharp limestone projections did not usually stay there long. Since anything that blew away would probably go over the edge into the gorge, we watched everything very carefully. We smoothed our sleeping places, set up the kitchen, and then turned to the serious business of margaritas. We consumed them with more than the usual amount of self-congratulation and relief at welcoming the end of the day all in one piece. Dinner was green chili stew—a favorite with all. Allen was clearly the hero of the day, and we all hugged him and congratulated him on a job well done. We were out and felt we had cheated the Grim Reaper once again.

Robert's Ascent Is Pure

"Robert was particularly pleased at the way the day had gone, but for a strangely selfish reason. He had not wanted to come with us up SOB, but neither did he want to go the long way around on his own. The reason he hadn't wanted to join us was that our planned use of preplaced bolts spoiled the purity of his venture. He wanted success to depend on man—him, preferably—and not on machine. Using bolts did not fit into his plan. The reason he did join us was that he was still seriously inconvenienced by the near-fatal fall he had taken more than a week before. So when Al was forced to climb all the chockstones, Robert's objections to the route vanished and his trip was 'pure' again.

"It is interesting to note that maintaining the 'purity' of his endeavor had already caused Robert to refuse to leave his recovery camp at Muav Saddle to seek medical help for his injuries. When Robert was examined after his trip, he was found to have had a cracked pelvis and some broken vertebrae. I should also point out that Robert's hike had begun near Green River, Utah, so his was a more serious expedition than ours.

The Drizzle Finally Flashes
"At dusk the sky began to lighten and the rain stopped. The skies cleared and we could see sunlight on the distant cliffs to the east. Then, suddenly, there were clouds blowing over the opposite cliffs and it was raining again, this time with greater earnestness and deliberation. We were exceedingly grateful to be under shelter and gleefully thumbed our noses at the storm. We were especially grateful to be out of the trench and if I didn't actually dance—and I think I did—at least I was dancing inside. While we were engaged in these displays of happiness, there was a roar and a waterfall gushed over the Redwall opposite us. There was a great deal of noise, and it drew us out in the rain in the gathering dusk to get a better look. I don't know whether it was the day's accumulation that was represented or whether it was just the heavier rains of the last hour or so—or both—but there was a lot of water in a great hurry to get somewhere.

"After about thirty minutes of this excitement, there was an even louder roar as water raced down the canyon itself. This we had to see, too, and we went over to the edge where it drops off in a 35-foot waterfall. There wasn't enough water to cover the chockstone, but at the edge it was about a foot deep where earlier it had only been an inch deep. The water hurtling into the gorge made an enormous noise, and we shone our feeble lights into the cauldron. It was frightening. The impression I still have is that of a pack of wild brown and white dogs in a feeding frenzy.

"When we returned to our shelter, I found it difficult to contain my ecstasy and I didn't try. Part of my excess of feeling was generated by having a very difficult and extremely important day end with success—without the necessity of bolts or body bags. In a very real sense, it was all downhill from here. The next month would have its difficulties, but at least it would 'go' one way or another. This day might very well not have 'gone' at all. We were fortunate that Al's capabilities were equal to the task. I doubt that I or Robert could have done it. Stan thinks he could have, but . . . In any case a great burden of uncertainty had been lifted from me and I needed to celebrate the release. I shouted obscenities into the darkness at the top of my voice and listened with awe as they bounced off the cliffs with a mix of wind and echo. My words must have served as nuclei for anti-raindrops, for soon the sky cleared again and the stars shone. The moon was in the east and shone upcanyon, illuminating our waterfall and flooding us with an eerie light.

NEED FOR A CLF COUPON

"Our clothes were not drying well. It was nearly dark and the humidity was high so we decided to use one of the cheery little fire coupons (see page 92) we had carefully saved for such an emergency. We built a cheery little fire. As we sat close around it, holding our wet clothes to the heat, we felt a slow ebbing of the intense emotion and began to think about what might have been if the waterfall and flash flood had been four or five hours earlier. Had we been foolhardy—and lucky—or rational and sensible—and lucky. The consensus was we would have been seriously inconvenienced—perhaps even have lost some gear—but we would not have been killed. I don't think the drainage would have had more than 2 feet of water in it at most, and we could have found refuge on a ledge or boulder in a place where the canyon widened, or even in the cave that forms under a chockstone—that would have been an exciting place to be.

"It was then we saw the *glob*—a gigantic mound of something pale white. It looked ghostly and sinister—it surely could have eaten Cleveland if it had so desired. It was some time before I recognized this glob as moonlight on a Redwall buttress—it didn't look like moonlight. I was manic on the events of the day and what I saw—until reason returned—was a *glob and it was slowly moving toward me.*

Gift of Water

"Another reason for ecstasy was the very real value of the rain. Our next three days would be on the Esplanade away from water except for the waterpockets shown on the map and Cork Spring—if we could find it. Now there would be plenty of water. Whenever-we-want-it water. Water for bathing, water for wasting, water for sacrifices to the margarita god, water for anything we wanted. Moreover, and this is critical for a complete understanding of our exuberance, we didn't have to carry it! It had been a good day." End of quote.

Back to the Future

In 1990 we were still able to use these bolts (with separate belay) for our descent of SOB. If you are a competent climber good at setting up rappels in awkward places, you won't need these bolts. However, future travelers down SOB should realize that eventually they will corrode to the point where they fail catastrophically.

Before I begin the description of the descent, let me insert a few words of caution. *Do not* attempt this Redwall route unless you or someone in your party is a competent climber. Despite the temptation to thread a rope through the hanger and charge down hand-over-hand, I recommend you proceed with more deliberation. Check the bolt and hanger and nut and use a sling. Above all, leave a rope behind in the hanger so you can prusik back up if something happens and you have to retreat. If you don't know what prusik means, you should be with someone who does.

Rappels Are Necessary

All the rappels are about 15 feet. The first two are onto gravel. The "extra" one, if it is there, is not bolted and must be downclimbed. The third and fourth ones are each onto a rock at the head of a pool—in 1990 this third pool was especially large and the fourth filled with gravel. If either of these last two chockstones has an over-your-head pool in front of it, I suggest the following: Rig a fixed line from the top down across the pool to the far side—it will have to be held tightly at both ends—and lower your packs down the sloping line by a second line attached to the first and to your pack by a carabiner.

Besides the chockstones there were several waist deep pools and one almost-over-your-head pool. Although we passed packs the length of this deep slot pool the first time we went down with packs, I have subsequently learned to place my feet on the sloping right side in waist deep water, lean across to the left side and inch my way through with pack on. It helps to be tall.

Two bypasses came soon after the chockstones. One was an easy traverse on the south side. The other, near the place where the side canyon from the north enters the main canyon, required a long traverse—perhaps 0.25 mile—on the north side to a bay, where you are aided in scrambling back down to the bed by a series of little ledges. From here it is not far to the River. There is a good campsite with flowing water—except possibly in very dry years—just above the final falls which bars easy access to the River. It usually takes me about eight hours to get through the narrows.

Descent to the River

The final descent to the River, which was not necessary because the routes up- or downstream leave from the bench we were already on, required some care—first, a contouring around to the bench on the upstream side, and then a descent through the final Muav layers on the stream side of the point, not the River side. This is steep; you may want about 100 feet of fixed line for the descent. Looking at it from the top—which is always the worst view—one companion was sufficiently intimidated to decide he'd rather have a beer. He was in luck. My son Stan had cached some on the bench for us earlier that summer. I found out a few years later on a River trip that there is a way to the River in the third bay upstream from the point.

A final word on the local fauna. The last few times I have camped here above the final drop to the River delta, I have been showered with pebbles as bighorns moved about above us. There seems to be a family unit living on the high bench. No big rocks have been knocked off, but there is always that possibility. In October 1989 there was a small rattlesnake sharing our water source, but the temperature was low enough that it couldn't even generate enough energy to rattle. The most noxious of the local residents are the ringtails. The frequent boat parties that camp on the beach below us apparently support a population of these nocturnal marauders. We had a bad night.

Ringtails a Pest

The first foray occurred shortly after dark. The ringtail that chose me as its target first took my pens—all four of them—one at a time. In the morning I found them all within 10 feet of my pack. Although I made no special effort to hide food, the creature seemed to have other things on its mind and left the food alone. It especially liked adhesive tape and toilet paper. I tried being a coiled spring with ski-pole walking stick in hand and struck several times, to no avail—the critter was too quick. Then I put my glasses on a ledge by my head hoping it might slow down to sniff them as it went by. It did, and my fist crashed onto its tail. I hope I broke it, because I almost broke my glasses.

Don and Gary had similar experiences; I could see light flashes and hear commotion from their campsites all through the night. As we were leaving the next morning, I saw something high up on a ledge and said, "Hey, Don, don't forget that bag of food you put up there on the ledge." He said, "What food? Where?" and then, "Hey, that's my tape recorder." It was strange. We had plenty of loose, unprotected food, but these critters were strictly high tech.

Section 2: Closing the Loop via Tuckup Canyon

> His way of explaining why off-trail route
> finding in the outback is so easy:
> "The route unfolds as it goes."
> AL STECK

Length
Allow six days, plus rest days, if any, to return to your car from the chockstone camp at the mouth of SOB Canyon.

Water
There is frequent access to water en route to Tuckup Canyon. The last water in Tuckup is about twenty minutes up Tuckup from the Cottonwood Canyon junction. This is a fairly reliable source. At least I do not remember there *not* being water there. I suggest a water and/or a food cache on the road near your exit point.

Quad Maps
7.5-minute maps
   Fern Glen Canyon
   Havasu Falls
   Hancock Knolls
   Hitson Tank
   S B Point

HIKING TIMES

The hiking times given here are a mix of those for the years 1986 and 1989. When the times differed over the same route, I give the longer ones. In general, those for 1989 were about 20 percent longer because daytime

A view of Mount Sinyala from the Esplanade between 150 Mile Canyon and Tuckup Canyon.

temperatures were higher. Estimated times are given in parentheses. "Toreva block" refers to a sort of rotational landslide.

Exit to the East (1989)

Use Areas	Location	Elapsed Times Between Locations (hours)
LB9	SOB Chockstone camp	2:30
	Start high over travertine	:30
	Descent opposite Toreva block	:30
LB9	Ledges Camp with waterfall	1:45
	Low bench to river talus transfer	1:30
LB9	Sinyala camp	:45
	Go up—then over—then high	3:45
LB9	Paradise	3:00
LB9	"2nd river access" camp	1:00
	Cork Spring Canyon	3:00
LB9	River camp beyond travertine	1:15
LB9	River access/beach	1:30
LB9	River access, beach, and shelter	4:45
	Upstream point at Tuckup Canyon	1:15
LB9	Bed of Tuckup Canyon	:45
LB9	Tuckup Canyon beach	(1:30)
	Side canyon going NE	(:15)

	Conglomerate Arch	(2:15)
	Redwall route to Esplanade	1:15
LB9	Cottonwood Canyon	2:30
LB9	Side canyon at the 4,000-foot contour.	1:00
	Base of Coconino Break	:30
	Cliff out	1:15
	Top of cliffs	1:00
	Rim	:40
	5,809-foot benchmark	1:15
	Road junction (signpost-but-no-sign)	1:30
	Cars	

Exit to the North (1986)

Use Areas	Location	Elapsed Times Between Locations (hours)
LB9	Side Canyon at 4,000-foot contour	2:30
	4,880-foot Chockstone	1:15
	Road	(2:30)
	Cars	

ROUTE DETAILS

Our objective was to follow the Muav ledges downstream along the River from SOB to Tuckup. As far as I know, this has only been done once before—by Robert. Fortunately, we had his meticulously detailed maps to guide us.

It is about 15 miles from SOB to Tuckup, a 15 miles worth doing, and I have done it twice—with quite different sets of memories. Even though the time for the "bed-to-bed" journey was close to three and a half days in both cases, I felt more rushed the first time—and intimidated. Robert's heavily annotated maps—"hi/lo access," "river access," "hi only," and so forth—gave me the feeling I was running a maze and might spend considerable time backtracking. I needn't have worried. Of all Grand Canyon hikes, this one probably best deserves my brother's assertion, "Not to worry, the route unfolds as it goes." Indeed it does. You don't need map notes to tell you to go up when that's the only possibility. This in no way means Robert's notes are unnecessary, however, because when you are tired and thirsty and your high bench is an oven, it is a great comfort to know that just around the corner is a ravine leading to the River.

Try for Low Water

The accompanying map with Robert's annotations is more or less self-explanatory. There are basically three levels of travel—along the water, on a sloping bench roughly 50 feet above the water (the "lo" level), and on another sloping bench roughly 150 feet above the water (the "hi" level). On these higher levels you may, at times, wonder where the next water is coming from, but except for the last day, there is frequent access to water. I found both the 1986 and 1989 hikes tiring, the first more than the second. I tend to get more tired for the same effort when I am separated from water, and we were along the River more the second time. This may have been possible because we could take advantage of low midnight water. The water travels approximately 100 miles a day so low water leaving the dam at midnight reaches mile 150 approximately a day and a half later—at noon.

Despite the fact that others may not be able to take advantage of low water in the early afternoon, I am going to base the route description on this second, pleasanter, experience. The participants were brother Allen, Allen's son Lee, Al's climbing friends Jim Wilson and Dick Long, Dick's nephew Brooke Long, my friends Don Mattox, Gary Ladd, and Katie Schmidt, and myself.

With all this climbing experience, it was no surprise that we all went down to the beach. We used the route on the SOB side of the upriver point and rigged a handline to make this descent easier. I used to scamper up and down without one, but no more. The boatman who helped me place a food and beer cache earlier in the year climbed to the bench on the River side of the upstream point—in the third little bay, I think. One advantage to putting in a cache is that you can have at least one elegant dinner. I forget what ours was—probably nothing too elaborate, since we had to carry out the trash. For the purists who are wondering, we also carried out the cache cans.

First of the Narrow Places
We left camp at 7:00 A.M. and immediately encountered the first of the four narrow places Robert noted on his map. It came between camp and the point. We had studied it the day before, so it didn't come as a complete surprise. Nevertheless, I moved with highly focused concentration. As soon as we got to the point a few minutes later, we could see the second narrow place. It was only a little worse than the narrow spot on the ledge trail out to the viewpoint above Deer Creek Falls. Certainly no real obstacle although a few of us dragged our packs a few feet because of the low clearance. We were on the low level and stayed there until we dropped to River level at 8:50. We went along the shore for 100 yards and then climbed high to get around a travertine cliff. This is just across from a 2,600 contour designation. A housesized slump (called a Toreva block) across the River marked the place where we could return to the lower bench via a boulder-filled ravine. The descent soon brought us to some ledges that quickly led downstream to what is known to boatmen as the Ledges Camp.

Ledges Camp
The Ledges Camp is a natural place for a rest, and we were certainly feeling natural. There is a small waterfall spreading its bounty and adding to the beauty of sight and sound. We soaked it all in for more than an hour and then moved downstream on the River talus, slowly going higher.

Transfer to Talus
Eventually we could transfer from the low bench to River level but there may be a problem if the water is high. When Robert was exploring for this route, he noted in his journal that the water was about 4 feet deep here. This meant he had to wade about 15 feet from where the talus was to where he

could climb up the cliff (he was going upstream). Water is at its lowest around noon and is already rising at 3:00 P.M. As we approached the transfer point, we could see the River talus where we wanted to be traveling. We started down off the bench in a bay about 75 to 100 yards upstream from the end of the talus. We went down about half way and contoured in to the final drop to River level. There is a messed up system of ledges here, so look around for the best way. At the final drop we chose to lower packs.

We had no problem with water level. We could climb down and step across 2 feet of water to a sandbar that was inches above it. But the water was rising. So, if you can, plan to get to this point early in the afternoon. If it should turn out that new dam release profiles deepen the water here, then we would swim, if we had to, and lower packs on a carabiner along a static line like we had already done in descending SOB.

Much of the way from this transfer point to our intended camp below Sinyala was on ledges. This meant we could travel quickly—and we were there in an hour. We had left camp at 7:15 and arrived at our destination at 2:45. There was nice sand, a small beach, and shelter for five or six people.

The next day we started up to the "lo" level, contoured a bit, and went up a Muav gully to "hi". Two hours later we were above what I call the Gillette rock—a sharp slab of limestone ready to slice an unsuspecting boat in two. It was hot and slow up on the high bench, but there was good shade in the many little limestone bays we contoured in and out of. We returned to the "lo" level when we could at the "river access" and contoured in to Paradise for lunch. Paradise Canyon joins the River at mile 155.4

Paradise

Because it is such a nice place, we stayed about an hour and a half. I would like to camp there someday. There is a beautiful pool right on the lip of the drop to the River, though it is hard to swim in it without stirring up great quantities of silt. There are also trees, shrubs, and grass as well as a sheet of slow, squiggly water flowing down a sloping wall with horizontal corrugations. The problem is that the water is only marginally palatable but, if you think it is too bad, River water is close by.

Paradise is almost on the eastern edge of the SB Point quad; the next landmark is Havasu Creek. When you are opposite it, you know exactly where you are for absolute double sure. Such certainty is infrequent along this route, so it is most appreciated when it happens. We left Paradise at 1:30 and started cooking in the hot sun. Soon we climbed to the "hi" level, just beyond a grove of ocotillos, where we could move fast. We even found occasional shade as we contoured in and out of a series of bays.

Havasu Creek

Very soon we had a view of Havasu Creek that few people have enjoyed. One of us yelled, but no one on the other side took notice. There were seventeen 18-foot yellow rafts snuggled in the estuary at the mouth. Allen likened them to a swarm of yellow jackets sipping at a tiny spring.

Sand for Sale

After passing Havasu we could descend to the low bench. Dick wanted to camp there, but I thought it was too awkward and dangerous to get to water, so we moved downstream 0.25 mile. We camped at the second of a pair of debris fans among boulders on insignificant patches of sand. Those who had extra sand "sold" it to those who needed more to smooth out their little nesting spots. Gary noted in his journal that there were "lots of bighorn droppings along today's route. High of 97 degrees in the shade on my thermometer."

The next day dawned as bright and clear as its predecessors and we were on our way by 7:15. We climbed the talus behind camp and in an hour were in the shaded confines of the Cork Spring drainage. There was no running water, but the seeps and pools created a special beauty of their own. After that, Robert's map said to climb to the "hi" level just before descending to the River, but we were so happy chugging along at the level we were on, that we decided to stay there as we passed a big travertine shoulder that I estimate to be at mile 159.1.

Travertine Shoulder

The slab we were on got steeper and steeper—up to 75 degrees—but we didn't care because we had a tiny bit of mountain sheep track to follow. Finally, the track disappeared and we were left on the edge of oblivion with only a rounded ripple to travel on. About this time a boater going by under us called out, "Is there a trail up there?" Mattox yelled back, "There is now." With great care and trepidation we managed to get to a chute which we followed up to where we should have been in the first place. From there it was up and over the top of the travertine, where we could immediately descend to a beautiful beach by the River—and lunch. I estimate this campsite to be at mile 159.2, and Robert noted another at mile 159.5. This spot had all the ingredients for a good camp—water, sand, and ample shelter—but it was only lunchtime. We managed to while away an hour and a half before gathering our wandering minds together and moving on at 12:45.

Along River

The next stretch was along the River. Our route was shady and scenic, but eventually the talus pinched out and we were forced up on the rocks against the cliff. On occasion these, too, disappeared and we were forced to wade short distances through water up to 2 or 3 feet deep. We did this a little after 3:00, but when Gary came through an hour later, the water was more like 4 feet deep—up to his crotch and he's a tall man. At 3:30 we made camp on a beach also furnished with an overhang. It was a good camp. It is opposite the "2,000" contour label and I estimate it to be at mile 161.2.

Whose Cairns Are These?

By staying so long along the River, we missed a cairn I had seen on the earlier trip. The notations "monument" on the map refer to cairns—one about 4 feet high that is built up against and on a large existing rock and another, slightly smaller and freestanding, about a mile farther downstream. We could find no evidence of authorship. They may be marking a mining claim, but I don't think so. Since his party was on starvation rations and he was "in a race for a dinner" when he passed here, it is unlikely they were built by Powell. For a while I thought they had been built by Stanton since he was planning to put his railroad tracks along this bench.

Stanton's journal, however, as edited by Smith and Crampton in *The Colorado River Survey,* notes they left Rapid No. 355 (presumably Upset Rapid at SOB Canyon) at 2:18; stopped at 2:28 and spent fifteen minutes at a large side canyon on the right (presumably Tuckup); stopped for another seventeen minutes at 2:53 to take pictures at Rapid No. 357; and passed Vulcan's Throne at 3:35. These times show that Stanton was moving fast through this part of the Canyon—less than an hour and a half from Upset to Lava—and I don't think anyone could build one of these monuments in fifteen minutes. So they aren't Stanton's, either.

Last Water
We left camp at 7:15 and moved downstream to the next boulder fan. This would be the last sure water until we reached the bed of Tuckup, so we filled both ourselves and our water bottles with the stuff before climbing up to the only bench available. Soon we contoured into the bay labeled "seep + waterpockets," and on the upstream corner we passed the second cairn we had found on the first trip. I forgot to look for it on this second trip.

We had camped in the "seep + waterpocket" canyon on the first trip. There were some bathtub sized potholes near the lip of the drainage and many thin seeps. There were also mosquitos, a very persistent ringtail, and much rain during the night. Shelter was at a premium. Two people could sleep lying down, but the rest had to sleep sitting up. Now, in 1989, there was no water of any consequence.

More Narrow Places
The high slope we had used on the earlier trip sometimes cliffed out, and we had to deal with narrow places in bays at the head of small drainages. At one the sheep had a "trail" along a ledge little wider than your boot. The stuff we walked on looked like hard mud pasted to the cliff and worn more or less flat by hooves and, indeed, that may be exactly what it was. But I prefer to believe it was a narrow Muav ledge covered with a thin layer of mud. In any case, we moved with great caution, trying not to put our full weight down. In one place I had to walk all bent over while trying to forget how heavy I was.

At this earlier time, we also encountered another narrow place that Robert mentioned. This one was, quite simply, too narrow for us. Fortunately, this happened to be the only bay we could cross by going down one side and back up the other. Pictures of us descending into this bay make us look as though we were standing on thin air. Actually we were standing on very narrow ledges—maybe half the width of our boot. Contouring around and down on a series of these ledges took us to a talus slope where life became much easier. Now, three years later, I encountered none of this that I can remember. Going along the River as long as we did must have meant we had bypassed the problems.

The Tedious Part

After we rounded the bend and began heading west-northwest, the way became particularly tedious. We could see the debris fan at the mouth of Tuckup but it seemed to take forever to get there—so much in and out, and it was so hot. Be prepared to have to go some distance into the Tuckup drainage to get down—it will seem like it takes forever if it is hot. We had to go by a rather large bay about 0.5 mile inside the canyon and then down minor cliffs and talus to the bed. It was all much harder and hotter than I expected, and I suffered. This "contouring around" was, in Gary's words, on a "trailless, ball-bearing-covered, loose, sun-seared, 45-degree slope." We had left camp at 7:15, were at the point on the upstream side of Tuckup by 12:00 and were in the bed of Tuckup by 1:15—just in time for a late lunch. This meant it took an hour to go 0.5 mile. After luxuriating in the shade and in the pools until 3:00 on cool, smooth Muav ledges, we headed on down to the beach.

For completeness, the next two paragraphs are copied from the route description for the Tuckup Canyon/Stairway Canyon Loop in chapter 5.

A few bypasses still remained before the final descent to the beach through the Muav and it was two hours before we reached it. If you have stayed in the bed, you will know you are almost there when you find a chockstone at the top of a 40-50 foot pour-off. If you reach the pour-off, back up a ways and take the trail contouring around on stream right. This trail is soon quite high above the drainage—a hundred feet or so—and if you are looking for an easy way down you will be disappointed. Instead, look for a very steep chute in the bedrock with a small ledge almost at the bottom. Once I missed it and went all the way out to the point above the beach. If that happens to you, retrace your steps with your expectations set a little lower.

The descent of the chute is fairly easy even though it is very steep and there is only one place—almost at the ledge—where I wish to pass my pack. Beyond the ledge there is an almost vertical 20-foot drop to the bed. At the beach side of the ledge, a small ramp provides access to the hand- and footholds that take you diagonally down across the face to where you can scramble to the bottom. This climb down the wall requires some climbing skills—it helps not to be acrophobic—and I recommend that you lower your packs and use a belay. This all takes time and the ten of us spent ninety minutes making this descent. Camp was on the beach along the River at the mouth of Tuckup.

A Jim Story

We retrieved the cache I had put here earlier by boat and began cooling the celebratory brews. Tomorrow would be a rest day, and the usual flurry of camp activity slowed considerably. Around supper time the tempo picked up somewhat and Jim Wilson volunteered to prepare the meal. This would seem to be a simple task—add water and warm—but there was one glitch. I should add that Jim lost his sense of smell when he was run over by a car in the early 1980s. Thus it was that our milk was reconstituted into a grim, gray, glob of gunk. When I saw the result and examined it, I could tell in a whiff what had happened. Jim had made up the milk by mixing it with our entire supply of Everclear—to the uninitiated, Everclear is 190-proof alcohol; dehydrated alcohol, as it were. Everclear looks like water and, to him, it smelled like water. Fortunately, the milk was so curdled we could put the mess in a nylon bag and squeeze 90 percent of the elixir out. Thus was the done undone. From then on, our margaritas had a milky cast to them, but who cared.

The Roof at Tuckup

A climbing problem was the focus of the next morning's activity. The upstream corner at the mouth of Tuckup Canyon is a small, friendly 20-foot cliff, and the top of that cliff is an overhang. Brooke set up a belay for those interested in climbing the overhang—aka "the roof." Everyone who tried could climb the cliff by bypassing the roof, but that wasn't true for the roof itself. Brooke could easily climb to the roof, reach out and up to a hold on the face of the overhang, put a foot up on the face as well, and then power himself up above the roof. It took great upper-body strength and skill to do this and he had plenty of both. Dick, Al, Lee, and Gary tried the roof several times and failed. George, Don, Katie, and Jim formed a cheering section. When the sun hit the wall at 10:30, the climbing nuts sought something else to do.

Mongolian Stick Climbing

Some sought shade, some went downriver, Gary went upcanyon and I went upriver to see how far the talus went. I went about 1.5 miles to the middle of the bend, decided that was far enough, and headed back to my lunch, which I had forgotten to bring with me. Everyone, except Gary, was inside the mouth of the canyon in the shade. After a while some of us ventured out in the sun and found other shade against the cliffs out by the River. As the shadows lengthened, Al and Dick gave us an exhibition of Mongolian Stick Climbing.

The cliffs that were affording us shade were limestone and, as such, were covered with solution holes—each 1 to 1.5 inches in diameter. Expert Mongolian Stick Climbers would tie sticks firmly to the soles of each foot, grasp others in each hand, and walk up the cliff by sticking the sticks in the holes. Our Stick Climbers were not so expert. They chose not to put sticks on their feet, partly because the sticks were driftwood, and hence fragile, and partly because their ankles might be damaged if the sticks did not come out of the holes when they fell. Still, the exhibition was a success. Pulling up and swinging on one stick while placing the next, our Mongolian Stick Climbers, with a certain flailing of the feet, managed to get several feet off the ground. It looked like fun, but the rest of us just watched. At dinnertime Al finally did the roof route while Lee and Gary failed again. Dick was saving his strength for another try tomorrow. I forget who put dinner together, but it wasn't Jim.

Another Jim Story

I should also mention that Jim is an astrophysicist. As such, he brings a special order to otherwise complex, chaotic tasks. One such task is that of commissariat—the person who creates the menu and purchases the food for a trip such as ours. Jim's first principle is to forget the menu; that is an unnecessary complication. To paraphrase Allen, Jim believes the menu "will unfold as you go." The purchasing of the food is also greatly simplified, although he does need an assistant. A calculator, which multiplies and subtracts, is also helpful.

As he enters the grocery store, Jim first calculates the Total Food Number. This number, call it T, is 24 times the number of people on the trip times the number of days for the trip. We were nine people for nine days so T would be 1,944. Then he starts at the far left-hand aisle so he can go clockwise through the store and begins pulling items off the shelves. As he does so, he calls out the number of ounces on the label; the assistant subtracts that number from T. Up aisle, down aisle goes the duo until finally there is a subtraction that gives a negative number. "Bingo," says the assistant, and the two of them pack it in and head for checkout. It should be clear by now that the ultimate cuisine will best be served if Jim's speed down the aisles is somehow proportional to $1/T$; that is, the less food needed, the faster the travel. Otherwise, the entire menu for a short trip might be breakfast cereal.

Can you see the menu unfolding as the trip progresses? The food is stowed away in several packs, and some is pulled out when it's time for a meal. No one has to dig very deep in his or her pack to find something appropriate for a given meal, and the right number of ounces is extracted. Sometimes, toward the end of a trip, we might have tuna fish for breakfast or cereal for dinner, but this will be rare and, besides, over the years it will all average out.

First Exit to Esplanade
The next morning we were ready to go at 7:00, but first there was more roof climbing. Dick, Gary, and Allen each tried one last time, unsuccessfully, and we finally left at 7:20. We had all climbed the Muav cliff by 7:45 and were back in the bed of Tuckup by 8:00. Then it was on to the Conglomerate Arch. This is a strange geological feature and the only such arch in the park that I know of. Right after it is a chockstone. I usually climb this obstacle by first climbing to the top of the bridge on stream left and then traversing to the top of the chockstone. In a little while we passed a slot canyon on stream right that went back 30 feet or so—at about the 2,700-foot contour. Between it and a big break on stream right there is a smaller break on stream left that ultimately takes you to the Esplanade—to the east.

Return via Esplanade
If we were returning to SOB Canyon via the Esplanade, we would leave Tuckup Canyon by that small break. However, since we had had no rain and I didn't want to count on finding water at Cork Spring, I decided to close the loop by another route. The route up the break is to climb 15 feet of cliffy ledges and then climb another 50 feet up a boulder-filled ravine to the base of the final 25 feet of Redwall cliff. There are enough—I won't say plenty of—holds to get up this sloping wall far enough that you can contour left over to the flats and up through a few broken cliffs to the top of the Redwall. Then the route takes you on a climbing curve around a Supai corner to the north and east and then southeast to a deep chimney that can be climbed to the top.

There will be two places to pass or raise packs. Once on top you can follow what is shown as the Tuckup Trail on the 15-minute quad maps.

Pictograph Camp

On this Esplanade return, I noted a "Pictograph Camp" near Cork Spring. This is a large flat-roofed overhang that we could see from afar as we approached it from the east in 1977 on our way to Lava Falls. The opening is about 5 feet high, and we found a stack of firewood, jars of white substances that I took to be sugar and flour, and a fire ring. It would sleep six or eight. I spread out my ground cloth, pad, and sleeping bag and lay down for a short rest before dinner. When I looked up I saw what looked to me like tapa cloth covering the ceiling. Looking closer, I could see that the whole underside of the overhang was covered with pictographs. My recollection is that it was an overall design rather than a collection of separate figures.

Route to Cork Spring

The only Cork Spring that Robert and I have found is at the top of the Redwall. Fortunately, there is a route to it from the Esplanade that I have tried to show on the map. Robert and I used it once when we came downstream from SOB Canyon to Cork Spring canyon on the Redwall and returned to SOB on the Esplanade.

Reentry to SOB

If you use the Esplanade for your return to SOB, you need to know you can get into the bed of SOB—and to water—three ways. First is via the canyon just north of Boysag Point on the Havasu Falls quad map—the spring is dry and a pour-off about half way down is bypassed to the north. You will have to contour into SOB on a bench for about 0.5 mile before dropping to the bed. The second way in is via the canyon leading to Hotel Spring. There is water and trail construction down this canyon. The third is via the Tuckup Trail that passes Buckhorn Spring. This is all I will say about the return to SOB Canyon via the Esplanade, except to add that I wouldn't do it until after a substantial rainstorm. Now, back to a better way of closing the loop in hot weather.

1989 Exit to Rim

Now that we had given up the idea of returning to SOB Canyon via the Esplanade, we decided to explore for a likely route up the canyon that goes almost due east of Schmutz Spring. Earlier I had been down a ravine about half way into the Coconino from the top and also about half way up into the Coconino from the bottom and thought I might connect these two routes. We made camp on the Esplanade at the edge of this canyon above Tuckup. The only problem was that I had not found water where I expected it below a chockstone at about the 3,400-foot contour. This meant we had to go back to the last water we had found which was about twenty minutes up from the Cottonwood Canyon junction. We were at camp by 4:00, but it was 6:30 before we had brought back all the water we needed.

Since we weren't going back the long way, we had extra food, extra margarita mix, and, the saints be praised, extra Everclear. Since it was our last night in the Canyon there was only one thing to do: Have a party.

Up and Out

We left about 7:30 the next morning and headed toward an obvious break in the lower Coconino that would take us up to a narrow band of talus. From camp to the bottom of the break and up it to the talus took about an hour and a quarter. We could follow this band of talus only a little beyond where I had already explored—perhaps a 150 yards—then it dead-ended in a cliff. But on our left, to the north, was a wide chimney leading to two 25-foot climbs. We handed up the packs and climbed on belay. One of these climbs, I forget which, can be bypassed by climbing a steep, crumbly, white, powdery slope a little farther east. To get up these two cliffs took about ninety minutes. Then we followed a game trail through more white, powdery dirt to an obvious exit ravine. Soon were on top—it was 11:00. Hiking east-northeast for another thirty minutes brought us to the road, and then it was only ten more minutes to our water cache at the 5,909-foot benchmark.

Brooke and Katie didn't wait for lunch but took off for the cars. The rest of us ambled through lunch before doing the same. The plan was they would be so fast they would reach the cars and get back to the signpost-without-a-sign junction about the same time we did. We were at the junction in seventy minutes, and they arrived twenty minutes later. And thus it ended, with neither a bang nor a whimper—just general happiness all around.

1986 Exit to Rim

If you choose to close the loop via the long north-northeast arm of Tuckup Canyon, the scenario is similar. At that time we had lunch at the 4,000-foot contour and left at 1:00 and were at the major chockstone near the top of the Coconino at 3:00. This obstacle can be climbed or bypassed to either side, but the rest of the way was slow—lots of big boulders and brush. The drainage splits just below the 5,600-foot contour, and the northerly half quickly ends in a box. We almost missed the other half that came from the east over an 80-foot dryfalls; in fact, part of our group had already started up some talus to the north. The rest of us went up some very steep talus to the south on the downstream side of the split. Since there were still several dryfalls in the bed of this arm, we wished we had climbed higher into the trees before contouring into it.

Soon the bed began splitting into myriad shallow drainages, and we decided to head east cross country to the road—calling out occasionally for our friends who had gone north. We found each other and the road at about the same time. We had left a car near here so we didn't have to go back to the trailhead. If we had, we would have found that it was about a mile to the aforementioned benchmark; then the route unfolds as before. If you leave a car here, I suggest marking the tributary drainages down 0.25 mile or more so when the bifurcations begin, then you will know which arms take you to the car. Alternatively, mark the road with small cairns in such a way that when you reach the road and find one, you will know which direction to take to the car and how far you have to go.

Section 3: Closing the Loop via Kanab Creek

> A general statement of condition on waking
> in the morning all bright eyed and bushy tailed:
> "Oh, God, to think by nightfall we'll all be invalids again."
>
> SARA STECK, day nine of a forty-two
> day hike from Lees Ferry to Lava Falls

Length
Allow six days, plus rest days (if any) to return to your car from the chockstone camp if you exit at Kanab Point. Allow two additional days if you return via the Esplanade.

Water
There is occasional access to water en route to Olo Canyon. There are occasional springs in Kanab Canyon en route to Scotty's Hollow. In an emergency you can purify the creek. Unless there has been a recent rain, you should not expect to find water beyond the small spurting spring just before the exit canyon in Scotty's Hollow. Do not count on Jewel Spring. The big pothole shown near Jewel Spring is a possibility, but not reliable. Cork Spring is more reliable, though you may have to go down to the top of the Redwall to find the water. If you return via the rim road from Kanab Point, you may find water in the stock tank by the road—but purify it.

Quad Maps
7.5-minute maps
Fishtail Mesa
Havasu Falls
Hitson Tank
Kanab Point
S B Point

ROUTE TO TRAILHEAD AT KANAB POINT

Mileage

0.0   This roadlog begins at the signpost-with-no-sign near the 5,757-foot benchmark. Leave the intersection heading north-northeast.

1.2   After 1.2 miles you reach a fork. Bear right. The left fork is blocked by branches for some distance.

1.9   After 0.7 mile a road comes in from the right. Go straight.

2.6   After 0.7 mile you reach a gate—probably open. Leave it as you found it. There are bad ruts through here, and it feels like they might tip you over.

3.2   After 0.6 mile a road comes in from the right. Go straight. Follow the sign—a weathered wooden arrow.

4.5   After 1.3 miles a rutted road comes in from the left. Go straight.

5.2   After 0.7 mile the road becomes badly rutted. We went around to the left.

5.6   After 0.4 mile you reach Merle Findlay Tank. If you close the loop by hiking along this road, you will want to put out water caches at easily found places. This is one such place. Where the fence crosses the road is another.

9.6   After 4.0 miles a faint road goes off to the right to a viewpoint. It is in

157

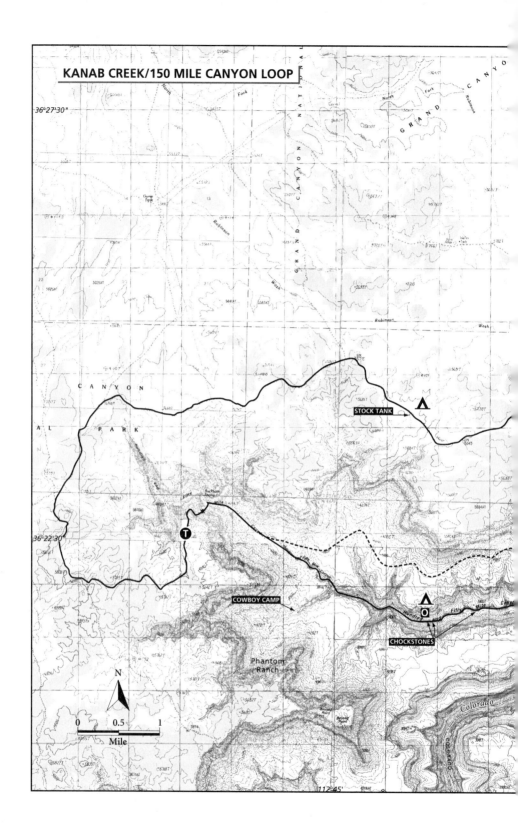

KANAB CREEK/150 MILE CANYON LOOP

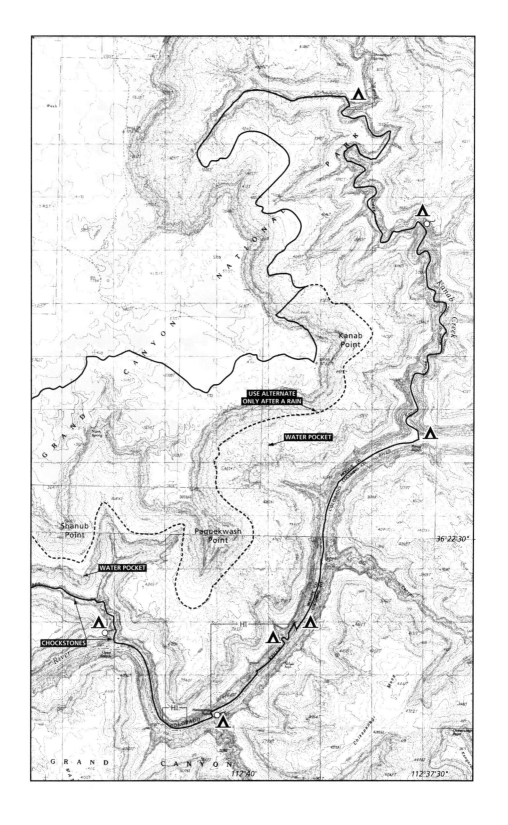

USE ALTERNATE
ONLY AFTER A RAIN

WATER POCKET

Kanab
Point

Shanub
Point

Paguekwash
Point

WATER POCKET

CHOCKSTONES

HI

HI

G R A N D   C A N Y O N

36°22'30"

112°40'

112°37'30"

good condition. We looked for the 5,712-foot benchmark but couldn't find it. Instead, we found an arrowhead—which we left in place.

10.3   After 0.7 mile a road comes in from the left. Go straight.

10.55   After 0.25 mile pass a survey marker on the left.

11.2   After 0.65 mile reach Kanab Point. There is a T here, and the road continues both north and south. The trail begins at the end of the northern stretch of road.

HIKING TIMES

Use Areas	Location	Elapsed Times Between Locations (hours)
▲ LB9	SOB chockstone camp	4:00
▲ LA9	Beach opposite Matkatamiba Canyon	2:45
▲ LA9	Water Bay	:30
	Bay with wisp of water	2:00
▲ LA9	Beach opposite Olo Canyon	2:45
▲ LA9	Mouth of Kanab Creek	1:45
	Big Travertine Spring	2:30
▲ LA9	Junction with Slide Canyon	2:00
▲ LA9	Point of False Scotty's Castle	2:30
▲ LA9	Junction with Scotty's Hollow	1:15
	Junction with Exit Ravine	1:15
	Top of Redwall	1:00
▲ LA9	Flash Flood Ledge	1:30
	Mushroom rock	1:00
	Passing first point	1:00
	Passing second point	2:00
▲ LA9	Helipad	1:15
	Top of talus	1:30
▲ NK9	Canyon rim	5:15
	Gary reaches car	1:30
	Gary returns to Kanab Point	

ROUTE DETAILS

The 150 Mile Canyon/Kanab Creek Loop, as originally conceived, consisted of segments I had previously hiked: trailhead to River down SOB drainage; upriver along Muav benches and river talus to Kanab Creek; up Kanab Creek to Scotty's Hollow; up it to Esplanade; back along Esplanade to SOB; up and out. When this loop was actually tried, the execution did not quite match the conception.

Value of Plan B

Don Mattox, Gary Ladd and I began our attempt to do this loop in late October 1990, but because Gary was the only one of us to complete it on foot, I consider the effort only a qualified success. However, despite this "defect" in execution, I am going to describe the loop as it happened and treat the return to SOB Canyon via the Esplanade as an alternate. There are several reasons for this. First, it was what happened. Second, it shows how significantly hiking times can be increased by the need for route finding—we spent considerable time scouting the river segment because I had left my notes in the car. And third, it shows the value of having a Plan B. Even though it was not our original intention to go out via the Kanab Point Trail, that exit was always a possibility. In fact, it is now my opinion that this routing is to be preferred; the Esplanade should only be used when a recent rain has filled the potholes.

Route to River Bench

Since I have detailed the descent of SOB separately, I begin this route description at the chockstone at the mouth of SOB. It is now the beginning of the third day of the loop. Getting out to the bench above the River on the upstream side, as we had to do, is always awkward—even without a pack. There is a fine wide ledge to walk on if only the ceiling were higher. Even though he was the tallest, Gary seemed to have the least problem—probably because he had the strongest back. Don took his pack off and dragged it a few feet at the worst places and I struggled along on one knee with the other foot searching for a purchase beyond the steeply sloping edge of the ledge. It was a great help to have Gary nearby to tell me when it was okay to stand up.

The route upstream to Kanab Creek is the reverse of a segment of my through-Canyon hike in 1982 with my son Stan, brother Al, and Robert. As such, it should have been old hat. It wasn't. One, my memory was incomplete—I could remember obstacles but not their location; two, route finding problems were quite different in the two directions; and, three, I had forgotten my notes. Then, in the good old days, it took us a day and a half from Kanab to SOB. Now, going the other direction eight years later, it took us two and a half. More precisely, it was more like three half days. Basically, I got us lost.

The "Impossible" Bay

I remembered two places from the earlier trip with exquisite clarity. One was a traverse high above the River on the narrow ledge that sometimes forms at the base of a cliff. The traverse was short—only about 0.25 mile—but memorable. The other special place was a small bay with an almost vertical semicircular wall—like someone had taken a big bite out of the bench we were on. Robert had told us about its looking impossible (from the upstream side) and he was right. He let us wonder a long time about what we could possibly do before showing us the trick. We climbed down to the base of the wall near the edge of a pour-off. From that vantage point it was clear the wall was not vertical, only very steeply sloping, and that it had many narrow steps on it. Soon Stan was on his way up with pack on; the rest of us quickly followed after he showed us the climb was easy. Easy, but not without features that stirred the adrenaline. At the start, you were above the bed before the pour-off and would fall only as far as you had climbed, but then, as you climbed diagonally out on the face, you were soon beyond the pour-off and would fall as far as you had climbed plus another 100 feet.

The author climbing "Impossible" Bay.

Going the other way I worried especially about this "impossible" bay. I worried about finding the place to begin the descent and I worried, too, about taking that first step off the flat onto the tiny steps. Would we need a belay? How would we lower our packs down the diagonal? As it happened, we did have two problems but neither was one I had worried about.

Go High Early

As we left the mouth of SOB on the low bench, we could look upstream a long way and see, a little over a mile away, a place where the River curved to the left around a point. We could see that our bench had pinched out by that time, but there was still the possibility that some tiny ledge might allow us to squeeze around the point. No such luck. But by the time we found that out, we had thrown much good time after bad and had to climb dangerously crumbly Muav cliffs. It was difficult and time consuming. We should have climbed to the next higher bench while the going was easy—I should say "easier"; it never was easy. My forgotten notes would have shown we should have climbed up about 0.8 mile upstream from SOB at a place east of the "4019T" elevation point. This would be just shy of the spot where the upper bench started around the corner. I estimate it took us three hours to the point opposite a canyon that drains Matkatamiba Mesa and one more hour to the beach opposite Matkatamiba Canyon.

Once high, we stayed high for about 0.75 mile and then moved back to the lower bench when we could see sunlight streaming down Matkat. From there we took a Muav ramp down to the water—and lunch. We were now about 0.25 mile from Matkat. Unfortunately, we had to go up again briefly through sawgrass around a seep and fight the attending vegetation—we tried the middle first, then low; finally we climbed around above it. We reached the beach opposite Matkat at 1250 and, although we had just had lunch, the thought of another rest was good for the soul.

The "Impossible" Is Invisible

As far as I knew, we had not passed the "wall" I had worried so about, and since I couldn't remember exactly where it was, I thought it was still ahead of us. But we wouldn't find it there, either. We had passed it by without recognition just after rounding the point. When I turned the critical corner just before it and caught up with Don, all I saw was a wall. I didn't see *the* wall, I saw only that our ledge had pinched out and wondered what were we going to do next. Don said, "If I hadn't seen Gary go across, I would have said it was impossible." What Gary had done was to start across the wall on the tiniest of tiny ledges. When that disappeared, he stepped down to another that, instead of disappearing in turn, only partially disappeared. It left behind a small rounded wave in the wall just barely big enough to offer traction. That and the handholds were enough to get him across—and us, too. It wasn't until we were at our Olo camp the next day and I realized we had not seen my "impossible" bay that it occurred to me perhaps it was the place I have just described. Even then I wasn't absolutely sure until I compared pictures of my two visits to the "impossible."

Early Camp at Matkatamiba

It had taken us almost five hours—including lunch—to go the 2 miles from the mouth of SOB to the beach opposite Matkat. That it had not been easy was due in large measure to my having forgotten my notes—that cost us an hour of wasted time. It also cost me something more than that: a measure of resolve. We had used up more than half a day to go less than half way to our proposed camp opposite Olo. Being demoralized and not knowing where the next water was, I declared the balance of the day to be a "rest afternoon". This would put us almost half a day behind, but I thought we could catch up.

After a short rest I began to get antsy about tomorrow's route. I didn't want to make a mess out of it, too, so I went on an exploratory mission. I had forgotten most of the details, but hoped the route would unfold as it was supposed to. I found my way to a high bench that I remembered as our previous route, followed it for a while to see how easy it would be tomorrow—the answer was "not very"—and then retraced my steps to the beach. I returned just in time to find a little sunlight left for a "swim" and found Don and Gary talking to Jim Slade, whom I had met ten years before along Shinumo Creek. He was with a group whose boats we could see across the River nestled in the tiny Matkat estuary. Included in that group were others I knew and some I only knew of—we were passing like ships in the night. Jim kindly offered us some beer, which was gently consumed with proper reverence, and we talked for half an hour or so before he had to move on. Then I took my swim.

How to Take a Swim

Swim is not the right word. In fact, I don't think there is a single word that accurately describes what takes place. I wade out to about my kneecaps and, as they are growing numb, I wipe myself all over with a wet facecloth followed by a quick and cursory rinse. Then I sit in the water, stretching out so I am completely below the level of the water. This is not the same as being "under water" because I am generally back on the beach before the water would have had a chance to close over my face.

Route Upstream from Matkatamiba

That night's sleep was very restful—Don said the place was too poor to afford either mice or ringtails—and the next morning we left at 7:40 and followed my route from the previous day. We went upstream fifteen minutes or so to a fine flowing spring—welcome today, as the River had turned muddy during the night—and then worked our way up the downstream side of that waterway. There was one big step up onto a boulder behind some sawgrass and I knew Don would make some sort of nasty remark about it—I was not disappointed. He broke the step off as he surged up the rock, so now it will be harder for those who follow. We climbed higher until it was convenient to cross the water and then went up more talus and a chute until we were on a rather steeply sloping bench. It was not easy to walk on, but at least the footing was mostly stable. Bighorns travel this route, too, though it is hard to follow their tracks for long.

A Bay with Water
In an hour we were opposite the first drainage that comes down from Chick-apanagi Mesa. In two more hours we were in a large limestone amphitheater with a little stream—at mile 146.6. This would have been a good destination for yesterday—only three hours from Matkat. But then we would have missed Jim's beers. We rested here in the voluminous shade by the pools and sound of falling water for almost half an hour before restless feet urged us onward to climb the powdery hillside and face the sun and my second intense memory from '82. This impressively narrow, steep, high stretch begins just after the Water Bay. Pictures from '82 give a false impression of a very precarious passage, but pictures don't show the sliver of flat ground we were following. Then I had been intimidated by Robert's description and had a nightmare about the "impossible" traverse. In my dream I crept along sideways by a place that required me to "belly out" around a protrusion when both my footholds pulled out—leaving me hanging by my fingernails. My brother said he couldn't help me because I was too heavy to lift, but Robert lifted me back on my feet with one hand. You can do that in dreams.

Finally, a Way to the River
Half an hour after the Water Bay we passed another small bay with evidence of water—damp sand and sawgrass. Robert's notes indicate he went down to the River here. He also mentioned a cave opposite, but, not having his notes, I didn't look for it. We continued upstream on the high bench. Olo seemed so close—less than 0.5 mile?—but we could not find a way down to the River. Finally, at 3:00, after extensive upstream scouting by Gary, we turned around to go back—to the Water Bay, if necessary. By 3:45 we were on a hospitable beach by the River just upstream from the spot where—on the other side—the lowest level of strata goes under water ending the riparian talus on that side. For the descent we took a talus slope—one of many— down off the high bench we were on to a lower one and then contoured a short distance downstream to a large brown buttress. From there it was a straight shot to the River and a short distance upstream to the beach where we camped. If I had brought Robert's notes, I would have seen his route leaving the high bench for the River southeast of Paguekwash Point.

It was a fine beach but we took our ritual swim without benefit of sunshine. The only sour note was that we should have been here for lunch; we were now a full day behind. We could see people camping upstream on the other side near the Olo entrance and wondered who they were. There was no company for us on our side, though, and we had another quiet night with neither mice nor ringtails.

Ranger Boat
It took us thirty minutes to get from camp to where we could look into the mouth of Olo Canyon. Then one of the boats we had seen there came across to investigate us. Fortunately, I had a permit as it was a park boat skippered by Head Boatman Mark O'Neill. Mark recognized our parched state and prescribed an appropriate remedy. We drank it with reverence, too. We visited with him, Jan Balsam, and another young lady named Holly for about thirty

minutes before the companion boats pulled into the current and their leader took off in pursuit. It was two more hours of boulder-hopping on slippery, slimy boulders to the mouth of Kanab Creek. Morning is the scheduled time of low water and by afternoon the rocks on which we were traveling would probably be under water. If, as is the case as I write, the water releases from Glen Canyon Dam follow an environmentally correct pattern of higher lows and slower increases and decreases, it might be necessary to retreat to ledges higher up, where travel would be harder and less certain.

Olo to Kanab along River
I found out from the park's River Subdistrict people when I got home that yesterday's intended flow was 4,000 cfs—this is low water. It was still low the next morning and we could get all the way along the River talus to Kanab Creek without needing to climb up on the bench above us. Several places were only 4 to 6 feet above water level, and one was only 2 feet above water. Because the River is so narrow here, I estimate a 2- or 3-foot rise in River level for each 5,000 cfs increase in flow. It might pay you to check with the Bureau of Reclamation people at Glen Canyon Dam to find out what the projected flow will be through here during your hike. That way you will know in advance whether you will walk, wade, or climb.

Our goal for tonight was the side canyon leading to the Slide of Susurrus—I call it Slide Canyon. We reached Kanab Creek a little before lunch. The way along the River talus was tedious, and the smoothly polished rocks were slippery. The wet smoothly polished rocks were *very* slippery.

Plovers Play Chicken (1991)
Although we weren't camping at the mouth of Kanab Creek, I wish to describe an incident that occurred there in 1991. Around suppertime a raucous assemblage of birds appeared by the River. There were too many to count, I would guess 100—perhaps 200. They were wheeling and squawking and I was reminded of a line in a John Updike poem in which such a movement of birds was likened to that of a scarf after being tossed into the air on a gusty day. Suddenly, though, these birds alighted on the water at the head of Kanab Rapids on the far side. They faced upstream and paddled fiercely. Nevertheless, despite their best efforts, the mat of birds slowly drifted downstream toward the white water—squawking all the while. At the last minute the flock burst into the air, circled once or twice, and then, once again, landed in the water upstream of the rapid to repeat their drift into the jaws of death. It was a game of chicken—bird versus rapid—and the bird always won, but just barely. This went on for more than an hour. The only variant I could detect was that sometimes the birds were more in the middle of the River, where the penalty for error was larger. One of us, more knowledgeable than the rest, said these birds were plovers. Whatever they were, they had apparently learned how to have fun.

En Route to Scotty's Hollow
Quite a bit of water was coming down Kanab Creek, and the many creek crossings were time consuming if we tried to keep our feet dry. I thought I

166

was one-up on the others with my hightop leather boots—I could wade through shallows up to 5 or 6 inches deep without a care. When Don and Gary followed me with their Hi-Tec lowtops, they got their feet so thoroughly soaked they could wade through deep water without getting any wetter. Bummer. Still reduced to rock-hopping and shallows wading, I was the person who was ultimately one-upped.

We reached Slide Canyon around 4:00 and didn't bother to go up to the slide. How often does this happen? We had spent a full day on the trail and it was time to quit. Don went up the canyon a few hundred yards for water as I don't trust the Kanab Creek water. When he came back it was time for the evening's libation. Still no mice or ringtails. What has happened to them all?

Our start the next morning was the earliest so far and we were at Water Canyon—aka Scotty's Hollow—in four and a half hours. We didn't have to hurry because Gary was staying behind taking photographs. This takes time, and we didn't want to get too far ahead of him. The way up Kanab is frequently tedious, with huge room-sized blocks barring the way. This is where people with wet feet can really move. I struggled and sweated and could catch up to Don only when he rested. We made the initial climbs in Scotty's and had lunch on the smooth rocks above the waterfalls.

No Hello for Hallowed Hollow

From here on, the travel was unhappily very easy. When I had last visited the hollow in the mid-1980s, it was a wondrous place—awash with beauty. Little waterfalls, ponds, ferns, marble bathtubs strung together with small trickles, even some up-to-your-shoulders pools that had to be waded. Now, only five or so years later, the place was a mess—nothing remained. All had been washed away or buried with gravel. Except for the chockstones, the entire route to the exit ravine—the major drainage from the southwest a little more than a mile up—was a gravelly path suitable for horses. The way is much easier now, but not as entrancing. Water still flows but it is not the same. The spring comes from under a chockstone, and there was a pencil-sized squirt coming out of the wall above it. As of October 2001, the pristine beauty of Scotty's Hollow has been restored by a flash flood, which has cleared away all the gravel. Soon after the water stopped, we reached the exit canyon.

The flash flood that had rearranged Scotty's Hollow beyond recognition had done the same to the exit canyon. Where water had been a constant companion, even sometimes a pain in the neck, there was now none—no pools, no waterfalls, no water, period. What had, in 1977, required a triumph of gymnastic skill to keep your feet dry—layouts, laybacks, chimneys—was a gravelly wasteland. A handful of chockstones—one at the bottom junction—continued to provide some excitement and diversity. If your party is of only average competence in climbing such things, let me suggest carrying along a small log at the end of a rope that can serve as a sort of grappling hook. None of the chockstones is very high—10 to 12 feet at the most—but they present a challenge. It took us a little over an hour to make our ascent of this exit canyon to the top of the Redwall, and in another hour we were at our camp on Flash Flood Ledge. I liked camping here again. It gave me a feeling of homecoming and continuity.

Flash Flood Ledge

This ledge is in the Lower Supai on stream right above a 75-foot dry waterfall. Climbing up the falls was a challenge—up a series of 4- or 5-foot ledges and behind fallen blocks wedged in a crack. In 1977, when I first exited Kanab via this drainage, we camped on this ledge to seek shelter from an impending storm. Beginning about dark, we were serenaded by distant thunderbolts— then rain. Even though our ledge began almost at the lip of the pour-off and stretched 50 feet or more beyond it, my nephew Lee was sufficiently concerned by what he considered to be our precarious location that he slept out at the farthest end of the ledge, where it was probably 80 feet to the ground— in his boots. Just where he was planning to go when our ledge went under water was not entirely clear.

My niece Sara squeezed under a low ceiling at the upstream end of the ledge and had a black widow spider within inches of her nose. She occasionally shone her flashlight on it to see that it wasn't any closer. She didn't worry a bit until she looked and the spider was gone. Later, when it returned, she squashed it. Uncertainty had been too much for her. The drainage flashed mildly twice during the night and, although the noise overwhelmed us, the water stayed away. More disquieting were the reverberating crash/rumble/echoes of rockfalls and landslides—some of them close. Even though the water coursing by was probably no more than 2 or 3 feet deep, the sound of rocks rolling along the bed, with its implied grinding action, made the excavation of the Canyon seem much less a distant theory and more an immediate fact.

Gary Backtracks for Water

Our problem in 1990 was not an excess of water—quite the contrary. I had expected to pick up water for the morrow on the way up, but none appeared, so after we established camp at the Flash Flood Ledge, Gary agreed to go back to the junction and gather some from the spurting spring. In an hour and fifty minutes he returned with four gallons plus a quart.

This was the end of day six and we had two more days of food. Climbing up to the Esplanade would take a few hours, and we would then have 16 "map miles" back to Buckhorn Spring. It would be relatively flat, but with lots of in, out, and around. And we were a day late. It had taken only two days in '77, but then we were blessed with rain and had an abundance of water without having to carry any. Also it was cloudy and we had been hiking for almost five weeks. Today we would reach the Esplanade with at least five quarts each, and there were five more waiting for us at our water cache 3 miles farther on. Whether we continued on around or took the caching trail to the rim depended on how many quarts it would cost us to go those 3 miles.

Mushroom Rock Marks Exit

The next morning unfortunately dawned bright and clear like the others. We started up the drainage at 7:30. There were more obstacles in the bed—one requiring a significant bypass to the right. Farther on, we climbed out toward the first ravine that showed access to the Supai rim, but we had to climb up some ledges by a small pour-off before we could contour onto the talus below the ravine. The top of the ravine was just left of a mushroom rock on the skyline. There were some hard moves. One in particular almost stopped me, and I was ready to call for someone to lower me a rope, but I called the engine room and asked for a little more steam and made it on my own. Gary said he found a seep in the main bed in line with the upstream side of the ravine. There was a small pool about 5 inches deep; if it is permanent, it could be very helpful. We reached the mushroom rock at 9:00.

Time for a Decision

We rested by the rock—it is probably 20 feet high—for half an hour before moving on. In an hour we passed the first point, and in another hour passed the second. We had lunch near a spot where there was a hole in the layer on which I was hiking. I was in Zen mode at the time and almost stepped into it. We reached the square flat spot that looks like a helipad from the rim at 2:00. We hadn't committed ourselves to going around to SOB yet, so I had been watching our water consumption very carefully. We had taken about four hours to hike 3 miles. Those 3 miles took three quarts of water from each of us. Those are map miles but so were the 13 still ahead of us. That meant we were traveling at a rate of about 1 mile per quart. If that rate persisted, we would each need thirteen quarts to get to SOB. We arrived at the helipad with two and picked up five for a total of seven. Unless we found potholes or a spring, we couldn't do it. There were some large potholes on the old Matthes map and I had marked them on my newer map, but I knew of no reliable springs. Continuing on the Esplanade to SOB seemed like a bad idea for two other reasons—food and time—so we decided to camp on the helipad and go out via the trail up to Kanab Point the next day.

The Kanab Point Trail

This is the trail that Don, Brad Schrick, and I had used to bring the water down to the helipad. The plan was to go to the rim and then hike the road back to the car. That meant we had extra water, and I used some of mine to take a shower with the spare perforated cap to my half-gallon water bottle. After serenades by coyotes and a strange large-sounding bird, we got to sleep.

We left camp at 7:15, were at the top of the talus by 8:25 and on top by 10:00. As I said at the beginning of the chapter, I strongly recommend driving out to Kanab Point before doing this loop, for two reasons. First, if you are going to use the trail, or even think you might want to use the trail, it is a good idea to know exactly where it is. I think I have shown it accurately on the map, but that is not the same as seeing it for yourself. Second, you can cache water for yourself along the road. It will be very comforting to know there is water waiting for you on the way back to the trailhead. There is a third reason as well, but not a very good one: If the sun is right, you can perhaps tell whether there are any potholes on the Esplanade by seeing them glinting in the sun.

Let me describe the Kanab Point Trailhead and Trail. The final bit of road is shown incorrectly on both the 7.5- and 15-minute Kanab Point quad maps. On the 15-minute map it should be shown as going north toward Kanab Point and then swinging west along the edge for perhaps 100 yards. On the 7.5-minute map, the swing to the west is missing. The trail, probably originally designed for stock, is now nothing more than a fairly good game trail. It starts down a small drainage a few yards west of the end of the road. The drainage steepens abruptly and the trail goes down sixty feet or so to a tiny valley parallel to the rim and follows its length until it, too, steepens abruptly. After a diagonal descent of 100 feet or so, we were faced with the problem of getting through about 20 feet of crumbly cliff. This was our first real obstacle. Get down it as best you can and, from my recollection, earlier is better than later.

From here we contoured/angled down to the northwest to a small promontory where there was an old weathered pickax. The route to the point is sometimes indistinct, but beyond it the trail is well defined. It continues steeply down a sandy hillside 100 feet or so to a small cliff and contours west on top of it to a break that leads down to a major cliff. The trail contours around on the edge of this cliff to the long talus runout leading to the Esplanade. I should add that when we reached the steep trail up the sandy hillside on our trips up the trail, it seemed easier to continue straight on a gentler incline and come up the east side of the small promontory with the pickax.

The Helipad

The trail is often on the edge of eternity and Brad moved with extreme caution—his whole world shrunk to the small area around his feet. Once on the talus, the trail proliferates into hundreds of fragments, but the route is clear. We angled down to the east, crossing several small drainages, to a square of bare Esplanade 50 feet or so on a side by a small hill—the "helipad." It will long have been visible as a seemingly man-made square down on the Esplanade. I think that is the hill shown with elevation 4,323 that is 0.6 mile northwest of the K in KANAB POINT near the roadhead on the 7.5-minute Kanab Point quad map, provisional edition 1988.

I described the Kanab Point Trail as we went down it. The only problem in going up is finding the right talus slope. You don't need to find the helipad unless you've cached water there, in which case you look first for the small hill. The talus slope you need is a big one—wide at the base—that goes almost through the Coconino. Look for a place on the map where the contours representing the Coconino cliff are widely spaced.

Gary Goes It Alone

Once on the rim, Gary decided he didn't want to carry his pack any farther—it was very heavy—and asked if we'd mind his going back to the car by himself. Neither Don nor I had any objection and off he went. I wish now I had suggested a compromise of hiking back to the stock tank. It was only about 6 miles and knowing there was water there meant we could get by with carrying very little. Although we didn't do that, it is still what I suggest to those doing this loop and exiting via Kanab Point. Gary took five hours and eight minutes to get to the cars. He zipped on by the stock tank without noting his time, but since it was almost 15 miles to the cars and 5.5 to the stock tank, it should be a little less than two hours to the tank.

ALTERNATIVE ROUTING ON THE ESPLANADE

In 1977, when I did the hike from the mushroom rock to SOB on the Esplanade, we were traveling twice as fast as I could this later time. There were four reasons for that: (1) I was fifteen years younger; (2) we had already been hiking for five weeks and were seasoned; (3) it was overcast and cool; and, most important, (4) the storm that sent the flash floods to scare us also filled potholes to overflowing. We never carried more than a quart of water, and that was only for convenience.

One of the large water pockets shown by Francois Matthes on his West Half map is located 0.3 mile south and 0.1 mile east of Jewel Spring. Robert noted it was 4 to 5 inches deep when he saw it and could hold another 6 inches, if necessary. The other is located south of Shanub Point at the southernmost tip of the broad flats of Esplanade. Robert noted that there was water in this pool two weeks after a rain. He also reported a slow dripping at North Spring close to Christmas 1980.

The route from the mushroom rock to SOB Canyon is one of many choices but no problems—except water. I have only a few things to say other than that.

- About the only place where you find a game trail is precisely where you need it most—around the head of a drainage.

- Somewhere in heading out the drainage below Jewel Spring, I came up out of a gully—on a small game trail—and saw a big overhanging rock directly in front of me. I went over to it and found a cowboy camp similar to the one between SOB and Tuckup—coffee cans, jars, chopped wood. I would have liked to camp here, but the others—I called them "the galumphers"— were long gone and I had no way to call them back.

- Robert has used the drainage 0.25 mile east of the western edge of the 15-minute Kanab Point quad map to get into SOB. Near the junction, he had to go upstream 0.4 mile on a ledge to get to the bed.

- In 1977, under the optimum conditions of youth, physical conditioning, cloud cover, water availability, and no food to carry, we went from the mushroom rock to Kanab Point in two hours and forty-five minutes and from there to a point east of Paguekwash Point in the same time. Five hours the next day took us to our next food cache at Buckhorn Spring. After a rain that same trip would take me three days today.

- From Buckhorn Spring you retrace your steps to the car. On the 1977 caching trip, my nephew took an old pickax from the spring as a souvenir. In 1989 I had him return it.

Lowering packs on the shortcut route to the mouth of Clear Creek.

7 Nankoweap Creek/ Bright Angel Creek Loop
Circumambulation of Walhalla Plateau

The recognition that even 7.5 minute maps do not tell all:
"Today looked so easy yesterday."

GARY LADD

Length
When I first did this loop it took twelve days, but several were short days so it conceivably could be done in less. The only difficulty with shortening the trip is the necessity to be at certain places in early evening to catch low water if you wish to maintain a River-level route. Another comment—to reduce the initial weight of our packs slightly, I placed a two-day food cache at Phantom Ranch before the trip began.

Water
Nankoweap Creek: There is a good spring below Kibbey Butte in Upper Nankoweap near the 4,800-foot contour. It is below the Tapeats in the Supergroup.

Kwagunt Creek: I have found water in Kwagunt Creek at the upper entrance to the narrows each of the four times I have been there.

Malgosa, Awatubi and 60 Mile Creeks: I have never found water where the Horsethief Trail crosses these drainages. Although I have not checked it myself, I have it on good authority that you can hike the Malgosa drainage from the Horsethief Trail to the River.

Carbon Creek: We found a small flow of alkaline water and some potholes near the upper end of the narrows in June 1989.

Lava Creek: In 1977 there was abundant water in Lava Creek from the spring near the 4,400-foot contour to its junction with Chuar Creek.

Chuar Creek: Intermittent surface water was found in the narrows in June 1989. It looked bad so we didn't drink any.

Unkar Creek: In 1977 there was flowing water amid a great deal of vegetation where side drainages come in about a mile northeast of the 5,072-foot elevation mark on the 7.5 minute Cape Royal quad map. A little smudge of green shows at a bend in the creek.

Asbestos Creek: There is sometimes water where the mine trail hits the creek drainage, but it is not reliable. I have never looked for the spring.

Vishnu Creek: I have always found water in the bed near the lower end of the quartzite narrows by the big overhang, although in June 1989 there was very little. There is sometimes water in the first drainage through which you

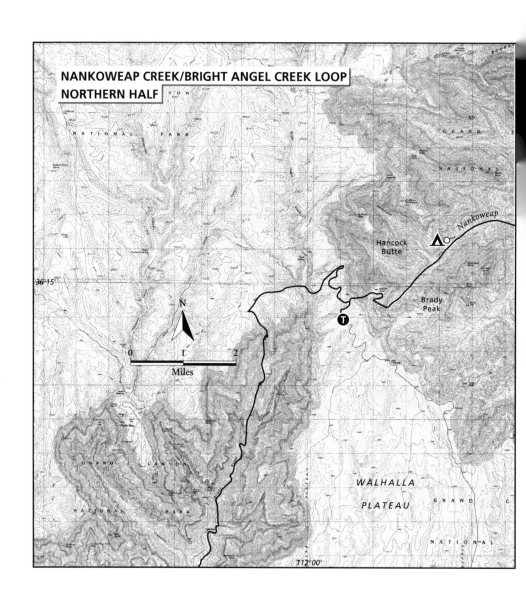

NANKOWEAP CREEK/BRIGHT ANGEL CREEK LOOP
NORTHERN HALF

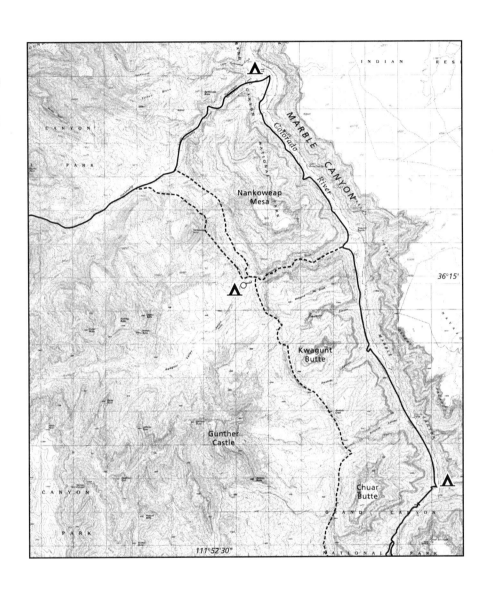

MARBLE CANYON

Colorado River

Nankoweap
Mesa

Kwagunt
Butte

Gunther
Castle

Chuar
Butte

CANYON

PARK

CANYON

PARK

INDIAN   RES

36°15'

NAVAJO

GRAND   CANYON

NATIONAL   PARK

111°52'30"

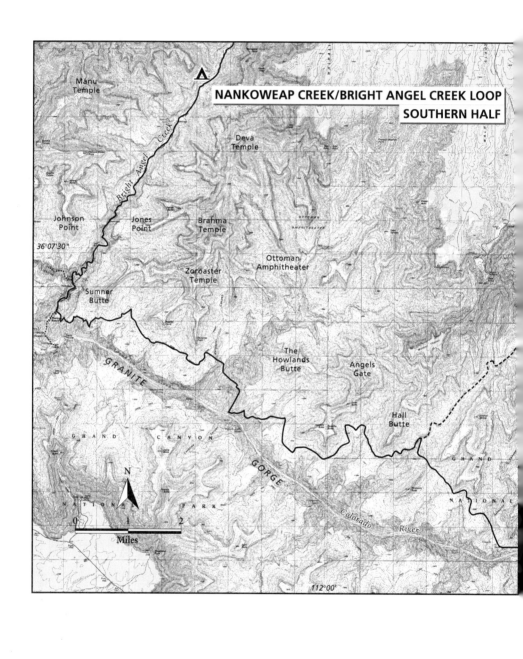

NANKOWEAP CREEK/BRIGHT ANGEL CREEK LOOP
SOUTHERN HALF

Manu
Temple

Deva
Temple

Bright Angel Creek

Johnson
Point

Jones
Point

Brahma
Temple

36°07'30"

Zoroaster
Temple

Ottoman
Amphitheater

Sumner
Butte

GRANITE

The
Howlands
Butte

Angels
Gate

Hall
Butte

GRAND

CANYON

GORGE

GRAND

NATIONAL

PARK

Colorado River

NATIONAL

N

0   1   2
Miles

112°00'

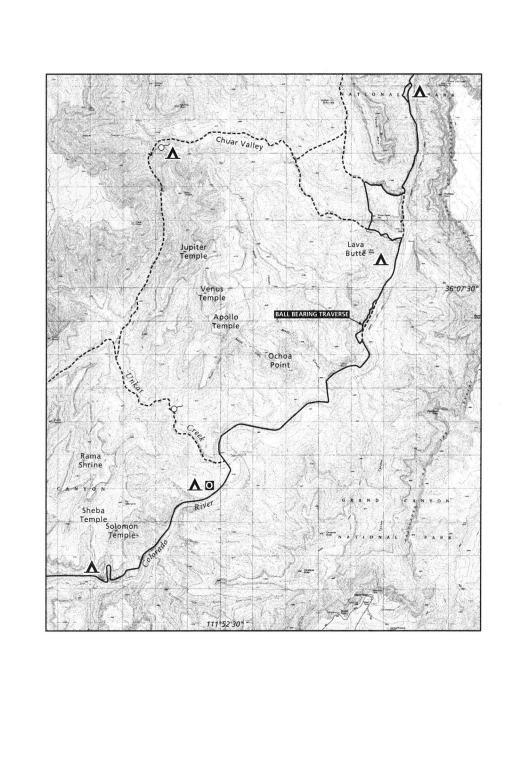

Chuar Valley

Jupiter
Temple

Venus
Temple

Apollo
Temple

BALL BEARING TRAVERSE

Lava
Butte

36°07'30"

Ochoa
Point

Unkar

Creek

Rama
Shrine

CANYON

GRAND   CANYON

Sheba
Temple

NATIONAL   PARK

Solomon
Temple

Colorado   River

111°52'30"

can exit the narrows to the west, but don't count on it. Even in June 1989 there was an abundance of water about 0.5 mile beyond the upper end of the Tapeats narrows.

Old Bright Angel Trail: The last water on the way up and out on the Old Bright Angel Trail is a beautiful little stream with a photogenic cascade in the Muav Limestone below Uncle Jim Point.

Quad Maps
7.5-minute maps
    Bright Angel Point
    Cape Royal
    Cape Solitude
    Desert View
    Little Park Lake (extreme lower right corner only)
    Nankoweap Mesa
    Phantom Ranch
    Point Imperial
    Walhalla Plateau

In my opinion the most convenient form of map to use, if it covers your area of interest, is a cut up version of the Grand Canyon National Park map. It will be smaller, lighter, and less expensive than any collection of the others.

Roadhead
Park at Greenland Lake automobile turnout. When you get your permit, it is a good idea to tell a road patrol ranger that you will be leaving your car at the turnout. This may prevent its being towed away.

ROUTE TO ROADHEAD
The Greenland Lake turnout is in the park on the North Rim of Grand Canyon about 2.5 miles down the Cape Royal road from its intersection with the road to Point Imperial.

HIKING TIMES
Most of the times given below were collected during a period of extreme heat in June 1989, but others were collected at other times, under other conditions and, in two cases, by another person. These times are denoted, in parentheses, by either a date, the letters "est." for "estimated," or the letters "Robt" indicating they are Robert's times.

Use Areas	Location	Elapsed Times Between Locations (hours)
	Car	:15
	Rim takeoff	1:15
	Kibbey Saddle	2:30
	Fault ravine	:45
	Bottom of fault ravine	3:15

178

▲ AE9	Nankoweap Spring (4,800-foot contour)	3:15
▲ AE9	Good pool for swimming	1:15 (1986)
▲ AE9	Bottom of Tilted Mesa Trail	1:30 (1986)
▲ AE9	Mouth of Nankoweap Creek	4:15 (Robt)
▲ AF9	Mouth of Kwagunt Creek	1:00
▲ AF9	Mouth of Malgosa Canyon	1:15
▲ AF9	Mouth of Awatubi Canyon	1:30
▲ AF9	Mouth of 60 Mile Canyon	3:30
▲ AF9	Beach upstream Little Colorado River	3:15
▲ AF9	Mouth of major drainage at mile 62.6	:20
	Wading place (low water at evening)	:10
▲ AF9	Beach below wading place	1:30
	Opposite Hopi Salt Caves	2:00
▲ AF9	Mouth of Carbon Creek	2:15
	Exit from Carbon Creek narrows	1:15
▲ AF9	Mouth of Lava Canyon	2:30
	Tanner cliff bypass (low water at evening)	:30
	End Tanner cliff bypass	:15
▲ AG9	Beach	:15
	Alternate bypass descent ravine, mile 67.5	5:00
▲ AG9	Mouth of Unkar Creek	:30
▲ AG9	Camp with small cave	2:30
▲ AH9	Bottom of quartzite ramp	3:00
	Descent ravine	2:00
▲ AH9	Colorado River	:45
▲ AH9	Campsite below Hance Rapids	:30
	Bottom of trail up to Hance mines	:45
	Bed of Asbestos Canyon	3:45
	Newberry Saddle	1:00
▲ AH9	Bed of Vishnu Creek	:15
	Water and shelter	2:00
	Bed of next wash (SW Wotans Throne)	2:30
	Saddle below west arm of Hawkins Butte	:45
	Top of Tapeats Break	3:45
▲ AK9	Beach near mouth of Clear Creek	1:00
	Leave Clear Creek drainage	2:45
	Bed of Zoroaster Canyon	:30
	Clear Creek Trail	3:00
▲ Bright Angel Campground Phantom Ranch		4:45
▲ Cottonwood Campground Cottonwood Camp		:30
	Bottom of Old Bright Angel Trail	2:00
	Muav Cascade	3:15
	Top of Supai Formation	2:00
	Rim—Junction with Ken Patrick Trail	1:30
	Ken Patrick Trail—Junction with Highway Car	:30 (est.)

High-Water Bypass 1:
Tonto Route from Mile 62.6 Beach to Carbon Creek
        Beach at mile 62.6   2:15 (Robt)
        Exit from Carbon Creek narrows

High-Water Bypass 2:
Difficult Dox Route from Mouth of Lava Canyon to River at Mile 67.5
        Mouth of Lava Canyon   1:30
        Ascent ravine lower end of island at mile 66.7 3:30
        Descent ravine at mile 67.5

ROUTE DETAILS

This loop was hard. Ordinarily, I try to avoid rating these loops, but I have to say this one was hard for several reasons. First, it was hot—Phantom Ranch got up to 115 degrees officially and more than 120 degrees unofficially; one day we measured 106 degrees in the shade. Second, the loop is long. Third, the flow of water in the River can be unpredictable. Under the current operating standards for the dam, the fluctuations in the water levels have evened out, but the water level can rise unexpectedly due to earlier power demands just when you need to wade a section of the River.

I had done all sections of this loop on other occasions, but I had never done it as a whole loop all at once until we made the trip described below. By "we" I mean Don Mattox and his stepson, Kyle Harwood, Gary Ladd, and myself. Our efforts began at the Greenland Lake turnout on June 14, 1989. I planned to leave my van at the turnout during the hike and so stated on my permit request. Nevertheless, the road patrol rangers almost towed it away as abandoned; so be sure to tell someone you intend to leave your car there. It is best to tell a road patrol ranger.

Rim Takeoff

After leaving our car, we had to go back down the road about 0.25 mile to a very sharp bend where the road turns to the west and timbers are set in the ground to keep cars from going off into the woods. We turned east into the woods here and contoured right and slightly up around a small knoll. This tiny upward portion of our descent precipitated the first of many criticisms of my leadership. "Hey, Steck, are you sure you know where you're going? We're supposed to be going down not up!" Mattox is always the most vocal of my critics and calls me by my last name when he is displeased. After we began our descent on the east side of the knoll, he was somewhat mollified and shut up.

We angled down and to the right and hit a deer trail. Actually, we found several deer trails, and people trails, too, so we often had a choice of routes. The Coconino has been broken down into many small cliffs by faulting and erosion. After one of these small cliffs, Gary contoured around while I went down—too far down—and had to fight my way back up through the brush to an awkward traverse to the saddle west of Kibbey Butte. It would have been much easier to have gone the way Gary did. We found much thorny vegetation along this descent, especially near the top, and I found it useful to wear gloves. I sometimes felt like Tarzan as I swung down holding on to the branches.

Kibbey Butte Saddle
Our descent to the saddle took about an hour and a half. While the rest of us sought relief from an already warm day—it was 9:30—in the shade of a ponderosa pine, Kyle took off to climb the butte.

Our next goal was to get in the fault ravine that goes off the south side of the saddle. However, the Esplanade Member capping the Supai forms a cliff so we had to sneak in from the east side of the ravine.

Route off Saddle
Harvey Butchart's route to the fault ravine, as given in *Grand Canyon Treks,* is to find a deer trail off the north side of the saddle down to the top of the Redwall and then to contour around the butte on it to the ravine. Someone I know who followed his advice found it excruciatingly difficult—brushy and dangerously steep—so I resolved when I first conceived of this loop to find another way if I could.

During an on-the-ground reconnaissance trip to Nankoweap Creek with my son Mike over Memorial Day in 1986, I explored the base of the cliff to the west of the fault ravine and found nothing useful. Aerial reconnaissance the next month with son Stan showed some possibilities to the east. The next year Randy Simons and I, starting from below, exploited one of these and found a relatively easy way up. In the process we found a small flowing spring in a grove of ponderosa pines at the base of the last climb. Later, I wrote Dr. Butchart to tell him of this easier way into Nankoweap off the Kibbey Saddle and he replied that he already knew of it, as well as of the spring, but hadn't thought to mention it in any of his books. My brother and I completed my explorations for a convenient way from the rim into Nankoweap via the Kibbey Saddle when we found our way down from the saddle in 1987.

Route to Fault Ravine
The descent through the Supai cliffs on the south side of Kibbey Butte begins at the bottom of a ravine 0.14 mile south of the summit of Kibbey Butte. Counting the main ravine going directly off the saddle into the fault ravine as number one, I count the descent ravine as number four. Another way to find it is to go up the ridge toward the summit until you can see a solitary ponderosa off to the right and then follow a line from that pine to the summit of Brady Peak—which has the distinct look of a middle finger extending from a closed fist. I have placed ducks along this line as well as one in the ravine and one at the bottom of the ravine at the pour-off.

We went west from this pour-off 150 yards or so to a large white free-standing rock tower and on the way passed a big overhang that could sleep twenty in a pinch. This is nice to know about if you are caught on the butte in a storm. From the tower I looked east toward the bottom of the cliffs and could see the very large ponderosa that marks the location of the final chimney. It is at least 150 feet tall and sprouts from a small spring at its base.

About 10 feet east of the tower, we passed our packs down a short six-foot cliff and proceeded diagonally down and east about 15 yards to a 15-foot chimney with a 3-inch thick fir branch hanging down it. We lowered packs here, too, and I used the branch as I would a fixed rope in scrambling down. From the bottom of this chimney, we headed for the big ponderosa and went to the point between two bays. On earlier occasions I have gone down the right-hand 30-foot chimney—actually two 15-foot chimneys with a small ledge in between—but this time Gary found a much easier way off to the left 20 feet or so where the cliff face was much more broken down. We were able to get down with a pack pass only at the top.

Kibbey Spring

After climbing down this break, we headed for the big ponderosa to rest by the spring. Unfortunately, it was only a small seep this time, but we rested anyway. Gary managed to extract some water from the damp ground, but the rest of us didn't bother.

One way into the fault ravine from the spring is to contour west and I once found a faint deer trail to help me. This time we couldn't find any trail and instead followed several talus slopes that took us diagonally down. As you round the point between the southeast and southwest faces of Kibbey Butte, you can look up and see the white tower where the descent started. We could also look across the fault ravine and see we were close to the top of the lowest Supai cliff—the Watahomigi. We went down to it, and Kyle dropped his pack and went on a bit to see if our ledge continued around a corner into the fault ravine. It did, and we followed his lead. After a short descent to find some shade, we stopped for lunch and Gary startled us by saying, "Do you realize that we've been hiking over four hours now and are still less than a mile from the car?" "Yeah, but we must be almost halfway vertically to where we'll camp." I threw this in to try and show that the morning hadn't been a complete waste of time.

Snow Job in June

The rest of the descent to the Nankoweap drainage was just down, down, down over rocky rubble that was, happily, so well stabilized that the rocks rarely moved when you stepped down on them. On the way down I caught a glimpse of a large dirty white slab in the ravine opposite and filed it in my mind as a piece of Kaibab, Toroweap, or Coconino that had slipped from above. It did seem a bit big to have survived such a long fall without breaking up, but I was concentrating on my feet and paid it no more attention until Don called out, "Hey, George, do you see that snowbank over there?" And instantly, without even looking, I knew he was right. "Yeah, I saw it," I called back. "Just imagine that. Snow at the bottom of the Redwall in the Grand Canyon in the middle of June. That means ice-cold margaritas tonight."

Nankoweap Creek

The fault ravine took us steeply down to its intersection with the west arm of Nankoweap Creek. This is an easy Redwall descent—remarkably easy—and from the intersection it was only three more hours of boulder-hopping until we reached the spring that feeds this arm of the creek. The spring is below the Tapeats in the Supergroup. You can tell roughly where it is—even, I think, from the base of the Redwall—by noting two large Tapeats blocks lying on the hillside on the north side of the drainage. The spring is near the closer of these blocks at about the 4,800-foot contour line.

When we reached the bottom of the fault ravine, Gary and Kyle climbed up to the snow bridge and had an icy shower in its dark interior. They estimated its size as 25 feet wide by 30 feet long by 8 feet thick in the middle—thicker at the edges. They gathered some snow for our water bottles and some for the margaritas. Kyle suggested the snow had survived because there had been a late storm and no warm spring rains to melt it away. He may be right, but it also helped that the snow was in a north-facing ravine and never saw the sun.

Nankoweap Spring

The last few hours to our camp by the spring passed without incident although it was now much warmer and we took frequent rests. There is a small bench of dark sand about 50 yards below the spring that we called home and a large sort-of-flat rock by the stream that we used as a dinner table. Kyle then showed his ignorance of the finer points of canyon camping. "Goddamn it, Kyle, what the hell do you think you're doing? Do you realize you're taking a bath in our drinking water! Now we'll have to go farther upstream for it." "Come off it, George," Kyle retorted—he specializes in retorts, though we could see he was embarrassed—"the tequila and Everclear will kill the bugs." Actually, we did use water from his pool because it was so convenient, but we teased him about his breach of etiquette by pretending to gag on it as we drank it.

I spent quite a bit of time by these pools watching the spiders when I was here with Randy Simons. Their webs spanned the open places between the rocks above the water. Each spider seemed to have its own web and defended it against trespassers with great ferocity. I am always surprised to see such fierceness in creatures so small that I could squash them between my fingers. Ardrey called it the territorial imperative and I have wondered how far down the scale of creatures it extends. Do flies defend a territory? Do they even have a territory?

Swimming Hole

We left camp at 5:45 the next morning. After spending half an hour at a "swimming pool" about half an hour above the Seiber Point drainage, we took off over the hill for Kwagunt Creek at 11:00. It was already hot, but not *hot hot*—yet. Our goal for the day was the mouth of Kwagunt Creek and we didn't make it. It became just too damned hot.

The only reason for going up and over to Kwagunt was because neither Don nor I had ever been down through the Kwagunt narrows. However, it was a error on my part not to acknowledge the heat and change plans. We should have gone down Nankoweap to the River and then down the River to Kwagunt. Don observed after the trip that I am not flexible enough—too concerned with staying on schedule. He said, "Do you think the park service gives a damn whether we're a day late as long as we're alive?" "Of course not," I said, "and I really don't mind being off schedule—though I'll try fairly hard to get back on it if I can."

I must interrupt the '89 narrative at this point. Since I am describing this loop as going down Nankoweap Creek and then down the River, I must delay my description of our excursion up and over to Kwagunt until it is time for that part of the narrative concerning the Horsethief Alternate.

Down Nankoweap Creek to River

The hike from the Seiber Point drainage to the mouth of Nankoweap is uneventful—just a few hours of boulder-hopping. For future reference you might wish to note the bottom of the Tilted Mesa Trail as you go by. Also, if you're nervous about drinking the creek water, you will find a good spring about 100 yards downstream from that junction—on creek left against the bushes.

I don't know whether they save any time or not, but when I am in a creekbed I look for trails going up onto benches. Sometimes the going is easier up there than it is by the creek, and there are several such trails-on-a-bench along the way down Nankoweap Creek. The longest one comes about a mile from the River. I'm guessing, but I place it by the bend at about the 3,100-foot contour. The trail goes up steeply on creek right; I know I have missed it when I come to a nice pool with Muav slabs to sun myself on. This trail wanders along quite high above the creek for a while and then settles down on a low-lying bench that ends at the River.

Hitchhiking

My first attempt to hike from Nankoweap to Kwagunt was with Don Mattox, Don and Adair Peterson, and others in the late 1960s or early 1970s. Don M was leading, and his plan was to go down the Tilted Mesa Trail and out the Salt Trail with a River crossing somewhere in between. Everything had gone reasonably well until the Nankoweap-to-Kwagunt stretch, where the rocks and brush along the shore were a real "pain in the bud," as Robert would say in his Germanic, learned-by-ear English. Eventually it was so bad that Adair went down by the River and hitched us a ride with a private boat trip. They left us at the Little Colorado.

Nankoweap to Kwagunt via Deer Trail (1982)

That was my first effort to get from Nankoweap to Kwagunt. The second was in 1982, with my brother, Don, Adair Peterson, and Robert. As the broad flat area on the downstream side of the Nankoweap delta began to slope up and narrow down, we looked for a deer trail 50 to 100 feet up the hillside that Robert had found on an earlier trip. This trail goes up and down a lot, but it is still easier than the rocks and tammies along the shore. Even after a late start—we had camped by the mouth of the creek—and a long consultation with a boatman about Robert's deteriorating gastrointestinal condition, we were at Kwagunt in time for lunch. This ends the short description borrowed from 1982. I'll skip the 1989 Nankoweap-to-Kwagunt segment because it is presented under the Horsethief Alternative.

Kwagunt to Malgosa

I had remembered from the 1982 trip that the route from Kwagunt on down had also been facilitated by a deer trail and I found one. But memory was misleading and it didn't seem particularly easy in 1989. After too much up and down, I abandoned it in favor of the rocks along the shore. It took us an hour to get from Kwagunt to Malgosa. Not bad considering we had long since left the shade.

Don was still suffering from his bout with heat exhaustion the day before and was talking about hitching a ride down to the Little Colorado. I was hoping, though, that by being along the river with its ample supply of cooling water and by going more slowly he could make it without a ride. I was ahead of him chugging along on my own when an oar boat came by and moved in close. Someone started yelling at me. At first I thought there had been an accident and that the person on the boat was telling me to go back. Finally, though, I heard some words more distinctly: ". . . I'll meet you at the Little Colorado." It wasn't until then that I realized the person yelling at me was Don. It hadn't seemed like Don—the Don I knew didn't wear a life jacket.

Malgosa to Awatubi

Gary and Kyle caught up to me shortly after Don passed and I heard the story of what had happened. As the first boat came by, Gary recognized the name of the company painted on the side and realized he might know some of the boatmen—two were named Jeff. He called out, "Is Jeff or Jeff with you?" Sure enough, Jeff Behan soon came along and pulled in. Gary visited with him and explained Don's problem and asked if they could take him to the Little Colorado. Jeff didn't think so but gave Gary some tomatoes, avocados, grapefruit, and beer—one for Kyle, one for Don, and one for me, Gary declining. Then the boat went off and soon caught up with Don. Contrary to the impression left with Gary, Jeff took him aboard. All that remained was for Don to tell me he was on his way to the Little Colorado.

Awatubi to the Little Colorado

We reached Awatubi only a short time after Kyle and Gary caught up with me and Kyle pulled out the three beers the boatman had given him. Guess what happened to Don's? We had a leisurely lunch in some shade by a beach en-route to 60 Mile and half an hour later reached 60 Mile.

Robert Is Sick (1982)

The mouth of Awatubi was also the site of a difficult decision made during the '82 trip. I have already mentioned the gastrointestinal difficulties Robert was having when we left Nankoweap. Well, as the day progressed his condition worsened, and by the time we got to Awatubi around 3:00, he decided he had had enough discomfort for the day. I felt at the time that if Robert had been his usual self we could have gone from Nankoweap to the Little Colorado in one day. Robert's condition did not improve during the night—still a mix of vomiting and diarrhea—and the next day we had to decide what to do about him.

In midmorning we flagged down a dory—Liz Hyman in charge, and she was very helpful. Besides leaving several big cans of fruit juice, various soft drinks, a loaf of bread, and assorted other stuff, she helped us implement our plan.

Robert Is Abandoned (1982)

Before our trip began, Robert and I discussed the problem of what to do if one of us couldn't continue. We had separate permits and agreed if anything happened to one of us, the other would continue. This sounds callous, but here is how it worked in this case. We would send a note to Dave Buccello, the head ranger at Phantom Ranch, asking him to initiate a rescue for Robert in four days' time if no countermanding instructions were received in the meantime. This was fail-safe. Either Robert would get better or he wouldn't. If he got better, he could send a note that he didn't need a rescue; if he didn't get better, he would be rescued. He had enough food and liquid to get him through five days, and none of us thought he was so sick he might die in that time. So we sent Liz off with the note and after lunch set off ourselves for the Little Colorado.

Back to 1989

Finally, after three and a half more hours of boulders and sand and friendly Tapeats ledges—maybe half that time if the weather were cooler—Gary, Kyle, and I reached the Little Colorado and were greeted happily by Don who hadn't expected us so soon.

Not far above the Little Colorado, my visor was blown off by a strong gust of wind. It sailed way over my head and way out over the River—at least 50 feet up and 50 feet out. Then it fell toward the water, but just before it reached its watery grave another gust caught it and carried it high again. It swirled around a bit and was finally tossed on the rocks 20 feet from me. A boomerang could not have been more precisely thrown.

There was plenty of time for a bath before margarita time. I should add that these are not true margaritas. I create a substitute from a mixture of lemon and lemon-lime Kool-Aid plus sugar with some lemon-lime Crystal Light added to reduce the weight. The alcohol is a mixture of tequila and Everclear.

Margaritas

I still vividly remember my brother's reaction on the '82 trip to this margarita nonsense. He is a wine man and viewed my happy-hour preparations on the first day of our eighty-day hike from Lees Ferry to Grand Wash Cliffs with ill-concealed disdain. "Why didn't you bring some wine?" he asked. But he drank the margaritas. When he saw me making the same preparations the next night, he said, "What, margaritas again?" with only slightly less contempt than the night before. The third night his remark, delivered with a hint of anticipation, was, "Are we having margaritas again tonight?" The fourth night he capitulated with, "How soon are the margaritas?" After all these years of margaritas, they have become a sort of tradition. However, on the 1989 trip our alcohol bottle developed a crack and much of the booze was lost. Kyle contributed some rum, but it was soon gone. For the rest of the trip we made do without the additive designed, according to my brother, to "dull the sharp edge of pain."

Mile 62.6 to Carbon Creek—First Try

The next day was horribly bright and clear just like its predecessors. This was unfortunate because we were going to climb up on top of the Tapeats and contour over to Carbon Creek. This meant we would be away from water for much of the day. This traverse would be new to me because in '82 we had enough sandbars to get past the cliffs we found here at water level. Unfortunately, the great flood of '83 had washed most of that sand away.

We climbed up to the Tonto level behind our camp—all was still in shade. After forty-five minutes we made a dip to River level to avoid contouring in and out of a small drainage, and an hour later did the same to avoid a larger one. A little after 8:00 we reached a major canyon. After we had all searched a bit for an easy way across it, Gary found a way off the nose to the beach at the mouth of the canyon. We went down and picked up some more water. It was 9:00 and already very hot. Gary soon found a way up the downstream cliff, but it was forty-five minutes before we were on the Tonto again—opposite the upper end of a large island.

After an hour and a half of contouring around, we were still only 0.5 River mile from the beach we had left more than two hours before. At this point Don decided he had had enough of the heat and announced he was going back to the beach and catch a boat to Phantom. The conversation went something like this.

Turning Back

Don: "Look, I'm by far the slowest one and I'm only holding you guys up so the only sensible thing is for me to go back to the beach and catch a boat. I'll leave you some of my water and you can all go on and be at Carbon in no time. Okay?"

He was very matter-of-fact and had worked out all the details—so he thought. It was true he had been going very slowly with frequent rests, and it was also true we had at least 2 river miles to go to get to the bed of Carbon, so what he said made at least partial sense. However, even though I've done it, I don't like to see a group split up.

George: "No, it's not okay." Don seemed surprised at my dissent. "You shouldn't go back by yourself. Someone will go with you."

This wasn't entirely a selfless remark. With Don gone I would be the slowest.

Kyle: "I could go back with Don, pick up some more water, and be back here in about an hour. How about that?"

George: "That's not a bad idea, but it would be an hour lost and the rocks are already too hot to touch. Gary and I could go on while you're gone but then, for a while at least, we would be split up into three groups."

Gary: "I'd sure like to go on, but not unless all three of us go."

Perhaps the three of us should have gone on. I could see a small hill about a mile away, though, in the shimmering heat, it looked much farther away than that, and that hill was about half way to where we could enter Carbon. But Don was depressed and that depressed me as well. Suddenly, all I could think of was the cold River and being in the shade. I did not want to go on. I wanted very much to go back.

George: "I think we should all go back, get up extra early tomorrow, and try this again then. It's after 11:00 now. Tomorrow we could be at this same spot by 6:00. It'd be a lot cooler then. Let's pool our extra water and cache it here."

Don: "George, I don't want you going back just on my account. You're not doing that, are you? I am perfectly capable of getting to the beach by myself."

George: "I know you can, but if you went by yourself and anything happened to you I'd never forgive my self. Besides, I'm happy to go back and try again tomorrow. Think how cool it'll be then."

Kyle: "Well, if you two are going back, so am I."

Gary: "Okay, but I'm going on a bit to see what tomorrow will be like."

So we cached half a gallon of water and started back. It was hot, and the rocks still too hot to touch, but, strangely, it didn't seem as hot as when we were going the other way. In an hour and a half we were back on the beach again—in the shade. That day the official high at Phantom Ranch was 110 degrees.

Mile 62.2 to Carbon Creek—Second Try

I am interested in when low water occurs at various places along the River so, during lunch, I put a stick at the water's edge to see if it was rising or falling. It was falling. In fact, when I checked it an hour later it had fallen quite a bit. Then it occurred to me that maybe it would fall far enough for us to get by the next cliff along the River. In late afternoon I went across the delta to the cliff to see how deep the traverse would be. According to my walking stick, which I jabbed in the water, it would be about up to my hips. Gary came over to take a look, too. "We can do that," I said. "Piece of cake," Gary added. This obstacle seemed to be the last one, though I couldn't be sure. As far as I could remember from the 1982 trip, the way was clear to Lava Creek once we passed this cliff. But as I've said, there was a lot more sand then. We went back to give the others the good news.

We started the bypass at 6:00 and were all across by 6:15. I was ecstatic. No more shish-kebabed hikers on the morrow. We made camp on a small sandbar opposite the bottom of the big island. We were all very happy at what we had accomplished. Kyle made his one and only offer to help with dinner, and Don even complimented me on thinking of trying for a low-water route. I slept very well without the specter of a sun-broiled Tonto traverse to haunt me.

Bypass Arithmetic

I found out from the River Subdistrict at the park, after I got home, that the average flows from the dam on Friday the 16th, Saturday the 17th, and Sunday the 18th were 16,944, 14,111, and 9,120 cfs, respectively. The cliff is at about River mile 63, and, adding the 14 miles from Lees Ferry to the dam

188

and assuming an average flow of 4 mph, this put us approximately nineteen hours downstream from the dam. Since we made the traverse at 4:00 on the 17th, this meant we were seeing water that left the dam late Friday night or early Saturday morning.

I include this numerical discussion to help others who are doing this loop decide whether to try this watery bypass or not. One additional piece of information is needed, however, and that is, "How much deeper will the water be for each 10,000 cfs increase in flow?" I don't know the answer, but I guess between 1 and 2 feet depending on how wide the River is here and what its velocity is. If I'm correct, this means a 30,000 cfs average flow would probably make the bypass impossible.

Environmental Impact Study

This is a good place for another comment that may make all this arithmetic discussion moot. An Environmental Impact Study is being made at the time I am writing this to assess the effect of flow variation on beach erosion. It is possible this study will result in permanent changes to the discharge pattern from Glen Canyon Dam. For example, it is possible that flows will be kept more nearly constant with changes being made only gradually. An experimental change to this effect is already in place. As a result of this uncertainty, if you plan on making this loop, I suggest you contact the Bureau of Reclamation people at Glen Canyon Dam to see what they expect the flows to be at critical times during your trip. Real-time river flow data is available from water.usgs.gov/realtime.html. Information on the ongoing study can be found at vishnu.glg.nav.edu/gces/newintro.html.

On to Carbon

We were up and away from camp before 5:30 the next morning. That was especially early for us. In two and a half hours, when we were opposite the caves housing the Hopi Salt Mines, we had our first view of the South Rim. Gary says these caves have pictographs in them. We were just above Carbon Creek when some Hatch boats pulled out from there—we missed a second breakfast by just a hair. (The Hopi Salt Mines are now closed to all access.)

Being an effective leader requires credibility and my supply dwindled further when we were forced into a small climb and a 200 yard traverse just upstream from Carbon Creek—a trivial matter I had forgotten about. But leaders aren't supposed to forget such things. Fortunately, there are several ways off the nose to the Carbon delta.

Carbon to Lava

Once we got to the mouth of Carbon, we took a break. Don said he would slowly move on down to Lava Creek—our destination for yesterday—and the rest of us took a brief tour of the Carbon narrows. It didn't take long for the tour to pall and we started back. Kyle made the prophetic remark, "I hope we don't see this place again." But we did.

We started down to Lava ourselves and met Don coming back. He was unhappy. "It cliffs out down there, and damnit, Steck, you said it would only take forty-five minutes to get to Lava from here. Now it's going to take hours."

An example of the depressing effect of unmet expectations. I didn't see any point in telling Don that I had never said any such thing. What I had said was that it took us forty-five minutes when we went down to Lava in 1982. Oh well, this way we would see some new country.

River Route

There is a River route from Carbon to Lava but we didn't know it at the time. The following year I made a trip downriver in Gary's dory and we camped at Carbon. During the afternoon I climbed above the low cliffs and found a deer trail going downstream. I followed it far enough to see that it would bypass all cliffs. If the steeply sloping knife edge just upstream from Lava turns out to be too steep, just go behind it. (See the Cape Solitude quad map.)

The Moebius Bend

Instead of being along the River, our route to the mouth of Lava Creek would take us about a mile up Carbon, about a mile over to Lava Creek, and about a mile back down the creek to the River. This is a common hike for boat people and there was a well beaten track up Carbon wherever one was possible. At the start of a big horseshoe-shaped bend in Carbon, Kyle noticed a track heading up the talus, but it was in the sun and by going up the bed we could stay in the shade. And besides the sunny way was steep. After almost closing the circle at the upper end of the bend we had to climb over a fall. We all climbed up on the left, but Kyle and Gary were ahead and out of sight. Don and I followed the path up to a ridge and saw that it went steeply down the other side. We were dismayed to find we had to climb down so far to get back into the bed. We were just ready to start down when we heard Kyle's voice behind and below us. "What the hell are you guys doing up there?" I was just about to ask him what the hell he was doing down there when he added, "The trail's down here."

Then our situation gradually became clear. There is a story about caterpillars crawling around and around the rim of a teacup until they die. Well, Don and I had almost sacrificed ourselves as human caterpillars on the Carbon Creek teacup. The trail we were about to go down was the same one that Kyle had noticed earlier going up. So much climbing is required to follow the bed of the bend, that the boat hikers have beaten a shortcut over the saddle at the neck of the bend. It is only a few feet from the saddle back down to the bed. Don and I had been about to do the opposite—take the bed around the bend then climb to the saddle and go down to the bottom of the bend in order to follow the bed again to the saddle. . . and so on ad infinitum. I felt very stupid at my mistake. But now, as an alternative to stupidity, I prefer to think it was just the heat affecting my judgment. In any case, we were lucky that Kyle was there to save us from a horrible fate on the Moebius Bend at Carbon Creek.

Just beyond the Moebius Bend the canyon goes mainly east–west and there is a short stretch of flowing water and some potholes. We didn't taste it, but I guess it is probably salty. Kyle was very solicitous and cautioned me several times, "Watch out for that pothole." It wasn't until we had stopped for lunch a few feet farther on that I noticed he was taking his boots and socks off to dry them. He had slipped into that pothole. Gary very carefully scratched the words Death Trek in the hard sand and took pictures of them "to use as a lead in for the slide show I'll be giving about this trip." I didn't feel exactly complimented. Then in the ensuing conversation he added, "Golly, you know, instead of being on this trip I could have stayed home and been audited by the IRS." I didn't feel complimented by that remark, either.

From Carbon to Lava
The exit from Carbon was very close to our lunch spot and fifteen minutes later we were heading over to Lava. The saddle between the two drainages is probably only 50 feet above the bed of Carbon and we very soon began our descent. Like the descent into Kwagunt, this one also reminded me of Hell. Pretty, but damned hot. And like Kwagunt, near the end when we thought we were home free there was a pour-off and we had to climb up and over a ridge to the left. I had seen this bypass trail from some distance away but thought it must be a game trail—it couldn't possibly apply to us. Wrong! We found no water in the bed of Lava when we reached it, but some soon emerged. It came and went and was gone by the time we reached the River. We took a rest in the shade of a gravel bank along the way and I took out my thermometer:

Ambient air temperature in shade 105 degrees F
Ambient air temperature in sun 111 degrees F
Temperature on a yellow rock 120 degrees F
Temperature on a dark rock 126 degrees F
Official Phantom Ranch high 115 degrees F.

Today was Sunday and the plan was to rest at the mouth of Lava until 4:00. Then we would head down to the cliff upstream of Tanner Canyon at River mile 67.2, about opposite Comanche Creek, to see if low Saturday water—transit time from the dam is about twenty hours—will allow us to get by at River level. In 1982 it didn't occur to us to even try and we made the traverse on the steep Dox ball bearings above the cliff. It seemed at least 45 degrees, and so hard you could not get the edge of your boot into it. It was also tedious and scary and I didn't want to repeat it.

Avoiding the Ball Bearings (1982)
Robert, who was a day behind us at this point, also made the ball-bearing traverse, but when he returned to the River, he went back up without his pack and found he could get by the cliff in the water. The water was only up to his waist, and high-water stains seemed to indicate the River level was seldom more than a foot higher. Since dam discharges are traditionally lowest for the week on Saturday and Sunday, we felt we had a good chance to get by at River level, too. Then we would be back on schedule.

Dave and Bec Kiel's Experience (1984)
As further evidence of how hard it is to make the traverse above the cliff, let me describe how the Kiels handled it. Dave and Bec Kiel set out in July 1984 to hike the length of the Colorado River from its source in the Rockies

to its terminus at the Gulf of California. This they did, though some of the lower part downstream of Grand Canyon was done by canoe. While they were still in the planning stages, they spent several days with me going over Robert's maps showing his route through Cataract Canyon and around Lake Powell. We also talked about this ball-bearing traverse and the possibility of a bypass at River level. I knew Robert had tried it, but I hadn't.

When they got to the start of the wading, it was too early in the afternoon and they thought the water was too deep and dangerous so they turned around and went back to tackle the ball-bearings. They tried that for a while and decided the River had to be easier and turned around for the second time. When they got back to the cliff, the water was much lower and they waded by without incident.

Lava to the Ball Bearing Bypass at Mile 67.2
We left Lava at 4:00 as planned and had only moderate difficulty in getting down to the cliff-out. The Grand Canyon Series strata tilt up and away from you so you are always following a rising ledge. But when you get too high, you have to climb down to the next rising ledge. Sometimes, when these ledges go around corners, they are skimpy and you find yourself with your feet on one thin ledge, your hands on another, and your pack hung out over the water. I was thus engaged when I heard a rattlesnake buzzing out of sight ahead of me. I moved very cautiously until I could see the snake posed no hazard. By the time the others arrived, the snake had gone.

Bypass at Mile 67.2
I arrived at the low-water traverse first, dumped my pack, and waded out along the cliff. There were plenty of rocks to walk on and in no time at all I was at the other end with the water never getting much above my knees. The others were already coming down as I was going back. The only problem was that my feet were aching numb. Still, I put my pack on and went back down. In half an hour we were all past the obstacle and at 7:30 we made camp on a nearby sandbar. Gary stayed behind to take some photos, Mattox went back to watch Gary, and Kyle went on downstream to see about tomorrow's route. All of a sudden it was getting dark and nobody was there to help put dinner together. To say I was grumpy would be an understatement.

The next day, Monday, Gary reported that at first light the River was even lower than the evening before and we could have sneaked by without getting our feet wet. Hooray for Sunday water.

Death by Erosion
By the time we left at 5:45 the water was rising but it was still lower than it had been at midnight. In fact, the low Sunday water helped all morning. There were many more ledges and sandbars to walk on. The ledges below Basalt Canyon were certainly easier at low water. It was still early when Gary found a beer floating in the water and gave it to us to share. About this time a fingersized rock fell from the sky and hit my boot. If it had been fist sized and had fallen a bit to one side, I would have been history. "Hey, whatever happened to Steck?" "Oh, him, he was killed by erosion."

Unkar Delta

We stopped at the upstream side of the great Unkar bend about 10:00 and were instantly covered with millions of tiny flies that were almost too small to see. They didn't bite but crawled out to the ends of the hairs on our bodies and moved around so the hair would move and tickle. As soon as I started hiking they flew off. Once as I was walking on some soft sand, I saw a lizard swim up to the surface through the sand and scurry off. What do they breathe under the sand? We had lunch at the Unkar delta by the rapids in case some boatman might make a mistake and flip, but no boats went by. Kyle said, "This is a no-good lunch spot—no shade and too much noise for conversation." I might add here that Kyle likes conversation. After lunch we went down a little way to the camp spot with the overhang at the very lower end of the delta. Lots of boats went by. A very restful afternoon.

Don must still have been bothered by something because he made a big deal about the clouds moving in. "A big storm coming. It could rain for days." But Gary observed, "I've never seen much of a storm come out of a sky like this." He wasn't worried and neither was I. Besides we had the overhang and the tarp. It did blow a bit, though, hard enough to blow the hot weather away and replace it with something slightly cooler. A cold front must have gone by.

Dinner was an experiment I hadn't tried for more than ten years. Now I know why. It consisted of crepes with brown sugar and freeze-dried cottage cheese. Not bad really, but more trouble than it was worth—especially considering the extra 8 ounces of frying pan.

Today was our sixth day—we were half way, and most of the uncertainty was behind us. Only four days to the flesh pots of Phantom Ranch, but there would be many climbs from River to Tonto and vice versa—1,200 feet. Tomorrow we would go downstream about 2 miles, take the rising Shinumo Quartzite ramp that emerges from the River, and follow it up and around to a steep ravine that would take us back to the River just above Hance Rapids.

Triple Breakfast Morning

We were late leaving camp—probably because it was still overcast and we overslept. Again, we had to take a series of rising ledges and then get down as best we could. Some of them were industrial strength ledges with downclimbs of 20 feet or more. In about an hour we came upon some Arizona River Runners (ARR) boats and were invited to help clean up the remains of breakfast. They didn't have to ask twice. Tomato juice, orange juice, eggs, and sausage. Then we hurried on and just happened to catch the Hatch boat party with their breakfast pants down. So we had three breakfasts that morning.

Shinumo Quartzite Ramp

With full tummies, we started up the quartzite ramp at 8:15. Mattox was still unhappy and mixed two indices for rating a trip when he said, "This trip is half as interesting and twice as hard as the Powell Plateau Loop." Another case of unmet expectations. He had expected this loop to be about as hard as the Powell Plateau one and packed accordingly—with more weight than he needed.

In ninety minutes we were at the promontory where Allen and I had turned around when we were exploring for this route many years ago. By this time the wind had picked up considerably and hiking was awkward. Sometimes heavy gusts forced me to hold onto the nearest big rock to keep my balance. Just down from the promontory and around the corner was the funnel-shaped descent ravine, and at 11:15 we started down. It was so steep and loose at the top that, for safety's sake, we went one at a time, or two close together.

Descent to Hance Rapids

Mattox went first. When he felt safe, Kyle and I started down. The far side of the ravine is a large steeply sloping slab set vertically, and I found it easier to go down with one hand on the slab for balance. There is a variety of small obstacles, but even the biggest one, which comes last, can be down-climbed easily enough if you lower your pack. In the flatter area before this climb we saw a fox saunter across in front of us. I wish I had noticed where it went.

Don was tired when we reached the River and there wasn't much shade—just some filtered sunlight under the tammies. It was almost 1:30 and very hot. Even cooling in the River helped for only a short time. Kyle was disgusted with the lack of shade and announced, "Hey, stay here if you want, but I'm going to find some shade." "Well, Kyle," I said, "I don't think you'll find any downstream that's any better than this." When he came back he was even more disgusted. "I hate it when you're right about important things when you're wrong about so many piddling things." In the meantime Gary had gone upstream and found big rocks that provided some shade—more as the afternoon progressed. We holed up there during the worst heat of the day.

To pass the time, Gary built a huge sand castle with a moat and a flat side toward the river on which he carved, in big letters, the single word BEER. He, of course, didn't drink beer, but I guess he thought the words CREAM SODA just didn't have the right impact. Around 4:30 we left this idyllic little corner of Hell. We went down past the dike and the big boulders along the north side of Hance Rapids to camp on a sandbar a little upstream from the spot where the trail leads up to the Hance mines.

Don Decides to Leave

Although we went only a relatively short distance—less than 0.5 mile—Don was totally wasted by the effort and by the heat. There was no longer any hope he could continue to Phantom with us, and the only sensible solution was for him to catch a boat ride down. If, after several days, no boats stopped and he was feeling no better then he would have to flash his signal mirror and hope for a rescue. Snagging a boat ride would be the least hassle, and Gary said there was a small inlet just downstream from our camp where boats pull in so passengers can explore the old asbestos mines. Don said he would wait there. He had food for several days and, of course, there was plenty of water. Feeling sure he would get a ride, the rest of us left our extra stuff with him so we could carry more water. Don's future being settled, we turned our attention to happy hour—sans booze—and dinner.

The River was falling when we arrived at camp around 5:00 in the evening, and it was still very low at 3:00 the next morning. By 5:00 A.M., however, it was high again.

Hance Rapids to Newberry Saddle

We left Don at 5:15—he later complained to the rangers that we had abandoned him—and had picked up water and started up the trail half an hour later. At 6:30 we were in the bed of Asbestos Canyon. On other occasions there has been water here, but this year was too dry and there was none. However, I did find some damp sand about five minutes up the bed. By 8:00 we were on the Tonto and could see Newberry Saddle very clearly—and close. (An interesting comparison—by 8:00 Mattox was already at Phantom Ranch.) All the wind yesterday must have meant a cold front came through. Even though there were only a few clouds, the air was relatively cool and the breeze wonderfully cool—sometimes even cold. It was an easy jaunt over to the saddle; we were there at 10:20.

Route Down from Newberry Saddle

When I was there last, with Robert, my brother, and the Petersons, I went left from the saddle while my brother and Robert went right. I forget where the Petersons went. But my way was not a good way, and I could look over to where Al and Robert were moving right along and wish I had gone their way. Now, seven years later, I was not going to make the same mistake again and looked for a way to start off to the right. A faint trail provided the key. It started us off in the right direction, and we contoured over and slightly down to a ridge that took us much farther down. Near the end of the ridge we dropped down to the right to a drainage that led eventually to the bed of Vishnu Creek. It was an easy descent.

Vishnu Creek

We were in Vishnu by 11:30 and the first order of business was to find water. We went up the creek into the Quartzite Narrows near a big overhang on stream right where there had always been ample flowing water before. This time there was only the tiniest trickle—two puddles barely big enough to dip a cup in. I could extract half a gallon from the larger puddle in ten minutes and in five more the puddle had filled back up. That meant a gallon every half hour. It would do, but more would be better, so we went upcanyon. Kyle explored the exit ravine, which sometimes has big bathtubs of water and Gary went way upcanyon to see if the spring at the base of the Tonto was operational. Both found some water. The bathtubs were empty but Kyle found a small pool of stagnant water up by a cottonwood. Gary found some shallow pools with flowing water "twenty-one minutes up" about 0.25 mile beyond where the canyon opens up.

In order to make tomorrow easier, we agreed to an early dinner after which we would load up with two gallons of water each and hike out to the point—in the cool of early evening—to camp. Accordingly, we snoozed away the afternoon. At 4:00 it was time for margaritas and then spaghetti. There was a bunch of that because we were only three eating for four, but Gary came to the rescue and ate everything in sight.

How to Destroy a Water Source

We might have been able to get all the necessary water from our puddle, but I had tried to "improve" its capacity by deepening it and, instead, destroyed it. I guess the bottom of the puddle had been sealed by fine silt; my digging disturbed the seal and allowed all the water to drain out the bottom. Also, I think the afternoon flow was about half that of the morning. In any case, we had to go up to Gary's water supply to get the required gallons.

Gurgling Water

Kyle and I hurried up ahead of Gary and found Gary's pools, but they didn't look as big as we expected. Kyle explored a little farther and actually found gurgling water. It was a deep pool, hidden in the reeds and rushes, with a small cascade at the inlet providing the gurgle. Our regular capacity was about five quarts apiece, but we augmented that by putting water in a gallon resealable bag and putting that in a pot to keep it from getting squashed. There were only two pots; however, Gary carried his gallon double bagged but otherwise unprotected. It worked fine.

We left the bed of Vishnu via the exit ravine at the 3,900-foot contour at 6:30 and made camp on a small knoll near the point at 8:00. Along the way I recited "The Raven," "The Cremation of Sam McGee," and "The Shooting of Dan McGrew." I don't know if the recitations helped the others pass their time, but I know it helped me pass mine. That hour and a half of evening hiking passed very quickly. As expected, the air was cool.

We had a very good opportunity for an early departure, but Kyle just wouldn't get up—"too cold," he said. No amount of coaxing, or shaming, or other forms of subtle coercion or humiliation seemed to work. Finally I remembered Kyle likes the direct approach and I proceeded to unzip his sleeping bag to extract the butterfly from its cocoon. That worked like magic—he was up in a flash. Too cold in the Grand Canyon in the middle of June! He's got to be kidding.

En Route to Clear Creek

It took us half an hour to get to the bed of the next drainage, but we went in an unnecessarily circuitous way. Instead of following the Tapeats rim, like we did, it is much quicker to follow the chocolate band of Bright Angel Shale. It leads directly to the rim of the descent ravine, which is 0.25 mile west-northwest of the southern tip of Hall Butte. The route out the other side is where the 3,800-foot contour crosses the bed—about 0.5 mile southeast of Dune Butte. The Fault Map does not show any faults here, but there are geological features that look like faults to me. In any case, the Tapeats is fighting a losing battle with the quartzite where you climb out. There is no obvious way up here and each of the three of us chose a different route. The way I prefer is to climb up on a rock and step across—carefully—to the mainland. Gary went up a crack a little to the north. I forget where Kyle went.

196

Camera Lost

After crossing the drainage west of Vishnu Creek, all we had to do was contour around to the Tapeats descent into 83 Mile Canyon. Except for one thing. I had lost my camera. I wasn't even sure I had picked it up after leaving camp that morning. I was willing to abandon it, but Gary said he would hurry back to a place where we had rested while he had taken some pictures. So Kyle and I rested some more while Gary went back. Unfortunately, he couldn't find the camera, so we continued on to find the Tapeats descent spot.

And Found

In the fall of 1990, I heard from my son Stan that some friends of his had hiked in the Vishnu area, and one of them had found a camera. Stan either hadn't known or had forgotten about my loss so he paid no attention to his friends' find until I brought it up. He eventually checked and found the camera was mine. The finder had developed my pictures and had the camera checked. The camera and case were out in the elements for fifteen months and were none the worse for wear, but the summer heat hadn't helped my pictures. At least I got back the only distant shots of the snow bridge.

Tapeats Break

The Tapeats descent into 83 Mile, which Don Peterson and I found in 1980, is about 0.6 mile west-northwest of the summit of Hawkins Butte. The descent is opposite a small arroyo on the other side. A large talus slope—more accurately a slump—comes up to within 20 feet of the Tapeats rim; I recognized it by the three small ducks I had placed on the platform on top of the slump in 1980. There is also a large cairn about 100 yards away on the Tonto, but I don't know the significance of it. The first time I went down here, we lowered packs and climbed down with a belay. This time Gary found a place where he felt comfortable going down without a belay and we found we could pass our packs down more easily than we could lower them. Each of us scrambled down without even a handline. The rest of the descent along the side of the slump also required care and more pack passing.

We decided to take a lunch break in the shade at the base of the Tapeats. It was going to be the last shade for a while, and we made good use of it. I offered the others some of my dried cuttlefish—I buy it in 1-pound bags at an Oriental food market near my home—and they both took some, though Gary said, "This stuff looks like something you can pull out of a mattress." "Well, if you don't like it, give it back." "No, I'll keep it. I like eating mattress stuffing." Gary said something else, too, that I liked better. In describing the trip, he said, "There are more neat little routes on this hike than any other I've ever taken."

Route to River

We went down the tributary drainage to 83 Mile Canyon and then down it about 200 yards. From there we went up the other side to the base of the Tapeats and contoured around to the point southwest of the "3938" elevation point. From the point we dropped down to the drainage to the west and went down it to the River.

Kyle was the first one in the bed and he ducked into the shade of a small rock to wait for the rest of us. The rock was so small that I paid more attention to where he could be hiding than to my footing and took a flawlessly executed head-over-heels tumble to the bed. I needed help in being extricated from my pack, but nothing seemed to be damaged. I proceeded with more caution after that. The descent to the River was typical—boulder-hopping and a scattering of pour-offs that called for minor route-finding and climbing skills.

Sharing the Beach at Clear Creek
We reached the River about three o'clock and made camp at the beach—now very small—just upstream from the schist ribs at the mouth of Clear Creek. Less than fifteen minutes later a private rowing party came by. Since they obviously wanted to camp there, we offered to share "our" beach with them. If they had been first, we would have been the supplicants. A good move even though we both had a right to be there. The beach is about one-third the size it was when I was there in 1982. More than that, all the vegetation that had provided shade was gone. The boaters were mainly from Los Alamos, and Gary knew the boatman who was rowing the dory—Merlin Wheeler was his name. He gave Kyle and me each a beer. Kyle had also baby-sat for friends of another couple in the party. Small world. They were very kind and invited us to dinner—cabbage rolls, Yugoslavian style, and fresh vegetable salad, with crepes for dessert. Excellent fare for three grungy backpackers. Another big plus for sharing a beach with boaters is the opportunity to use their Porta-Potti—no small blessing on this tiny beach.

The Horizontal Waterfall
The route from the mouth of Clear Creek to Phantom Ranch consists in going up and over to Zoroaster Canyon and then climbing out of Zoroaster and aiming for the Clear Creek Trail. But first we had to get over to Clear Creek. Fortunately, there is a trail that even continues up the creek once it gets there. We went up Clear Creek a little more than 0.5 mile to a point just above the "Horizontal Waterfall"—a spot where a vertical falls is taken by a rocky scoop and flung sideways. We bypassed this falls on the left and were at a big bay where we could see the ridge to which we had to climb. I found it convenient to climb the drainage that kept to the right. It is solid rock and is in the shade longer than other routes. When we got near the top, we found we had the choice of several ways to climb to the ridge.

Clear Creek Trail
We climbed to the ridge, went north, turned left at the base of the Tapeats, and contoured in to the bed of Zoroaster Canyon. There was plenty of shade through here, and we stopped and ate the oranges that some thoughtful woman had given us. In no time at all we had climbed down 15 feet or so to the bed of Zoroaster, crossed it, and climbed out to the Tonto on the other side. Then we finally came to the trail. With it under our feet we could really zip along—maybe even 2.5 mph. Once on the trail it was only three hours to Phantom.

Phantom Ranch

The first thing we wanted to do when we reached Phantom was find out what had happened to Don. But as we passed the Phantom Ranch dining room, I thought we should go in and see who was manning the lemonade stand. Good luck, it was a friend, and we were each treated to two glasses of that most excellent elixir. They claim it's the best lemonade in the Canyon. Then we went down to the ranger station to see about Don and to start in on my beer. It was locked so Gary went down to the Rock House to see if anyone was there. Kyle and I took the uppermost campsite and were cooling ourselves in the creek just above the bridge when Sjors, a NPS volunteer I know, came by and called out to me. Then the three of us went back to the ranger station and the beer cache. Sjors told us that Don had received a ride about ninety minutes after we "abandoned" him. He had reached Phantom about the same time we reached the Tonto. From there he hiked up to visit Bruce Aiken at Roaring Springs and then up the North Kaibab Trail to the rim. The only problem was that he had to carry all the extra stuff we had given him.

Party Time

Besides the beer and margaritas I had cached at Phantom in April, there was also a case of beer that I had arranged for Vern Bessey to buy for me, so there was plenty of stuff for a party. We also invited Sjors to dinner and gave him the one we didn't eat when we were guests of the boat party. Sjors had a problem. His funding of $5.00 a day as a volunteer had run out, so he had to provision himself. Shortly after that happened, Sjors was awarded a plaque by Secretary Lujan himself—for extraordinary achievement as a volunteer. What's that about the right hand and the left hand? Later, though, during a prolonged search for a missing hiker, Sjors was hired as a temporary ranger, which more than made up for his loss of funding.

It was quite dark by the time the festivities were over and Kyle and I went down to the campsite. I shone a light on the ground before putting my ground cloth down, and lo-and-behold there was a scorpion wandering across. I waited until it was in the bushes before putting my stuff out. All night, each time I turned over, I wondered whether or not I would get stung.

A Rest Afternoon at Aiken's

I don't know why it took us so long to get to Roaring Springs the next day, but it did. Six hours for 8.5 miles. We did spend forty-five minutes with Janice, the ranger at Cottonwood, socializing over a cold soda, but still it shouldn't have taken as long as it did. It might have been the fact we were carrying two sixpacks of beer. We were going to meet Bruce Aiken for lunch. Bruce is the NPS person at Roaring Springs and his job is to keep the pumps going that push water up to the North Rim. The South Rim also gets Roaring Springs water, but that water flows by gravity to Indian Garden and is pumped to the rim from there. Bruce has had this job for almost twenty years, and the house he uses is in a special spot. It is so pretty there—and cool, only 82 degrees. I had to put something on to keep warm in the wind. I guess that proves I had acclimated to the heat.

It was Saturday so Bruce didn't have to work and we just lolled around on his veranda and had iced tea and visited. We tried waiting for Janice before drinking the beer but it was a losing battle.

Greg Eats a Scorpion

Bruce has named his lizards and one named Greg surprised us by killing a scorpion. I didn't actually see him kill it, but I did see him eat it—and burp at the end after he had swallowed the stinger. We got to look at Bruce's new Redwall Cavern painting-in-progress—this one from the inside looking out— and cheerfully gave it our critical eye. I was able to see the finished product when a reproduction of it appeared in the October 1989 issue of *Southwest Art*. I like his style.

Janice finally arrived for a few rounds of beer and then Bruce created supper. The room vibrated with the sounds of Mozart, Beethoven, Vivaldi, and Brahms, among others. It was too bad that we would be up and out on the morrow. Back to civilization. Sadness.

Our plan was to take the Old Bright Angel Trail to the rim and then take the Ken Patrick Trail to the highway near Greenland Lake where we would walk to my van. The Old BA used to be shown on the 15-minute Bright Angel quad map but the 1962 edition eliminated it because someone didn't want people using it expecting it to be maintained. It is not shown on the Bright Angel Point 7.5-minute quad either. However, it is still shown on the 1962 Grand Canyon National Park map.

My Life on the Trail Crew

Knowing I wanted to use it for this loop routing, I spent parts of three years as a trail maintenance volunteer brushing out this abandoned trail. I pruned up to the top of the Redwall and down almost to the bottom of the Coconino. For some reason, I could never find anyone to help me twice. Even though the work was done several years ago, those parts are still in good shape. But the Supai and Hermit parts that I never got to are very overgrown. The Sierra Club also spent parts of several years brushing out the Ken Patrick Trail and cutting through all the downed logs. It is now in good shape, too.

Even though I worked hard and long at the job of clearing trail, I didn't always proceed according to the rules. When I visit the South Rim I usually visit my friends in the ranger operations building, and on one occasion I dropped in on Butch Wilson, who at that time was the Canyon district ranger. It wasn't all social because I wanted his okay for my last bit of trail clearing. Before he gave it he said, "You know, I've had a bad report on you." I couldn't believe he was serious and thought he was pulling my leg. So I went along with it. "Okay, what did I do this time?" "No, I'm serious," he said, "I've had to answer a nasty letter about you." And he went on to say that someone had written the superintendent a complaint letter to the effect that someone had cut the spines off an agave by the Old Bright Angel Trail and rendered it defenseless against the predators that wanted to eat it. It was true I had done that, but it surprised me greatly that anyone cared. I had considered that particular plant a danger to passing children because it was at an awkward, hard-to-avoid place on the trail; the spines would have been at eye level. What I should have done, if I really thought it was a danger, was take out the whole plant.

Another part of my experience as trail crew led me to consider the agave as a real villain in the outback. I was working from the bottom up by myself and using the bunkhouse at the Roaring Springs Ranger Station as headquarters. One day I slipped, put my hand out, and slammed it onto an agave spine. Only a tiny spot of blood showed the entry but the fact that I could not begin to make a fist without great pain told me part of a spine was still in my hand. I was $800 poorer by the time that spine was removed. I have a Zorro-type z in my palm and I know two others who have similar marks for similar reasons. The surgeon who operated wasn't really convinced anything was there, and I still think I might have saved the $800 with an offer of double or nothing.

Old Bright Angel Trail
Someone has ducked the Old BA and it is easy to follow. The trail begins just east of the iron footbridge at the mouth of Manzanita Canyon across from the Roaring Springs Ranger's house and crosses the steep hillside with the springs. After about a mile we crossed the creek and took the trail up the west side. I once found a railroad watch in the mud by the creek crossing— I still use it. In the shale, the trail goes up and down twice. After following a skimpy trail along a steep sidehill, we were at the Muav cascade east of Uncle Jim Point. This is a good photo opportunity for the water does beautiful things. From here the trail ascends the Redwall in one long arc with only a few switchbacks. When it reaches the Supai drainage, the trail goes up it for maybe 0.5 mile, and we had to be alert to catch the spot where it leaves the drainage.

Ken Patrick Trail
We had lunch on top of a limestone pillar, but a fierce wind blew my pack over. We might have stayed there longer if it had been more pleasant. Instead, we went on and soon were on top at the junction of the Old BA and the Ken Patrick Trails. I found out later from a plaque at the head of the North Kaibab Trail that Ken Patrick was a ranger SLAIN IN THE LINE OF DUTY AT THE POINT REYES NATIONAL SEASHORE AUG 5, 1973. ASSIGNED TO THE NORTH RIM FOR SEVERAL SEASONS, MR. PATRICK KNEW AND LOVED THIS ENVIRONMENT.

A sign at the Old BA/Ken Patrick junction reads: N KAIBAB 4 MI.—ROARING SPRINGS 7 MI.—PT IMPERIAL 6 MI. The trail spends too much time going west and even a little bit south but don't despair. Eventually, it will head in the right direction. In an hour we reached the meadow that goes up to the intersection of the highways to Point Imperial and Cape Royal. A sign there read: PT. IMPERIAL 4 MI [with an arrow to the left]—N KAIBAB TR 6 MI [with an arrow to the right]. As we approached the meadow, I noticed a building in the woods that I didn't remember having seen before. As I got closer I realized it was only a big limestone block with a dark blotch on one side in the shape of a door.

The trail climbed steeply on the east side of the meadow and in half an hour we encountered a confusing arrow pointing left. Since we went on a bit and then doubled back beyond a big downed snag, I think the arrow meant "go off at right angles here and you will hit the trail after a bit." The trail spends far too much time going north; I'm sure that if we had known exactly where we were, we could have gone cross country and hit the highway much closer to Greenland Lake. Finally, ninety minutes after reaching the top of the Old BA, we reached the highway. There was a car parked in a turnout there, and we startled Duane and Beverly from New Jersey out of their nap. Nevertheless, they very kindly gave me a ride up the road to my VW bus. That saved me 1.5 miles of walking. In this fashion the loop was closed after twelve days of hiking—some of it rather strenuous.

ADDITIONAL USEFUL INFORMATION

Date	Average Flow from Dam (cfs)	Max. Temp. at Phantom Ranch	Campsite
Wed June 14	14,978	106	Upper Nankoweap
Thu June 15	14,978	113	Kwagunt Creek
Fri June 16	16,944	108	Little Colorado
Sat June 17	14,111	110	First Bypass
Sun June 18	9,120	115	Second Bypass
Mon June 19	15,487	113	Lower Unkar
Tue June 20	16,284	109	Hance Rapids
Wed June 21	15,094	106	Vishnu Point
Thu June 22	15,845	109	Clear Creek
Fri June 23	16,143	104	Phantom Ranch

Horsethief Trail Variant: Nankoweap Creek to Lava Creek

Length
I would allow two days for the trip from Nankoweap Creek to the mouth of Lava Creek via the Horsethief Trail.

Water
The only reliable water between Nankoweap Creek and the River at the mouth of Lava Creek is at Kwagunt Creek. I worry about Kwagunt, too, but it has been flowing the four times I have been there. Although I have not checked it myself, I have it on good authority that "Malgosa goes." If you are hurting for water when you cross Malgosa, I suggest going down it to the River. I would also expect water up the Lava Creek drainage in what the quad map labels CHUAR VALLEY.

Use Areas	Location	Elapsed Times Between Locations (hours)
	Nankoweap Creek near 3,600' contour	1:30 **
	Nankoweap/Kwagunt Saddle	1:30 **
AF9	Kwagunt Creek	1:30
	Kwagunt/Malgosa Saddle	2:15
	Malgosa/Awatubi Saddle	1:45
AF9	Saddle by Awatubi Crest	1:30
	Chuar Saddle	1:00
	Carbon Butte	1:00
	Junction East and West Forks Carbon Creek	:30 (est.)
	Top of Carbon Creek narrows	1:15 (est.)
AF9	Mouth of Lava Creek	

** In the heat of mid-June 1989 these two times were 3:30 and 3:00, respectively.

ROUTE DETAILS

I return to the 1989 narrative. The up and over from Nankoweap to Kwagunt involved climbing 1,000 feet and, although it wasn't yet very hot when we started over at 11:00, I didn't allow for how much hotter it was going to get. This decision to take the harder, hotter route would affect Mattox's physical—and hence mental—condition for the rest of the trip.

Rock Art

Having tanked up with a gallon of water each, we left the Nankoweap drainage at about the 3,600-foot contour and cut across to the drainage coming north from the west side of Nankoweap Butte. Then we went up the south side of the ravine just to the south of the knoll with an elevation of 4,241 feet and found some shade beneath an overhanging cliff. Among the big blocks that had fallen, we found one that had quite a few petroglyphs on it. The worked face was almost horizontal. With magnificent shade in abundance we had lunch.

It was noticeably warmer when we again ventured onto the sunlit hillside and climbed up to the flats south of knoll 4,241. Here we had a choice. We could either lose some hard-won altitude and go southeast up a draw just north of the contour designation 4,200, which in turn is north of Nankoweap Butte, or we could continue to climb and contour around and up to the saddle between the "4810T" and "5052T" elevation points. Gary had already chosen the former when I reached the ridge and, while I was making up my mind, Kyle chose the latter. Kyle hoards his altitude like Midas did his gold and was not about to lose any even though the contouring looked tedious. Because going up the drainage below me looked easier than contouring around into it, I chose to follow Gary, and Mattox followed me. In the end I think Kyle was right.

Nankoweap/Kwagunt Saddle
Soon after we reached the drainage, it split, and we had another choice. The left-hand branch would likely have been better, as it climbed more evenly, but since Kyle was off to our right somewhere I thought it better to take the right-hand branch. The way up to the saddle was obvious enough, but Mattox was suffering from the heat and starting to show symptoms of heat exhaustion. Gary, who was still considerably in front, looked back and saw we were moving very slowly, so he dropped his pack and came back for Don's. By the time Gary had carried Don's pack to where his own was, Kyle was coming down from the saddle and carried Don's pack up the rest of the way. Bless them both. We were all on the saddle by 2:30. But there was still the long descent to Kwagunt Creek.

Downhill through Hell
The way down is to play "follow that drainage." A few bypasses were required that were aggravating. It was the hottest part of the day, and even though we were going downhill, it was slow going with extended rests when we encountered shade. A variety of drainages merge as you near the creek and they were all in dark rock that radiated heat with a fierce intensity. Because our water was running low and because of the chance that Kwagunt Creek might be dry, I listened with eager ears for the marvelous sound of running water but heard none. The rocks were too hot to touch, and the sand I was walking on was crusted white with various salts. I remember thinking Hell might well consist of hiking like this for eternity. Gary and Kyle were ahead; Don was behind. I had waited for him a few times but then went on ahead to be sure that someone went back for his pack. And just when I thought I was home free, I came to a 50-foot pour-off.

Encounter with an Unexpected Cliff
I have written about the psychological importance of expectations, and this encounter with an unexpected obstacle, when I was very tired and hammered down by the heat, was demoralizing. I sat down in the partial shade of my pack and sipped some water. During this rest I collected my wits enough to notice a small duck and a faint scuffed trail leading up the right-hand slope at the edge of the pour-off. It was probably only 10 feet but going up it was like the final assault on a fiery Everest.

From the top I could hear the welcome gurgle of water, and it was a walk-off down to the creek. Gary was there, already preparing to go after Don's pack, but there was no sign of Kyle. I figured he had hit the creek in a different spot and was already submerged.

After I rested a bit and saw Gary off on his errand of mercy, I went down to the creek to submerge myself. That was easier said than done; I had to do some Corps of Engineers–type streambed modification to be able to submerge even half of me. The water was warm, but it was cooler than the air and certainly felt good.

Heat Banishes Judgment

Kyle came by while I was thus submerged, and I loaned him my spot. I asked him where he had been; he explained that when he came to the final pour-off he had been even more wasted than I and was similarly shaken by the unexpected obstacle. He, unfortunately, had not seen the duck that would have guided him to the right, but instead went left to a crack at the edge of the pour-off and threw down his walking stick and dark glasses. Throwing down your walking stick before descending a cliff is natural, but throwing down your dark glasses is not. That simple act shows he was not totally rational—the heat had affected his judgment.

He climbed down the crack to about 10 feet from the bottom where he got stuck. Then he fell/jumped the rest of the way. Fortunately he landed on steep sandy talus. He retrieved his walking stick and dark glasses and continued down the drainage. He followed it to the creek and found a small spring in the process.

Too Many Salt Tablets

Don's experience was different. He had taken too many salt tablets and did not have enough water. His tortured stomach went into writhing spasms, which incapacitated him for a short while. He was ambulatory by the time Gary caught up to him.

Ants but No Mice

After Don arrived and had a chance to recuperate somewhat, we moved camp down to a sandy bench near Kyle's spring. The bench was hard and cracked. I was standing over one of these cracks while I set up the kitchen and soon had hundreds of tiny ants crawling over my legs—they were swarming out of one of the cracks. Fortunately, all the cracks weren't so occupied. From long habit we hung our food to keep it from the mice. The scraps we left out as decoys were untouched the next morning. Gary remarked, "Kwagunt is so poor it can't even afford a mouse."

Don Became Sensitized to Heat

I'm sure Don had been in the first stages of heat exhaustion that second afternoon—very tired and often faint and dizzy. But frequent, and sometimes extended, rests in the shade and having his pack carried partway for him got him to the creek. Although he had recovered to a degree by the next morning, his weakness would return whenever he became overheated. He later thought he had become sensitized to heat that second day by my error in taking us on that very taxing up and over.

Kwagunt Narrows

We were late the next morning and didn't leave camp until 6:00. The trip through the Kwagunt narrows was uneventful. I expected some obstacles but found none and we were on the Kwagunt delta by 7:30. Gary and Kyle went down to the River to get some water as preparation for our hike along the River to Malgosa. This I have already described.

Horsethief Trail

The only time I have followed the Horsethief Trail—along the Butte Fault—from Nankoweap Creek to Lava Creek was in 1977 and the following notes date from that time. We were on our way from Lees Ferry to Lava Falls, a journey that would take us forty-two days. Besides Don Mattox, who joined us at Nankoweap Creek, there were niece Sara, nephew Lee, sons Mike and Stan, young friends, Greg Edgeington and Dale Finn and myself. When I need to refer to the younger members of the group collectively in what follows, they will be called simply, "the kids."

Because of my bias in favor of camping by water, our plan was to camp at Kwagunt Creek if it were flowing. But the weather was overcast and we were there by 11:00 which is time for an early lunch but not for an early camp. We had left Lees Ferry thirteen days before and were travel hardened and, after a rest day, champing at the bit. Besides, Don Mattox had paid more attention to the map than I had and suggested continuing on after lunch toward tomorrow's goal—Lava Creek—so that, as he put it, "tomorrow will be not only easier but possible."

So we continued on after lunch, and all we had to do was go up and down. Up and down to Malgosa Creek. Up and down to Awatubi Creek. And finally up to the saddle alongside Awatubi Crest that we called the South Col. During the afternoon the sky cleared but the air was muggy and at one rest stop where I arrived late and found the last shade taken up by Lee's pack, I lost my temper. I don't remember what I actually said, but what I intended to convey was that as a general principle packs don't need shade, people do. What I said made Lee angry, but he moved his pack anyway and Stan suggested I take a salt tablet. I did and began to feel better. That incident took place almost fifteen years ago, but Mattox still reminds me of it whenever I put my pack in the shade.

As we came down into the Malgosa drainage from the Kwagunt/Malgosa Saddle, I stumbled upon a horseshoe and a large collection of rusty tin cans by what must have been an old cowboy (horse thief) camp. In a similar position on the next saddle, I found an old coffeepot. I believe the existence of these items supports the view that horse thieves used this part of the fault.

Our camp on the South Col was a beautiful place. The world fell away on two sides to create a splendid isolation. The wild geology of Awatubi Crest added spectacle, and when the moon came up, close to full, its soft light suffused all this with an otherworldly quality. Unfortunately a cold wind came up that would last all night. It coated everything with noise and misery.

This was the night of September 28, and we were still using our summer gear. Luckily for me, Greg loaned me his windbreaker. It was still cold the next morning, and our routing was now the opposite of what it had been the day before—it was now down and up. Down and up to the saddle west of Chuar Butte. Down and up to the ridge overlooking the greenery of Lava Creek. Since we were taking the High Road to Unkar Creek, we went southwest from the nearby junction of the East and West Forks of Carbon Creek and dropped into Lava Creek near the 3,360-foot contour.

If you are following the Horsethief Trail to the mouth of Lava Creek, you will want to continue down Carbon Creek from the East Fork/West Fork junction to the beginning of the Carbon Creek narrows. Here you will find the boater trail going over to Lava and then down Lava Creek to the River.

High Road Variant: Lava Creek to Vishnu Creek

Length
2 days.

Water
Water is available at the camping spot near the c in LAVA CREEK. Next water is at the tangle of tributaries shown as a smudge of green about 0.5 mile north of the U in UNKAR on the Cape Royal map. First water in Vishnu is at the top of the quartzite.

HIKING TIMES (1977)

Use Area	Location	Elapsed Times Between Locations (hours)
	Junction East and West Forks Carbon Creek	4:30
AF9	Camp by the 4,200-foot contour in Lava Creek	2:15
	Saddle west of Juno Temple	2:30
AG9	Unkar Creek at 4,000 feet elevation	2:30
	Saddle between Vishnu Temple and Freya Castle	2:00
AH9	Top of Tapeats in Vishnu Creek	

ROUTE DETAILS

There is a low ridge between the Carbon and Lava drainages, and route finding is not a problem. It took only ninety minutes across there and we had a long rest/lunch by the pleasantly gurgling water of Lava Creek. The trip up the drainage to the small waterfall at the spring and the Indian ruin beyond it was not so pleasant. It must have rained hard recently because we had a great deal of mud to contend with, and travel up the creek was quite slow. We made camp by the spring—near the 4,200-foot contour south of Chiavria Point. The next day we climbed through the Tapeats opposite the ruin and headed south up the drainage toward the saddle between Juno Temple and Cape Final. It was a long brushy climb to the saddle.

Unkar Creek
It was an easy drop into the Unkar drainage. Although we looked for water we could not find any. Eventually we sent the kids down to the River for water—possibly a 10-mile roundtrip—expecting them back the next morning. In fact, however, they found lots of water in the tangle of tributary canyons at about the 3,320-foot contour. They goofed off for a while and were back just after dark. We camped close to the place where two branches of the creek are close together for almost 0.5 mile. The springs are about 1.4 miles

207

An Indian ruin in upper Lava Creek near the place where one goes up and over to Unkar Creek on the high road to Vishnu Creek.

downstream of this junction. The next morning we headed north up our bit of Unkar and then turned abruptly to the southwest just north of the 4,400-foot contour designation toward the saddle between Vishnu Temple and Freya Castle. The route up was easier than the one to the Lava/Unkar Saddle. We had a beautiful view of the South Rim from the saddle, and I took a lot of pictures. Unfortunately, when I changed film I left the old roll on a rock.

The route into the Vishnu drainage is directly down the fault line through big Supai boulders and then limestone ones. Finally we reached a slot canyon and elected to contour around to the north on a bench to a talus slope that took us the rest of the way down. (See *Grand Canyon Treks*, page 58.)

When my brother and I went back a few years later looking for the lost film canister, I couldn't find it. What Al did do on that trip, however, was climb the Redwall slot just below the saddle on the Vishnu side. I again took the talus.

Vishnu Creek
Below the talus Vishnu opens wide, and we went down to the Shinumo Quartzite by a spring and took a siesta. The plan was to have an early dinner and then go out on the Tonto and camp somewhere on the point below Hall Butte.

A Way to Moderate Conflict

The High Road from Lava to Vishnu has now been sketched out and I consider this chapter officially closed. But before it is de facto closed, I want to elaborate a bit on how to increase the chances of success of a long trip. Books abound on how expeditions have been blown apart by internal conflict. I have been on two long trips now—one of forty-two days and one of eighty days—and although conflicts arose, they never got out of hand because of the moderating influence of an "outsider." On the eighty-day trip Al, Robert, and I had company on almost every segment of the trip. This meant new jokes, new foibles, new interactions. All these new people helped keep us on an even keel. On the forty-two day trip in 1977, Don Mattox and Mike were the outsiders. They joined us at Nankoweap on day thirteen and left us at Phantom on day twenty. Don was the "good cop" to my "bad cop" and could have fun with the kids.

8 Tatahatso Wash/ Eminence Break Loop
Circumambulation of Tatahatso Point

> Another realization that maps do not tell all:
> "It always surprises me that so many 25 foot cliffs
> can be hidden among 80 foot contours."
> JIM SULLENBURGER

Length
Four days, plus rest and/or exploration day(s), if any.

Water
I found a small amount of flowing water at the Tatahatso/Leche-e junction in late October 1987 but none in late August 1985. I have found pothole water farther down the drainage near the Redwall pour-off the three times I have been there—once in April, once in August, and once in October. In addition, Robert found big pools there in May 1983, and Rangers Crumbo and Quiroz found some there in January 1985. There is a Redwall break leading to the River 1.5 miles upstream. It will take about three hours from the Tatahatso drainage to the beach there. The next water downstream from Tatahatso Wash is at the River at President Harding Rapids. This is also the last water for the climb out.

Quad Maps
7.5-minute maps
    Tatahatso Point (for roads)
    Buffalo Ranch (tiny bit)
    Shinumo Altar (for roads)
    Nankoweap Mesa (bit of road)

Roadhead
The route starts along the Eminence Break about halfway across the neck of Tatahatso Point where the road makes a sudden swing from northwest to southwest. This loop is on reservation land so two Navajo Permits are needed as well as one from the National Park Service.

ROUTE TO ROADHEAD
The route to the trailhead for this loop begins at the Cedar Ridge Trading Post near mile marker 505 on US Highway 89 north out of Flagstaff.
Mileage
   0.0   Head west from Cedar Ridge on a dirt road just to the south of the burned out remnants of the buildings that used to be the Cedar Ridge Trading Post.
   6.9   After 6.9 miles you reach a major fork just to the north of Bodaway Mesa. Road 6120—the numbers 6120 are inside an arrowhead—goes to

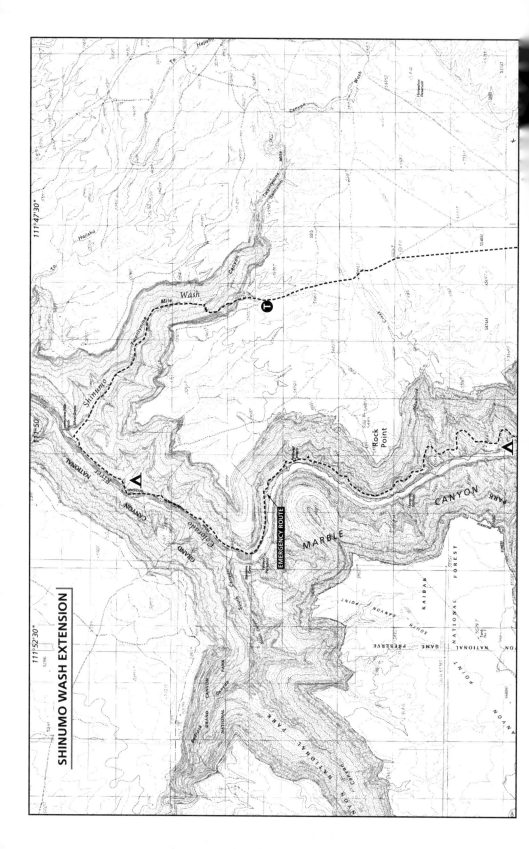

SHINUMO WASH EXTENSION

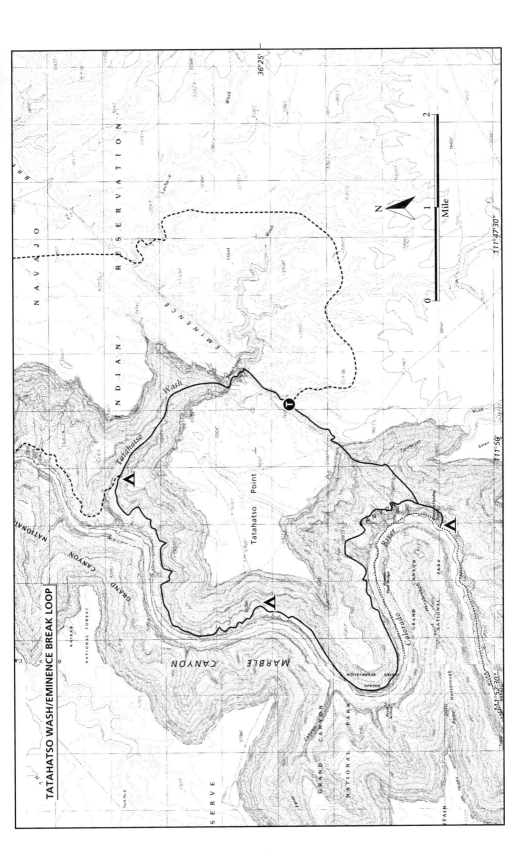

TATAHATSO WASH/EMINENCE BREAK LOOP

the left between Bodaway Mesa and Tooth Rock and is my preferred route to the Salt Trail Trailhead. Road 6110 goes to the right—take it.

7.5   After 0.6 mile turn left down off the shoulder onto an almost insignificant track—at least it seems insignificant considering the fine road you have been on. You will soon pass Corner Rock Reservoir on your left.

8.3   After 0.8 mile you reach a fork. Go right.

8.6   After 0.3 mile you reach another fork with a faint track going left. Go right.

9.6   After 1.0 mile bear left at a fork.

10.3   After 0.7 mile bear left at a fork. The right fork takes you to some buildings.

11.5   After 1.2 miles bear left at a fork.

11.7   After 0.2 mile you cross a faint road. Go straight.

13.0   After 1.3 miles you reach a fork. Go left on a road that will take you down and across Black Spot Reservoir.

14.4   After 1.4 miles—during which you have gone down one side of the reservoir, across, and up the other—go straight at a fork.

15.0   After 0.6 mile a road merges from the left. Go straight.

15.6   After 0.6 mile bear right at a fork.

15.9   After 0.3 mile bear left at a fork.

16.3   After 0.4 mile a road merges from the left and your road swings abruptly from west to northwest.

17.1   After 0.8 mile you reach a sign that reminds you that you are still on Road 6110.

17.3   After 0.2 mile you pass a road T-ing in from the right.

20.4   After 3.1 miles you round the point of a hill and can look out across Tatahatso Point. As you contour left out on the top of Eminence Break, note the drainage you have been following continues on west. This is where the route to Tatahatso Wash begins.

21.0   After 0.6 mile the road turns steeply down to the right. If you take it out to Tatahatso Point, be aware you may need four-wheel-drive to get back up the hill. The Eminence Break route is in the ravine just below you at the base of the Break.

Reservation Mud

Those who have driven out on the Navajo Reservation when the roads are muddy—after rain, for example, or as snow is melting—can all testify it's a mess. Twice I have gone to the Eminence Break Trailhead without crossing Black Spot Reservoir, once because I was lost and once because I could not cross the lowlands by the reservoir because of the mud. I think I turned south each time onto the road from Black Spot that runs past the "5780T" elevation point. After about 2 miles south on this road I turned west to a dwelling and then north again eventually reaching Road 6110 just before it makes its sharp turn to the northwest. The time it was wet I slipped and slithered in my VW bus—with snow and mud tires—and was very glad there were two cars. We didn't get stuck, but we almost did—several times.

A very unnerving thing happened to me during the slithering when I was trying to decide whether to turn left or go straight at an intersection. It was very foggy with a light misty rain and I asked my son Stan his opinion. He said, "Why would you want to go left—that's south." I was sure it was north and told him so. There were no clues. The sky was evenly lit and the sur-roundings painfully flat but as we argued, I got a brief glimpse of Shinumo Altar. Stan was right and I can tell you it is very wrenching psychically to discover you are turned 180 degrees around when you thought you had a good head for such things.

HIKING TIMES

Use Areas	Locations	Elapsed Times Between Locations (hours)
▲ Reservation	Car	:30
	Top of descent ravine	1:15
	In bed of wash	1:45
	Hermit dryfalls	:30
	Tatahatso/Leche-e junction	2:00
	Top of Redwall	:45
	Upstream point	2:15
	Top of access ravine	:30
▲ SF9	On beach	:30
	Top of access ravine	3:00
▲ SF9	Bed of Tatahatso	:30
	Downstream point	1:30
	Window	1:30
▲ SF9	Tram-site camp	:30
	Opposite Buck Farm Canyon	3:15
	North side of Eminence Break canyon	1:15
	Top of descent	:45
▲ SF9	On beach at President Harding Rapids	3:30
	Road	:15
Reservation	Car	

Campsites upstream from Tatahatso Wash, including those in the wash above the Redwall, downstream from Tatahatso Wash are in the Eminence Break Use Area (SF9).

There has been a dispute between the Navajo Nation and the U.S. gov-ernment over the ownership of that part of Marble Canyon north of the Lit-tle Colorado River and between the middle of the River and the eastern rim. The Navajo claimed west to the middle of the River, and the government claimed east to the rim. This controversy left the inner canyon—where we hike—claimed by both. The controversy was finally decided in favor of the National Park Service, with the boundary being the Canyon rim. Just to be safe though, you may want to get permits from both jurisdictions.

ROUTE DETAILS

The loop hike down Tatahatso Wash and out the Eminence Break route is mentioned by Butchart (*Grand Canyon Treks*, page 76), who said it would probably take two days. The first I heard of its being done was in a report

215

of a trip taken by Rangers Kim Crumbo and Joe Quiroz during January 21–23, 1985. When I did it, I followed their directions for the descent into Tatahatso Wash rather than Butchart's because I found them less ambiguous. Crumbo told me their whole trip took one and a quarter days. However, they did not go down to the River.

If you have only one car and leave it at the start of the hike, you will notice from studying the map that the final closing of the loop requires walking about 0.6 mile from where you *wish* the car was to where it actually *is*. Even if you have left water at the rim exit point, you may feel burdened by this additional walk at the end of an already strenuous day. The only solution I can see to this problem is to deliver hikers and packs to the rim entry point, have one person drive the car back to where you would like it to be and then return to the entry point on foot. One other thing to be careful about: The National Park Service has received reports of cars being vandalized when left in this area.

Counter-Clockwise Loop Is Best
I will describe the hike as going down into Tatahatso Wash—for three reasons. First, and most important, it gives you a chance to discover the extent of your water problem, if there is one, while you can still do something about it. Second, it saves the delightful time—two days would be nice—to be spent on the beaches alongside President Harding Rapids until the end of the trip. And third, this was the way we did it in October 1987. There were four of us: son Stan, son Mike, friend Christine, and myself.

I am interested in place names and their origins and have long wanted to know what the Navajo names on the maps mean. To this end, I asked Ed Chamberlain—the curator at the Hubble Trading Post Historical Site—to ferret out meanings of some words for me. One of these was Tatahatso. The first thing I found out was that meanings are hard to come by for the reason that the spelling of a word on the map leaves out many symbols essential to meaning. Thus, Ed could report back to me that Tatahatso meant, possibly, "big wash," "the wash over there," or even "the narrow place by the steep place that goes down." Gary Ladd's contact gave him "big rim" and Nancy Brian gives "big crevice" in her book on Grand Canyon place names, published 1992. All of these names are appropriate. Take your pick.

Water Availability Critical
The feasibility of this loop depends on the availability of water in the Tatahatso drainage, and the nearer the water is to the Redwall lip, the more convenient it will be. There has been water at the lip the five times I know of: once in January, once in April, twice in May, and once in October. But the October visit and one of the May visits were times when the water supply in the whole drainage was skimpy. There is an inaccessible plunge pool about 20 feet down the beginning of the Redwall gorge where skillful and precarious dipping with a pot on the end of a string could possibly net you enough water. A rappel and subsequent prussick could do the same thing. I have never had to use this water supply, but the possibility of tapping it exists if you are prepared. For the moment, I will assume that there is some, probably grungy, pothole water in the bed of Tatahatso Wash near the Redwall lip.

Rim Takeoff

The route into Tatahatso Wash starts down a small ravine 0.1 mile northeast of the "5662T" elevation point just above the 5,600-foot contour. Then it goes down another, very steep, ravine—45 degrees but it seemed steeper—about 0.15 mile southeast of the "5442T" elevation point. This ravine takes you through the Kaibab Limestone to the Tatahatso bed.

Descent Ravine

We parked near the spot where the first small ravine, if extended southwest, would meet the road and went down that ravine until we were through the fault. Then we went northeast alongside the base of the cliff to the descent ravine. It is right beside the cliff and has a cairn to mark it. There are a few chockstones to block the way but only one is of any consequence. Once, coming up, I climbed up on the west, but now, going down, I thought it easier to climb down on the east. I climbed down to within 6 feet of the bed—where Mike had jumped the rest of the way—but I was afraid to jump. There was a boulder in the middle of the bed and no good place to land. I sat there facing out thinking about jumping for some time before I remembered my climbing skills, faced the cliff, and climbed down.

We completed the descent from the car to the bed of Tatahatso in just under two hours. The footing was generally stable in the steep ravine but you must descend such places with care to avoid rolling rocks on your companions.

Garden of Room-Size Rocks

Once we were in the bed, the going became quite difficult. Many room-size rocks blocked the way, and ingenuity was required to find a way around and through them. The only major obstacle came in the middle of the Hermit where a substantial pour-off blocked the way. We bypassed it by going up to the right (east) and contouring north to a descent. There is a more direct bypass down a small ledge on the right. But there isn't always room for a person with a pack on so it is quite a struggle. I have come up that way and Mike went down that way, but I find the up-and-over technique less intimidating.

Flowing Water

The wall-to-wall collection of big blocks thinned out after the bypass, and it was a relatively straight shot to the confluence of Tatahatso Wash and Lechee Wash. We got to this junction in midafternoon and, since there was water and since one of our party was a very tired puppy, we decided to camp on the pleasant Supai ledges we found there.

Pothole Water at Lip of Narrows

It was an easy two hours the next morning down to the top of the Redwall narrows. There was ample pothole water for all our needs so we didn't have to make any change of plans. If there had been no water and if we couldn't have retrieved any from the plunge pool, we would have abandoned the loop and, instead, contented ourselves with extending the upstream part of our hike before exiting the Canyon the way we entered it.

Our plan now was to explore upstream for three or four days so I could show the others the Redwall routes Robert found there.

River Access at Mile 35.8

There are two river access points upstream from Tatahatso Wash, and the first one is a worthy goal for a hike. It is a steep chute at river mile 35.8 about 1.5 miles upstream from Tatahatso—at the 2,855-foot river elevation marker and about a mile west of the 5,558-foot rim benchmark. When you descend to the River here you are almost exactly opposite what is called the Bridge of Sighs because of the resemblance to its Venetian counterpart.

River Access at Mile 32.6

A more dangerous river access point is about 0.5 mile up from Redwall Cavern, at River mile 32.6. I consider it sufficiently dangerous that it should be used for emergency purposes only. This is an access with a history dating at least to the time when Marble Canyon was being studied for possible dam sites. Metal rods in the limestone and remnants of the manila rope that connected them still exist. I'm sure it was used by people living in the tent city on the nearby Redwall rim. I can imagine cook's helpers making their several daily pilgrimages to the River for water.

Route Upstream

After taking on some water at Tatahatso Wash, we began contouring around to the descent ravine opposite the Bridge of Sighs. It took us three hours, in addition to lunch, to get there, but that included almost an hour just to get from the bed of Tatahatso to the point overlooking the River. It wasn't strenuous but all the ins and outs made the journey tedious.

About ninety minutes after we left the bed of Tatahatso, we were opposite the mouth of 36.7 Mile Canyon and, about forty-five minutes later, crossed 36 Mile Canyon. It was still another forty-five minutes before we were opposite the Bridge of Sighs Canyon. There are two drainages 0.2 mile east-northeast of the "Natural Bridge" on the 7.5-minute quad. The northernmost, and lower, of these two drainages drains the bowl via a precipitous pour-off. The other, the higher more southerly one, is the descent ravine.

Descent to River at Mile 35.8

The route down was straightforward and, even though it was very steep, all the rocks were well consolidated in a conglomerate matrix. The only route finding needed was the final descent to the Muav ledge on which we contoured upstream to the small beach. This final descent was along a narrow ramp just downstream from where we began looking for it. I have been told to look for an Indian ruin in this vicinity, but I have not seen it. It is apparently visible from the other side of the River. The time for descending the chute is about twenty-five minutes and the total time from Tatahatso Wash was three and a half hours.

We had a comfortable camp on the beach and planned for the next day to be a rest day. We were going to try to get upstream to the next river access point at mile 32.6. Our "very tired puppy" was now a "very tired and very stiff puppy." The totality of descent-with-pack over the last two days had just about destroyed that puppy's quadriceps.

We were not able to get up to the river access, but in three hours we did get to the bend below Rock Point where we had lunch and then headed back to our camp by the River. The description of what's farther upstream is given in the Tatahatso/Shinumo Extension at the end of this chapter.

Prehistoric Indian Route (?)

The canyon opposite the descent ravine at mile 35.8 has an exceedingly interesting Redwall route. It seems to be an ancient Indian route and was accidentally discovered by Dave Dawson in 1984. It involves going into a cave and down a spiral tunnel to another cave together with a path on the cliff face formed by laying rocks on logs stuck in a crack. I describe it more fully on page 228 under Emergency Route to River.

We were back at camp by the River a little after 3:00, none the worse for our six hour "rest day." This gave us time for a quick dip in the glacial pool at our doorstep and for a very leisurely dinner.

Back to Tatahatso Wash

The next day we left camp at 8:55 and were in the bed of Tatahatso at 12:20. The route from there to our eventual camp at the tram site was very pleasant. "Overcast and cool with a 10 percent chance of rain within twelve hours." The way was easy, and it always took considerably less time to get from the point we were on to the one we could see than we thought it would. That is certainly part of the definition of a "pleasant" walk.

Hole in the Redwall

The only noteworthy feature of that walk was the Redwall "window." I would have walked right over it but Mike asked, "What is that big hole over there? It looks like a mine shaft." On close inspection the "hole" was a tube going down and then out to the Redwall face so you could see light when you looked at the bottom of the hole. The hole connects with the cliff face about 50 feet below the rim.

About half an hour later, when we were opposite the "fin" that figured in our Lees Ferry to Lava Falls hike in 1977, I deposited the contents of my little box of Robert's ashes on an overlook. This fin, which is a thin ridge of rubble extending from the Coconino to the Redwall, is an interesting geological feature and is described more fully on page 256 under River Route: Lees Ferry to Nankoweap Creek.

Tram Site

There was not much left to mark the tram site. The tram was operational in the early fifties and supplied the camp that supported the activity concerned with the proposed Marble Canyon dam site. The major man-made features still remaining were level places for tent platforms. Close inspection of the ground revealed a few nails and a few hinges and some fragments of broken crockery, but that was about it. All in all, it was rather disappointing to find that the prior occupants had removed all their trash.

About the time we made camp it began to drizzle so up went the tarp. By the time we went to bed, however, it had cleared enough that Mike and I chose to sleep outside with the tarp only as backup. About 5:00 in the morning, we needed that backup and moved in with Stan and Christine.

Rubble Trouble

The next day went quickly, too, until we rounded the corner and had to deal with all the rubble produced by the faults. Crossing the canyon produced by the first fault was a major undertaking and I think each of us took a different route. The next pair of canyons with the little nubbin of 3,600-foot contour between them was easier but still strenuous. We had lunch on the flat place just east of the 2,845 benchmark surveying the final jumble in front of us very carefully. Unless we could go down and then back up, we were in for a very difficult time.

A short segment of Redwall Narrows in the bottom of the drainage was all that gave us pause—if we went that way and it hid a nonnegotiable pouroff, we would be in even bigger trouble. But Stan thought it would go and, indeed, it did—quite easily. In fact, we were on the opposite ridge in just forty minutes.

Descent to Beach

In fifteen more minutes we were ready to start our descent to the beach. There is a rudimentary trail and it would be troublesome to make the descent without it. The descent took forty minutes—just six hours from our tram-site camp.

We made two excursions in what remained of the afternoon. We went upstream to try—unsuccessfully—to spot the Bridge of Poles somewhere on the other side, and we went downstream to try—successfully this time—to find some beer. We found three. We also put up the tarp as a storm was coming. In fact, it rained hard for about eight hours that night.

Butchart mentions the Bridge of Poles at mile 43.3 many times in his last two books, describing it as a rickety platform of fitted poles that can be walked across if you are of an adventurous frame of mind. Carbon dating of one of the poles gave an age of 1,100 years. Several people, including Butchart, have climbed up to it and Kenton Grua and a companion climbed past it up to the Redwall rim. The conventional wisdom, however, is that the bridge is not part of a path to the rim—as are the poles in Bridge of Sighs Canyon.

The next day we explored farther downstream—found more beer—to the big beach where the deer trail takes off on its way high around the corner downstream to connect with the River route to Nankoweap and Kwagunt Rapids. I had come up that way from the Little Colorado with Robert in 1983.

After lunch and some recreational bathing, I went back upstream for another unsuccessful attempt to find that elusive Bridge of Poles. I also wanted to see the Hansbrough Inscription, but I didn't know where that was, either. What I needed to do, obviously, was to come to this place with someone who knew where these two features were. This I did in 1990 when Gary Ladd accompanied me on the Shinumo Wash/Eminence Break extension of this loop.

220

Location of Hansbrough Inscription

The Hansbrough Inscription is under an overhang at the downstream end of an outcropping of Muav Limestone next to President Harding Rapids. This outcropping is visible from the beach at the bottom of the trail and has a talus "hat" above it. There is also talus on the upstream side, and the dihedral angle under the overhang is visible from the beach. As a final clue, the inscription is almost directly away from the River at the rapids. Among the locust on the flats below and in front of the inscription is another grave. It contains the remains of a Boy Scout who drowned in Glen Canyon in the days before the dam was built.

Location of the Bridge of Poles

The Bridge of Poles is opposite a point about 0.25 mile upstream from a Redwall tower—actually a slump or Toreva block—that is 100 feet high and 25 to 30 feet in diameter. There is talus on both sides; an energetic person can pass behind it about halfway up. This tower is not visible from the beach at the bottom of the trail but I estimate it to be about 0.5 mile from the rapids. Once you are in position, look on the opposite wall for a place where a person can climb several hundred feet up rock and talus. More scrambling up to the right leads to a cleft and the Bridge of Poles is in that cleft.

What Happened to Hansbrough and Richards

In Marble Canyon, humanity lays a light hand upon the landscape. Rather, it is form and beauty that are hard to ignore. There are a few places where tangible artifacts of human presence intrude sufficiently to trigger an awareness of history, but here in Marble Canyon this awareness comes only when summoned. So let us summon the ghosts of Peter Hansbrough and Henry Richards and hear of their fate.

Hansbrough and Richards were members of the Brown-Stanton expedition of 1889 whose purpose was to survey the Colorado River to check the canyon's suitability as a railroad right-of-way. Hansbrough, who had worked for Stanton as the foreman of some project in Idaho, was an oarsman and Richards a black "steward." They had started at Green River, Utah in May 1889, and after running the survey to Hite (then called Dandy Crossing) the party split up. Some were left behind to run the survey to Lees Ferry, some went home and the rest hurried to Lees Ferry to continue the survey from there, leaving on July 9, 1889. Brown drowned the next day as his round-bottomed boat flipped at an eddy fence just below Soap Creek—at a place now known as Brown's Riffle. Brown had not allowed lifejackets to be used and it is somehow fitting that he was the first victim of that stupidity. Hansbrough chiseled an inscription to Brown's memory on a rock face at Salt Water Wash.

Five days later Hansbrough and Richards were the next victims. They drowned when their boat capsized in the fast water just below 25 Mile Rapids—Rapid No. 133 in Stanton's notation. Smith and Crampton, who edited Stanton's field notes and published them in *The Colorado River Survey,* say in a footnote that they studied the maps and the notes and concluded that No. 133 was 26 Mile Rapid. Others, particularly Crumbo, studied the River and the notes and conclude that No. 133 was 25 Mile Rapid. I agree with Crumbo for the following reason.

Marble Pier Canyon

By studying the North Canyon Point quad map, the new 7.5-minute map that covers these rapids, I conclude that 24.5 Mile Rapids is at the mouth of what Stanton called Marble Pier Canyon—Sheep Spring Wash on the map. Stanton gave the name Rapid No. 132 to the one created by this wash and described in some detail a 70- by 80-foot remnant of marble cliff 40 feet high standing in the middle of the wash. The North Canyon Point quad map shows just such a feature as a nubbin of the 3,040-foot contour on a promontory of the 3,000-foot contour below it almost in the middle of the wash where it opens out to the debris fan.

This limestone block, with a "well proportioned cutwater on the upper end," was exactly what Stanton needed as a central pier for a bridge spanning the wash—hence his name "Marble Pier Canyon". Stanton's party camped—his phrase is "went into camp"—by this pier at the head of Rapid No. 132 late in the afternoon of Saturday, July 13, 1889. I conclude from this that 245 Mile Rapids is Rapid No. 132, and this implies that the next rapid, 25 Mile Rapids, is Rapid No. 133. Sunday they rested and by noon Monday Hansbrough and Richards were dead.

In the late 1970s, 25 Mile Rapids was officially renamed Hansbrough-Richard Rapids; that new name appears on recent editions of the Emmett Wash 15-minute quad map. Note, though, that Henry Richards's last name is misspelled as "Richard" on the map. Note also that the name 25 Mile Rapids is still used on the 7.5-minute North Canyon Point quad map.

What exactly happened on that Monday morning, July 15, 1889? Up at 4:30 A.M. which would be first light in the absence of Daylight Saving—and breakfast at 5:00. Sunday had been a day of rest and rain showers but no mention was made of Monday's weather. They left camp at 6:40, and almost at once had to deal with the rapid at the mouth of "Marble Pier Canyon"—this is No. 132. They lined the boats through although one was damaged, and they pulled in at the head of Rapid No. 133 about 8:00 A.M. to repair it. Stanton notes that No. 133 was as bad as the previous one.

In his book *Down the Colorado*, Stanton refers to events suggesting Brown's premonition of death. He does the same with Hansbrough and Richards. Stanton notes that Hansbrough woke him up at 4:00 Sunday morning "terribly frightened" with a bad pain in his big toe. Stanton also notes that Hansbrough followed him around all day Sunday very troubled and talking about his life, death, Heaven, and the possibility of future life. Stanton finally read some verses of the Bible to him. This seemed to quiet some of Hansbrough's agitation.

The two blacks, Richards and Gibson, had camped by themselves some distance from the others, and after Richards's death, Gibson told Stanton that Richards, too, had exhibited a state of mind on Sunday similar to Hansbrough's.

The water was an ugly thick brown soup after all the rain of the past days. They lined the boats around the top of the rapid and were ready to start down though the fast water—no waves—about 10:20. Richards wanted his boat, with Hansbrough at the oars, to accompany the first one, but the consensus was that it was better for the first boat to go alone to see how it went. The first boat did not go out far enough and was forced to make another landing a few hundred feet farther down and start over. With some effort they were finally able to pull in to the sandbar below to wait for the others. Watching them, Richards suggested that he and Hansbrough line their boat down. Stanton said it didn't look bad but it was their decision. Hansbrough was ready to row and persuaded Richards to come, too.

Hansbrough and Richards got into their boat and Stanton pushed them off telling them to stay well out in the current away from the rocks near shore. For the first few hundred feet they were doing fine; then the current forced them against a cliff on the left that was about 25 feet high and undercut a few feet off the water. They tried to push off to keep from going under the overhang, and at first it appeared that they had succeeded. Then suddenly their round-bottomed boat flipped. The people in the first boat went after the struggling Richards, but he was sucked under before they could help. Stanton and another man ran downstream, but by the time they got down to the River it was too late. Hansbrough was not seen after the boat capsized. Shortly after these two deaths, Stanton abandoned the expedition, to take it up again in December 1889 with better boats *and* lifejackets.

Richards's body apparently was never found. However, the following January, during the second expedition, Hansbrough's skeleton, identified by peculiarly made shoes still on his feet, was found on the rocky cobbles of a beach near what was later to be called President Harding Rapids. The inscription I was seeking memorializes his death as does the name Hansbrough Point, given to the 2-mile-long promontory opposite.

The *1989 Grand Canyon National Park Calendar,* published by Dream Garden Press, notes that Hansbrough's bones were found on January 17, 1890 at mile 43.5. Stanton's Field Notes for that day, as edited by Smith and Crampton, say only that at "7:30 A.M., after breakfast this morning we took the remains of P. M. Hansbrough and buried them in a mesquite grove under the marble cliff on the left side of canyon just below where a side canyon comes in, directly opposite Rapid No. 160" (President Harding). The inscription P.M.H. 1889 was cut in the cliff beside the grave.

While it was possible that the bones were found before breakfast, it is more likely they were found the previous day during the portage. In a footnote to Stanton's entry for January 16, Smith and Crampton write that on the 16th Stanton was so busy with survey calculations for the railroad that he forgot to mention in his notes that Hansbrough's bones had been found. So I can only conclude that the calendar entry is off by a day. The calendar is also off by a day in noting the deaths of Hansbrough and Richards. These observations probably qualify as nitpicking and I mention them only to show that when you try to reconstruct what really happened, you often find discrepancies among the sources.

More Death and Near Death

Besides the Hansbrough-Richards tragedy, death and near death have figured in the history of this part of the River on other occasions. In August 1923, having heard on their radio a few days earlier of President Harding's death, a USGS survey expedition chose to take a layover day as an "Official Day" of mourning at what the leader called Boulder Rapid. Crumbo, in his book, *A River Runner's Guide to the History of the Grand Canyon,* implies the name was changed to President Harding Rapids later during the map making process.

In 1949 in 24.5 Mile Rapid—Stanton's Rapid No. 132 at the mouth of Marble Pier Canyon—Bert Loper, a veteran canyon river runner, apparently died at the oars while rowing through it—he was seventy-nine. What are assumed to be his bones were found at the mouth of Cardenas Canyon in 1975. His boat can still be seen at the mouth of Buck Farm Canyon.

A near death occurred in 1955 at the big boulder in the center of President Harding Rapids. John Daggett—who, with his companion Bill Beer, were the first to swim from Lees Ferry to Lake Mead—got caught under the rock and almost drowned. That was their only brush with death and they eventually finished their swim without further mishap. The story of their epic swim is well told by Beer in his book *We Swam the Grand Canyon,* published by The Mountaineers, Seattle, in 1988.

Route to Rim

The route from the beach at President Harding Rapids to the rim was generally to the northeast and steep and strenuous. After retracing our steps up the trail to the top of the Redwall, we worked our way over to the drainage coming around from the southeast. After crossing it we climbed up through the lower Supai cliffs until we couldn't climb any higher. Then we contoured over to the fault ravine leading to the rim. Along the way there is a mushroom rock 10 feet tall, or so, and I am always comforted when I finally see it. I know then that we will soon be starting up and out. Soon after encountering the mushroom rock, we had the option of climbing the Supai alongside the fault ravine or taking a narrow ledge over to it. I took the ledge, as I always have, but the others chose to do the climb.

At first I could continue up the drainage, but then it became too steep and I climbed out on the left (north). From there it was a straightforward scramble to the top. But I must emphasize that it was a very *steep* scramble and every rock I stepped on or held on to seemed eager to continue its journey to the sea. I have never had a problem there, but I am always very cautious. Finally I reached the Fallen Tower Bridge, as Butchart calls it, and knew I was just about out so I stopped to wait for the others.

By climbing the Supai ledges on the right, they had eventually reached the drainage above the steep place that caused me to leave it. From there they continued more or less right up the drainage. They found very precarious footing in many places—especially in the Hermit where the crumbly shale threatens to act like ball bearings under your feet. I went up that way once and decided never to go there again if I could help it.

Mike agreed with me. He thought the way they went was the scariest ascent he'd ever made. He described it as being so steep it was a four-point—sometimes six-point—ascent. By that he apparently meant he was on all fours most of the time with the knees thrown in occasionally for extra friction. He says he moved slowly with great care and advises anyone else going that way to do the same.

After a reunion at Fallen Tower, we continued uneventfully to the rim and then up the Tatahatso Point Road past the very rocky part to the "good" road. Since we had two cars, we didn't have to walk over to where the other car had been left. But I have walked it and anything level is a piece of cake after the climb up the fault.

Extension: Shinumo Wash to Tatahatso Wash

Length
If the loop begins and ends at the Shinumo Wash Trailhead, allow a minimum of six days. This includes a day for hiking the 9 miles or so back across the top from the Eminence Break Trailhead to the Shinumo Wash Trailhead. Rest days, if any, are extra.

Water
The first water is at the River at mile 30.2. The only dependable water between mile 30.2 and Tatahatso Wash is at the emergency Redwall route at mile 32.6 and the Redwall break opposite the Bridge of Sighs at mile 35.8. There may be pothole water in the bed of Tatahatso Wash near the Redwall lip, but you shouldn't count on it.

Quad Maps
Additional map required: North Canyon Point

Roadhead
The roadhead for the Shinumo Wash Trail is at the rim of Shinumo Wash 0.1 mile south of the 5443T elevation point.

ROUTE TO ROADHEAD
Mileage

0.0   This road log starts from the highway by the burned out wreckage of the Cedar Ridge Trading Post just north of mileage marker 505.

6.9   After 6.9 miles you reach a major intersection. Road 6120 goes left and Road 6110 goes right. Go right.

7.5   After 0.6 mile you pass the road going off to the left that you would take if you were going to the Eminence Break Trailhead. Go straight.

9.5   After 2.0 miles you reach a fork. The road to the left goes to a hogan. Go straight.

13.8 After 4.3 miles you have passed many small roads and are now passing some stone ruins on your right. Keep going straight on the good road. You are also passing Shinumo Altar.

17.0   After 3.2 miles you have gone down a wide cleft through the upthrusted part of the Eminence Fault to the flats below. A good road goes left at a fork. Go straight.

17.4   After 0.4 mile the good road makes a sweeping turn to the right from northwest to northeast. You do not want to make that turn. Turn off onto a small road continuing northwest. In 1989 this was a very minor turnoff up and over the shoulder left by a road grader. From this turnoff it is 3.5 miles to the trailhead.

17.9   After 0.5 mile a road merges from the right. Go straight.

18.3   After 0.4 mile you reach a fork. Go left.

19.0   After 0.7 mile a road Ts in from the right. Go straight.

19.1   After 0.1 mile you reach a fork. Go right.

19.6   After 0.5 mile a road merges from the right. Go straight. You are going down a rocky grade.

19.9   After 0.3 mile the road forks. The better road goes left to a viewpoint. Go right up a hill.

20.3   After 0.4 mile you reach a fork. The right fork goes to the edge of the wash, but it is too soon. Go straight.

20.4   After 0.1 mile a road merges from the right. It is the road you would now be on if you had gone right at the last intersection.

20.9   After 0.5 mile you reach the trailhead. You are now 20.9 miles from the highway. After another mile the road disappears.

HIKING TIMES

Use Areas	Locations	Elapsed Times Between Locations (hours)
	Car—Shinumo Wash Trailhead	3:45
	Top of Redwall	1:00
▲ SG9	River—mile 30.2	2:00
	Opposite South Canyon—mile 31.6	:30
	Opposite Vasey's Paradise—mile 31.8	:30
	Top of emergency descent ravine— mile 32.6	:30
	Construction site—mile 32.8	1:30
	Below Rock Point—mile 34.0	1:00
	Nautiloid Canyon—mile 34.7	2:00
▲ SG9	Top of descent ravine—mile 35.6	2:15
	Opposite 36.7 Mile Canyon	1:15
▲ SG9	Bed of Tatahatso Wash—mile 37.3	

All campsites are in the Shinumo Wash Use Area (SG9).
Remember, you will need permits from the Navajo Nation in addition to the one required by the National Park Service.

ROUTE DETAILS

It was April 1, 1990—April Fool's Day—but there were no tricks as we got ready to leave the cars. Maybe we were too busy or maybe we just didn't know each other well enough yet—or maybe we forgot. The group—son Stan,

Marce, Leslie, Bert, Mark, Peggy, Kat, Ginger, Gary, Jarold, David, Karen, and myself—left the cars at 8:30 and were in the Shinumo Wash drainage an hour later. There is a reasonable trail; the only problem is making sure you cross the Wash when the trail does. We took a long rest on the shady Supai ledges and were on top of the Redwall in time for lunch. After that we took the trail about a mile downstream on top of the Redwall until we could get to the River at the breakdown created by the Fence Fault.

Besides the obvious access to the River down the Redwall break, there is another one, requiring some minor climbing, about 100 yards upstream. There are also warm springs, which are near, at or below River level depending on the River flow.

Downstream Trail
We camped near the River and had to search the downstream hillside for the trail the next day. We found it by angling up the hillside until we crossed it. It was not much but it speeded our downstream progress considerably. We stopped to look down on the beach at the mouth of South Canyon and one picture I took gave the distinct impression I was on the other side of the River.

Emergency Route to River
We were at the top of the emergency descent ravine by noon and ate lunch before we started down. This descent ravine is 0.4 mile south of the "5357T" elevation point. A bulge of 3,600-foot contour supports a tower and I would use that tower to judge my location.

Robert discovered this route for himself in 1983 and later, during a hot August in 1985, I used it to make a quick roundtrip for water. Taking time only for a short rest and a long drink, I made the roundtrip in fifty-five minutes. I quote now from Robert's journal as he approached from downstream.

Robert's Journal Entry
"June 3: Once I got around the point out of the Nautiloid Creek drainage, I returned to a good and steady pace along the edge of the Redwall rim. Still 0.75 mile away, I recognized Redwall Cavern up ahead where the gorge turns to the left. But the best view came about 0.5 mile farther upstream. The next drainage north of the Cavern had numerous relics of a construction site— cables, ruins of a wooden cabin and small concrete slabs with bolts—all probably related to the proposed dam site. I picked up a constructed trail here heading my way toward Shinumo Wash. From this site I noticed 0.5 mile upriver that the lower half of the Redwall face below a ravine did not have the normal sheerness but angled off toward the River. Without really considering it seriously, I had the idea that it might be possible to climb up there with friction. Unfortunately, I could not see the upper half of the wall since it was hidden from view, but since I had the time I decided to have a closer look.

Robert Finds Route Used by Construction Crew
"From the top of the ravine it looked like two impassable falls in the bed, but a duck farther down got me interested enough to continue climbing down. I passed an anchor bolt—a 1-inch-diameter iron hook embedded in cement—

and what appeared to be the first falls turned out to be a series of limestone steps—steep, but only half as bad as it looked. More anchor bolts gave me a clue that I might be on to something. The second falls was real but off to the right I noticed a narrow ledge—just the right size to accommodate a trail, 1 to 2 feet wide with 70-degree walls above and below.

Route Details

"This ledge soon pinched out, and it took me a second to recognize a broken section angling down in the form of a steep ramp. Taking each step with extreme caution, I got down to some talus below. It would have been nice to have had a few more steps near the bottom. The talus did not go to the River. Instead I had to go right again onto the tilted Redwall face where there was a row of 3-foot iron rods with a 3-inch loop on top. There were small fragments of rope attached which indicated that a rope railing once was here. I could go down the wall—from rod to rod—with my hands behind me for friction. Except for the last 30 feet—that looked too steep. Instead I tiptoed to the right on a tiny ledge—maybe an 1 or 2 inches wide—to where the river talus reached higher.

"I was so fascinated with this route that I climbed back up, got my camera and tripod, and did it all over again shooting a complete sequence of traverses and climbs. I assumed this route was established for water supply for the construction crew. I wondered if 'Old Joe' was assigned or had volunteered to run up and down this place. The route has plenty of exposure but the footing is safe. After a few shuttles it probably becomes a simple routine walk." End of quotation.

Rope Advised

Robert didn't use a rope, and I didn't either when I tried this route two years later. But now, in 1990, it looked harder than I had remembered. Besides, in bringing eleven people—one stayed behind—down this route, which is not quite as steep as the Redwall Route in Upper Phantom, I felt obliged to use a rope—not as a belay, unless requested, but as a handline.

We had two ropes. We used a 50-foot piece of 0.5-inch webbing on the steep ramp—tied off on an old drill jammed in a crack at the top—and we strung the 75-foot piece through the loops on the iron rods.

This is a dramatic Redwall route and a must for people who collect such things. Nevertheless, I call it an emergency route for the purposes of this book because it has its risks and is not necessary. It is possible to get from a camp by the River at the access provided by the Fence Fault at mile 30.2 to the easy access at mile 35.7, opposite the Bridge of Sighs, in one long day—provided, of course, you don't dilly-dally too much along the way, and don't try the emergency route.

Although I support Robert's hypothesis that this route was used to provide water to the crew at the construction site, I don't think that was its only use. Boaters have noticed a series of boards, arranged in a kind of walkway, leading from near the iron rods at least halfway toward Redwall Cavern. These boards are quite high on the cliff and may have led to Redwall Cavern, which I doubt, or they may have led to drill holes in the wall.

228

We carried about ten gallons of water back up the "Iron Rod Route" to use for dinner and to get us to the next River access. We camped on the flats just downstream from this access ravine and were at the construction site after only a few minutes the next morning. The inscriptions there date from January and February 1951 and immortalize Edna, Rod, Osborne, Bud, Dan, and Slim Jack Ballew. Like Robert, we could see just a bit of the Iron Rod Descent upstream.

This was an especially easy morning for me. Stan was heading back today so, during the morning before he retraced his steps, I carried his water and he carried my pack. I could really move. He went as far as the point below Rock Point where you can see quite a way downstream. He turned back about 10:00 and I turned back, too—into a turtle. Stan had not intended to hike back to the cars all in one day, but the going was easy enough and he managed to get back there by 4:30—six and a half hours and 5 miles plus the Shinumo Wash Trail from when he turned around.

Nautiloid Creek
We were at Nautiloid Creek about an hour after Stan left. It drains the south side of Rock Point and is named on the 7.5-minute Tatahatso Point quad. This drainage gets its name from the nautiloid fossils found in its bed near the River.

My 1990 notes say, "Enter the drainage via the first talus slope that is opposite a possible exit and at the bottom contour into the bed on a narrow ledge." My 1987 notes, made when we were going the other way, are more specific. They say "Go down the gully that touches the top of the first C in COLORADO on the east and then go around and out the gully just across from that C." I also noted that it was harder to find this route from the north. I think these gullies are due north of the elevation mark denoted "3534" on the 7.5 minute Tatahatso Point quad map.

Descent Ravine at Mile 35.7
It took us almost an hour to cross the next big wash—brute force, no tricks possible, and in another hour we were at the top of the descent ravine opposite the Bridge of Sighs at Mile 35.7. It was midafternoon and we all went down for R&R at the River. We also made a water run. Some of this water was for dinner and breakfast and some was to get us over to Tatahatso Wash, but most was to augment the supply in Tatahatso should it be too meagre.

We camped in the drainage just upstream from the descent ravine because we could spread out more there. We were off and running by 7:30 the next morning and in about an hour we were at the next major drainage. Those of us who were behind at the time took what we called the Mr. Spice Route, though the reason for that appelation escapes me at the moment. It involves going down the nose toward the point for the view and then backing up a bit before angling down into the drainage.

Surprise Canyon Formation
As you make this crossing, note the rocky knoll of Surprise Canyon Formation. It is a dark brown pebbly conglomerate that lies in old Redwall streambeds. George Billingsley discovered it sometime between the 1976 and

1986 versions of the beautiful Geologic Map of Grand Canyon so that the later map shows some and the earlier one doesn't. Billingsley uses this formation to trace the drainage patterns on top of the Redwall before there was any Supai deposition.

We were opposite the canyon at mile 36.7 by 9:45 and in the bed of Tatahatso Wash by 11:00.

Route into 36.7 Mile Canyon from Rim
It is possible to get down 36.7 Mile Canyon from the rim to the top of the Redwall on River right, and you can see the route as you go by. Along the rim on the north side about half way along its length is a freestanding column of Kaibab Limestone and its pedestal extends to the Toroweap. The route leaves the rim in a cleft just to the west of this pillar and heads diagonally down and east to the base of it. A small talus chute leads to a thin band of Coconino Sandstone and then expands to cover the rest of the Coconino and the Hermit Shale. The route then contours east for some distance on top of the Supai Formation to a chute that is out of sight from this viewing angle, but which takes you directly to the bed of the wash that is the top of the Redwall.

Extension: Eminence Break to Shinumo Wash on Rim

HIKING TIMES

Eminence Break Trailhead	7:00 (est.)
Shinumo Wash Trailhead	

ROUTE DETAILS
The fee for beginning this loop hike at Shinumo Wash and enjoying all the wonderful sights between there and Tatahatso Wash is now due—the hike back. The straight-line distance between the two places is 6.6 miles and a convenient ground distance that bends to the east in a circular arc and allows for crossing Tatahatso Wash and Leche-e Wash is approximately 8.5 miles—say 9. If you can maintain a speed of 1.5 miles per hour, this will take six hours—say seven.

I have not hiked this return, but when I do I will try to follow the map routing from the top of the Eminence Break to the cleft, formed by Lechee Wash, that takes you down through the break. Then I would head north to the route I had already driven. I would also consider making this return a few days before a full moon—so the almost full moon is already up in the sky as darkness approaches—and go about half way after an early dinner. This dinner and associated beverages, together with food and water for the next day, would have been cached at the top of the break just before the start of the hike.

With Shinumo Altar clearly visible in the moonlight off in the near distance to keep you on track, it would be feasible to continue hiking through part of the night.

9 Rider Canyon/ South Canyon Loop

> The reason why people who hike
> with Bert Fingerhut carry such heavy packs:
> "You can never have too much gasoline . . .
> or too many stoves."
>
> BERT FINGERHUT

Length
Seven days, plus layover days, if any.

Water
There will be no water on the rim except what you have in your car or have cached. You can probably find occasional pothole water in the bed of Rider Canyon, especially in the narrows close to the River, but the only sure water will be from the River. Below Cave Springs, when the Redwall becomes a serious obstacle to river access, the only ways to the River before South Canyon are in the ravine opposite Tiger Wash and along the Fence Fault at Mile 30.4.

Quad Maps
7.5-minute maps
    Bitter Springs
    Buffalo Ranch (upper right)
    Buffalo Tanks
    Emmett Hill
    Emmett Wash
    North Canyon Point
    Tatahatso Point (upper left)

The 7.5-minute maps show the roads best.

Roadheads
    Rim of Rider Canyon.
    Rim of Bedrock Canyon.
    Turnaround on rim above 27 Mile Rapids.

ROUTES TO ROADHEADS

Log to roadhead above Rider Canyon
Leave Marble Canyon going west on US Highway 89 Alternate. After almost 19 miles, turn south just after passing mileage marker 557. If you pass a turnoff for a historical marker, you have gone too far—go back about 0.5 mile.
Mileage
    0.0   Leave the highway and go south through a gate.
    0.2   After 0.2 mile you pass a loading chute and stock tank on the right. There is a road to the left. Go straight.

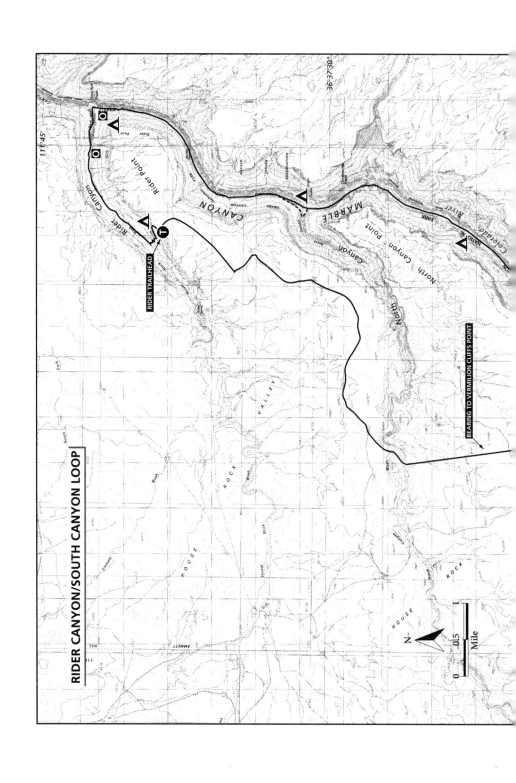

RIDER CANYON/SOUTH CANYON LOOP

RIDER TRAILHEAD

Rider Point

Rider Point

Rider Canyon

RIDER CANYON

MARBLE CANYON

Colorado River

North Canyon Point

North Canyon

ROCK VALLEY

HOUSE ROCK

HOUSE ROCK

BEARING TO VERMILION CLIFFS POINT

111°45'

36°37'30"

N

0   0.5
Mile

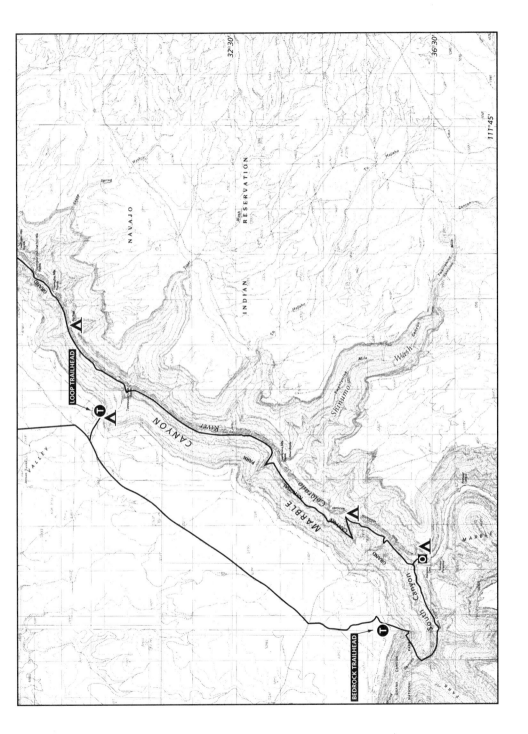

0.7   After 0.5 mile the road splits to avoid muddy ruts. Go whichever way seems best. Shinumo Altar can be seen straight ahead.

1.5   After 0.8 mile you pass a road going to a corral on the right. Go straight.

2.0   After 0.5 mile you cross a cattle guard and reach a fork. Go left.

3.0   After 1.0 mile you are going down a hill along a ridge in the direction of Shinumo Altar.

3.3   After 0.3 mile you go through a cattle guard.

3.8   After 0.5 mile you reach a place that can be very muddy after a rain.

3.9   After 0.1 mile you cross an arroyo—solid footing even when wet.

3.95   After 0.05 mile you cross a narrow "isthmus" of dirt connecting the arroyo to higher ground that bridges a ditch in the process.

4.3   After 0.35 mile turn left in front of a fence.

4.5   After 0.2 mile turn right through a fence. A corral and buildings will be on your left after the turn.

The road becomes better, and speeds of 30 mph are occasionally possible.

5.2   After 0.7 mile you go through an opening in a fence.

5.4   After 0.2 mile you reach a fork. Go left. The right-hand road goes to the North Canyon crossing, requiring four-wheel drive.

6.3   After 0.9 mile you go through an opening in a downed fence and reach a fork. Go straight. The road to the right goes 0.5 mile down a shallow drainage to the North Canyon crossing road already mentioned.

8.6   After 2.3 miles you reach a road T-ing in from the left. Go straight.

9.6   After another mile you can see the cliffs on the far side of North Canyon in the middle distance.

10.8   After 1.2 miles you are going down a hill into a valley leading to the rim.

11.5   After 0.7 mile you cross the wash. There is a fork. The right-hand road continues down the wash a short distance to an overlook. The road to Rider Canyon continues left up a draw.

11.8   After 0.3 mile you reach a junction with a loading chute on the left. Go right. If you continue straight, you will soon be going down a steep gravelly hill to a large metal stock tank. Until recently, this was my roadhead for the Rider Canyon descent.

12.1   After 0.3 mile you pass a faint road to the right. Go straight.

12.5   After 0.4 mile you pass a faint road to the left. Go straight.

13.4   After 0.9 mile you reach a knoll overlooking the descent ravine. You can park here and hike a short distance down to the trailhead, or you can drive an additional 0.3 mile and circle around and down to the same place. It is about a thirty-minute hike back along the rim to the large metal stock tank already mentioned.

The descent is the second ravine—parallel to the rim—that you come to as you hike down from the knoll.

Log to roadhead above Bedrock Canyon via North Canyon Wash
Mileage

0.0   Take the right-hand fork at a junction 5.4 miles in from US Highway 89 Alternate on the road to the Rider Canyon Roadhead.

1.0   After 1.0 mile you join the other road coming down from the Rider road. Go straight.

1.3   After 0.3 mile you pass a stock tank in the wash on the right.

1.5	After 0.2 mile you have gone down a steep grade and are crossing North Canyon Wash. There's another tank in the bed of the wash. Four-wheel drive is highly recommended for getting up the rocky hill on the other side.
3.1	After 1.6 miles there is a fork. Go left.
4.1	After 1.0 mile there is a junction. Go right.
4.8	After 0.7 mile a road merges from the left at a gate. Go through the gate.
5.0	After 0.2 mile you reach the road to the overlook above 27 Mile Rapids. It is 0.35 mile out to the overlook; you may wish to camp there.
5.4	After 0.4 mile you pass a road to a stock tank. Bear left.
5.7	After 0.3 mile another road to the tank merges from the right. Go straight.
7.5	After 1.8 miles a road goes off to a tank on the right. Go straight.
9.1	After 1.6 miles you reach a major intersection. Left takes you to the rim. Right takes you to Cane Ranch. Go across.
10.3	After 1.2 miles the road ends at the point between South and Bedrock Canyons. The rim entry/exit point is approximately 300 feet east of the western edge of the North Canyon Point quad map and 0.44 mile north of the southern edge. There is a cairn, and you start down a steep narrow defile.

Log to roadhead above Bedrock Canyon via Cane Ranch

Go west from Marble Canyon on US Highway 89 Alternate. Go 0.7 mile past mileage marker 559 and turn south onto the well graded Buffalo Ranch Road.
Mileage

0.0	Leave the highway.
10.4	After 10.4 miles go across a cattle guard and turn left. Going straight takes you to the Cane Ranch.
10.6	After 0.2 mile you reach a fence corner. Turn left.
14.5	After 3.9 miles the road forks. Go left.
15.1	After 0.6 mile you reach a gate.
15.7	After 0.6 mile the road curves by a stock tank and forks. Go left.
18.8	After 3.1 miles you reach the main intersection referred to earlier where a left turn takes you to the overlook camp 4.1 miles away, straight ahead takes you to the rim and a right turn takes you to the Bedrock Canyon roadhead.
20.0	After 1.2 miles you reach the Bedrock Canyon roadhead. Four-wheel drive is not needed to get to either the overlook or the roadhead by this road.

HIKING TIMES

Use Areas	Locations	Elapsed Times Between Locations (hours)
▲ AC9	Car at turnaround above 27 Mile Rapids	1:45
	Bed of North Canyon	3:15
▲ BLM Land	Rider Canyon roadhead	1:00
	Bed of Rider Canyon	4:00
▲ AB9	Mouth of Rider Canyon—mile 17	3:15

	Boulder Narrows—mile 18.5	1:00
▲ AC9	Base of rim route at mile 19	3:30
▲ AC9	Mouth of North Canyon—mile 20.5	3:00
▲ AC9	Double-decker sandbar—mile 21.8	2:30
▲ AC9	"Indian Dick" Pinnacle	2:15
▲ AC9	24 Mile Rapids	1:00
▲ AC9	24.5 Mile Rapids	2:30
▲ AC9	Beach at Cave Springs Rapids—mile 25.4	2:00
▲ AC9	River access opposite Tiger Wash	3:15
	Opposite To Hajisho—mile 28.4	1:30
	Opposite Shinumo Wash—mile 29.2	3:00
▲ AC9	Beach at Fence Fault crossing—mile 30.4	2:30
▲ AC9	Mouth of South Canyon—mile 31.6	2:30
	Bedrock Canyon	3:15
▲ AC9	Rim	2:00
▲ AC9	Car at turnaround above 27 Mile Rapids	

Remember: The times given include rests but not lunch.

ROUTE DETAILS

The rim return between Bedrock and Rider Canyons closing this loop is roughly 13 miles so I am beginning this route description approximately in the middle at the overlook shown on the 7.5-minute North Canyon Point quad map on the rim above 27 Mile Rapids. Before setting up camp at the overlook, we had already placed two caches. One, on the rim at our exit point above Bedrock Canyon, consisted of water and treats. The other, on the rim of Rider Canyon at a roadhead near our entry point, consisted of all our dinners for the rest of the trip as well as libations of various kinds, including water. This Rider Canyon cache was supposed to lighten our loads for the first day's hike.

I had picked the overlook as the place to leave our cars partly because it is a little closer to Bedrock than to Rider, making the last day's return to the cars a little less taxing, and partly because I thought it would be a beautiful and scenic place. The eleven veterans of much previous Grand Canyon looping who gathered at that scenic place all looked ready for the first hike of the season—except me. After a winter of unimpeded sliding toward total decrepitude, I am never quite ready for the Grand Canyon. We were, in alphabetical order, Bert, Bob, Caroline, Don, Gary, George, Hansjorg, Jane, Jim, Leslie, and Marce. Last names are omitted to protect us all.

Rim Hike to Rider Canyon

The agenda for the first day was to hike across the top to our cache on the edge of Rider Canyon. To do this we first had to cross North Canyon and exploration a few days previously had shown the easternmost crossing to be along the eastern edge of the big bend just east of the word WASH in NORTH CANYON WASH on the 15-minute Emmett Wash quad map. This same bend is shown under the word WASH in NORTH CANYON WASH on the 7.5-minute North Canyon Point quad map. The route to this crossing is basically north from the cars, though more careful map study on the 15-minute map showed using

Spiderman Lee Steck exercising on a Rider Canyon dihedral.

a bearing on the closest point of the Vermilion Cliffs to be not only better but easier.

After about 3 miles of travel on this bearing, Don, who was in the lead, crossed a drainage and went up the other side only to find he had another drainage to cross. He directed the rest of us to go down to the junction of these two drainages before climbing up. After correcting for this detour, we found ourselves at North Canyon within 100 yards of where we wanted to be and were in the bed of North ninety minutes after leaving the cars. Bert and some others crossed North Canyon somewhat farther to the west. It was only a short distance from the crossing place to the road, but then it was something over 5 miles to our cache. After two hours of road walking and a break for lunch, we were at our cache by the big water tank.

Bert believes in traveling in style, and part of that belief is expressed in the adage, "You can never have too much gasoline." He used to add, "or too many stoves" but I beat him down from three to two for this trip. At dinner he found he accidentally beat himself down from two to one. My stove is a Whisperlite and needs a fuel bottle with a special top, but having six full quarts of his own he left mine behind at the last minute because I kept saying two quarts would be enough. I feigned sorrow for his hardship but was secretly delighted. As it turned out one stove was plenty and I will never know how much fuel was dumped or carried out.

DOWN RIDER CANYON

While we were putting in the Rider cache, Bert and I spent some time exploring and found the road that goes directly to the rim takeoff point, but we had already placed the cache and the distance saved was minimal so we left the cache where it was. Nevertheless, next time I will take the closer road. It was cold this morning so I, for one, was glad to be moving. The baby rattlesnake Jim found yesterday afternoon coiled tightly near his sleeping place had also moved. It was about half an hour over to the descent ravine and an hour more to the bed of Rider. The whole route down is steep but well marked and there are two places, just below the rim, where we had to squeeze under a chockstone. One such place was roomy enough to negotiate with pack on but the other wasn't and packs were lowered. There were still a few awkward places below the limestone cliffs but, except for the possibility of rolling rocks, the way down was without hazard.

Rider Obstacles

Searching my memory banks for obstacles in the bed of Rider, I can count six—there may be more, and I may have them in the wrong order. The first is an 8-foot pour-over that often has a 5-foot log leaning against it. Most of us used the log, but Hansjorg and some others took a somewhat longish bypass on stream right. Next came a pool with easy, albeit slippery, access to the upper end. The alternatives to wading were to go along the edge on stream right until you had to jump out and down perhaps 7 feet to fairly dry mud, or continue on a smaller ledge using fingerholds above eye level until you could jump directly down to dry ground. A solitary hiker with no one to help would have trouble doing the climb and would probably have to wade here.

The next pool required wading and the bottom is gooey mud with sharp rocks. There are advantages to being first to cross such a pool. Don knew the bottom becomes gooier with each passing person and he was first. The way down to the pool is on stream right, and a mud ledge forms under the pour-off as the pool dries. Although this ledge was now under water, Don knew it was there and used it. Some of the others also went that way, and I think those who didn't wished they had. While we were engaged in the crossing maneuver, two people from the River came up and passed us. It appeared we would be sharing the beach with a boat party.

Two major bypasses are required after the pool. The first on stream left and—shortly after—another on stream right. The first of these took us quite high on a ledge until we were able to climb steeply down to a pack lowering place. The second took us on some sloping ledges but we could keep our packs on. A final, minor, bypass on stream left takes you along a ledge behind a big sloping rock where you can climb down. Shortly after that we were on the beach. It had taken us three and a half hours plus lunch to come down the bed of Rider to the River. It was 2:15.

We found some marginally warmer water in the estuary at the mouth of Rider and washed up. I even submerged briefly—very briefly. The boat party had the main beach for its camp; we were left with the sand among the rocks up against the cliff. I picked the long shallow cave for my camp spot and slept especially well with the roar of Houserock Rapids drowning out all extraneous noises—like Don's snoring.

Ringtail Thievery

A furry marauder—ringtail?—had a good time at our expense during the night. Leslie was the most devastated—all her peanut butter was gone. As I was packing up, I noticed a big stuff sack at the back of my cave where the top sloped down to meet the floor. I crawled back to retrieve it and found a plastic bag with it. These items belonged to Bob and the plastic bag held the rest of his supply of sausage balls—a delicious biscuit item flavored with sausage. As my eyes adjusted to the darkness while getting Bob's stuff, I noticed some other things. With more wriggling and use of my walking stick, I retrieved them as well. Hallelujah. One of them was the bag of Leslie's peanut butter tubes—undamaged. I thought I might be rewarded by a spoonful, but how soon she forgot. The other bag belonged to Jane.

On our way out of camp, I stopped and visited with our boating companions, who were taking a layover day. There were six of them for four boats—two from Albuquerque, two from Los Alamos, and two from Durango. One of the Coloradans reminded me we had met before—ten years ago when we shared the beach at South Canyon on my long hike. Small world.

Route to North Canyon

Our goal for today was modest—3.5 miles to North Canyon. But we couldn't do it. One reason was a late start, and the other was that the River route just upstream of North Canyon was under high water and we spent much valuable time trying to push a low- or medium-level route.

It is only 1.5 miles of boulder-hopping from Rider Canyon to Boulder narrows, but that short distance took us more than three hours. There were some stretches of fast ledges but generally it was a question of big, sometimes slippery, rocks. After an early lunch at the narrows, it was still an hour for the next 0.5 mile to the rim route at mile 19. Bert and Jim took off to test it and the rest of us went on. It was close to 1500 by the time I caught up to the others waiting at the impasse where our River route had vanished. Caroline volunteered to check the next ledge up and when that didn't go, she and Don tried the next—and highest—one. They were gone a long time and came back without a definitive answer. Finally, the decision was made to retreat to a small bit of sand a few hundred yards back upstream for camp. Gary and Caroline stayed to push the route through to North Canyon for us to follow tomorrow. This they did via that uppermost bench. Bert and Jim also succeeded in pushing their way to the rim at mile 19—Gary says the hardest part of that route is the part at the bottom.

We aimed for an early start the next day and were on our way by 7:00. We were on the high bench forty-five minutes later and in the bed of North, which rose to meet us, by 9:00. We had descended to a lower bench about 400 yards upriver from the North Canyon delta, but this was not necessary. Both benches continue on around the corner to the big talus slope leading to the bed of North about 400 yards in from the mouth. This is the same talus as that ascended by the trail to the North Canyon Pool, a frequent destination of River runner hikers.

We Meet Larry Stevens

We rested for some time on the comfortable Supai slabs because a boatman who came by told me that Larry Stevens was upcanyon and I had wanted to meet him for some time. Larry is the author of *The Colorado River in Grand Canyon—A Guide.* His group was studying riparian vegetation as part of the Environmental Impact Statement being prepared on the effects of various protocols for water releases from the dam. Larry eventually came by and we had a nice visit. Then it was time to move on. We were still moving very slowly; it took six hours, plus half an hour for lunch, to do the 2.5 miles from North Canyon to our camp where the Redwall emerges near mile 22.7. Part of the reason for our slow progress was a talus runout of roomsized boulders. My guess is that it was about 50 yards wide. It was such a jumble that it took us about half an hour to cross.

A Killer Vise

It took me a little longer because I took a bad tumble in the process. I hung on to a crack and swung around a floor-to-ceiling corner of rock, stepped on empty air, and fell lengthwise into a tapering crack about 10 feet deep and 20 inches wide at the top. With my pack on I fit snugly in the rocky vise. With each exhalation, I slipped a little deeper. With each struggle to extricate myself, I slipped a little deeper. I could not reach the hip-belt release. I could not reach anything useful with either hands or feet. I have the feeling that had I been alone, I might have suffocated as surely as though I had been in the grip of a python, anaconda, or boa constrictor. Fortunately for me, Jane came by, took my outstretched hand, and pulled me out far enough so I could shed my pack. And then Gary came up and complained he was too late for a good picture. Photographers are all alike—vultures, every one.

Behind Schedule

Gary marked this talus jumble at mile 21.7 on his map. I should have done the same, but I was too shaken to remember to do that. I have subsequently gone over my notes from two other trips along this route, and neither one makes any mention of such talus. Either we had zipped by it earlier without noticing or it is newer than September 8, 1982. We went on about another mile before making camp a little upstream from Indian Dick Rapid—as named in Larry Stevens's guidebook. Today we have gone only 3 miles. We had planned to be at Cave Springs Rapids. It is likely that if we had managed an early start from Rider and reached the North Canyon impasse two hours earlier, we might have been at North Canyon last night and made it to Cave Springs for tonight. We are now a half day behind schedule. The point is, I expected no problems in reaching North Canyon. I had forgotten that routes can change and hadn't allowed time for handling such changes.

Persistence Pays Off

We managed a fairly early start the next morning and were at Indian Dick Rapid in about twenty minutes. It was in this neighborhood that Gary showed Don and me a Supai boulder that had 0.5-inch deep groove worn in it by a branch of a bush. The twig—still growing—had produced scar tissue to protect itself, but the message was clear that persistence pays off. Sandstone is no match for water or twig or bicycle tire. In the bed of the Little Colorado, Gary once showed me a Supai boulder that had a bicycle tire wrapped around it like a necklace and the tire had worn a deep groove in the rock—deep enough that I could not remove the rubbery noose without expending more energy than I was prepared to use.

Powell's Marble Sidewalk and Stanton's Marble Pier

Soon our small select, physically retarded group—Don, Bob, and I—caught up with the rest. This usually meant trouble and it did this time, too. The marble sidewalk we were on had suddenly developed a wrinkle—another impasse. Some had climbed up to the next level, and some were undecided about what to do next. Gary dropped his pack and went on far enough to decide it was worth a try. Don and I also decided to push on over the wrinkle on our hands and knees. Others followed. Eventually we reached a bigger wrinkle and even Don and Gary climbed up a level. I am sure that on my earlier traverses, we had descended to sand at River level at this point—sand washed away by the flood of '83. This was another route change, but one that didn't really matter much since we were within just a few feet of river talus at 24 Mile Rapids. We rested a bit and then saddled up for the move to 24.5 Mile Rapids for lunch. That put us about opposite the Marble Pier, described in the previous chapter, which Stanton intended to use as support for his bridge across the surrounding wash. After lunch we moved down to Cave Springs Rapids.

Cave Springs Rapids
This took two hours, to which I must add the half hour it took to descend to the wash leading to the rapids. We climbed down an erosional slot in a 10-foot wall of coarse sandy rubble. This slot—maybe 8 inches wide and 12 inches deep—had one step in it. We lowered packs and people more or less sequentially without incident—Jim providing the anchor for a bit of webbing that served as a handline. Gary insisted on lowering his own pack and that leads me to a comment that I have so far resisted making. Gary's pack is heavy beyond belief because, besides the ordinary stuff we all carry, he also has 20 pounds of camera gear. He is one of the few people I know who realize the burden that superheavy packs can put on the people who are not carrying them. In recent years I have come to the point where I refuse to handle them in pack passing situations when wrestling them puts me at risk.

Even More Behind Schedule
When we had all gathered in the shade of some tammies, we had a high level meeting. We were behind schedule yesterday and getting farther behind today. Shorn of their pros and cons, these were our options: One, camp where we were tonight and be a full day behind; two, go on and use a poor camp at the River access opposite Tiger Wash; three, the slow group take the first option and the fast group, the second. Today was Wednesday and several of the group had commitments that required them to exit the Canyon on Friday, if at all possible. There was general reluctance to splitting the group; besides, only the slow ones knew the way out. The ultimate consensus was to camp where we were at Cave Springs Rapids, get an especially early start the next morning and camp Thursday night at the big beach at mile 30.4, where the Fence Fault crosses the River. On Friday the fast group would go up and out and the slow one would camp at the South Canyon beach and go up and out Saturday morning.

Caves
There are, indeed, caves at Cave Springs Rapids, although the spring is upstream a little way. One cave had mostly driftwood in it, another not much of anything, and a third a collection of relics—the business end of a shovel and a basin full of small rusty traps. There was also an innocent looking hazard—a sloping rock along the River. Don ventured out on it to fill his water bottles and started slipping into the fast water. He said later he was lucky to get enough traction to save himself. He felt, too, that had he slipped in, his shouts might not have been heard above the noise of the rapids and we would never have known what happened to him. It can happen. A few years ago a hiker slipped into the rushing water alongside Havasu Rapids while trying to get a drink and was sucked down and never seen again.

Our afternoon at Cave Springs was most restful, which may have accounted for our being able to get a very early start the next morning. We were gone by 6:10—the earliest start yet—and were on top of the Redwall half an hour later. The next 1.25 miles to the wash opposite Tiger Wash took an hour and a half—pretty good time—and Bert saved us a trip to the River for water by finding a pothole with at least twenty gallons of water. About a mile downriver from the pothole, the River makes a slight turn to the east, and we found ourselves once again in shade—most welcome. We also were the target of sharp, piercing screams from a pair of peregrine falcons. If the delicious descending trill of the canyon wren is soothing and restful, then the call of these falcons is the scraping of fingernails on a blackboard.

The Eternal Dilemma
In the main, the hiking on top of the Redwall through this part of the Canyon was fairly quick and easy—until we came to side drainages. Even the small ones looked enormous to tired eyes and the need to choose whether to contour in and back out or to go down and back up seemed almost too much to deal with. It always surprises me that these drainages are never as deep as they look from the edge and it is almost always the case that going down and back up is easier than contouring around. I think the reason is that, although going up the far side is an aerobic struggle, the going down is not and the average stress is less than that of contouring over what is usually a longer distance.

Opposite the Silver Grotto
The fast and slow groups rarely had lunch together. This particular day, though, we did use their shade after they finished with it and pushed on toward camp as we approached. Around 12:30 we were opposite the wash between Tiger Wash and Shinumo Wash—it is nameless on the 15-minute map but is called To Hajisho on the 7.5-minute map. In another hour and a half we were opposite Shinumo Wash and could see five boats tied up at the delta with people heading for the Silver Grotto. A little later we could see half a dozen hikers striding purposefully over to the edge to look down into the grotto before heading back to their own boat farther downstream. We were disheartened by their speed of travel even though we knew they had a trail.

I didn't write down the time I was at the edge looking down on the beach that was to be our home for the night. I should have because, even though I could see that Bert and Caroline were already there, it was to be a long time before the rest of us could join them.

The Way to the Fence Fault Beach
In 1982 I was also in the slow group, and standing in approximately the same place I could also see two of my companions on the beach. In this case it was Robert and my brother. Since they were almost under me—and not on the far beach where Bert and Caroline were—I naturally wondered how they got there. Some frantic hand signals led me to believe I should back up some before starting down. I later wrote in my journal that I must not have backed up far enough because the route I picked was too exposed for me to feel comfortable. I had enough hand- and footholds but I moved with extreme caution trying not to look down. I'm sure I asked, but I don't remember what route Allen and Robert took except it wasn't the way I went. All I knew was I didn't want to go the way I went ever again.

A decade later, I remembered my previous vow, and Don, Bob, and I contoured into the immense bay created by the Fence Fault and found only cliffs below us. Crossing a rise we could look across a big gully and see Gary making what looked like a difficult traverse of a rubbly cliff. Soon others followed him. Don decided their route was too risky and crossed that gully higher up, where it was easier. Gary and the others had gained access to a ridge and headed down. Don, with Bob and me in tow, started down the ridge, too, and saw the others coming grumpily back up. Leaving Bob and me to follow as best we could, Don hurried on to see where Gary and his crew were going. When there was a sure way to the bed of this awful canyon, Don waited for us, and we were all soon down in the drainage. Gary had yelled at us, "Do you want a fireball?" and I had yelled back. "Yes." I wasn't sure I would find them but soon I saw three round red candies. Not knowing he was included in Gary's largess, Don had hurried by—so I had two and Bob had one. I would have bet real money there was no saliva left in my body, but that red-hot cinnamon candy teased some from I don't know where, and soon my spirits were lifted considerably.

The Best Way Down?
A final note on the descent—if I ever come this way again, I will try the direct route near the point that I said I never wanted to see again. Maybe it wasn't so bad after all. A final final note. In 1992, while on a River trip with my daughter and grandson, we camped on the Fence Fault beach. I had time to go over to the spot where a descent, if there really was one, would come down. There is a small pinnacle—maybe 30 feet high with a cairn on top—at the upper end of the beach. This pinnacle is connected to the cliff by a small rocky isthmus, and the route begins on the cliff side of this isthmus. It did not look easy, but it looked possible provided your boots had adequate friction.

Caroline as Heroine
Caroline was the heroine of the day. She and Bert had visited with the woman whose boat had carried the hikers we had seen in the vicinity of Shinumo Wash. Bert was in the process of saying good-bye when Caroline nudged him in the ribs and whispered, "Ask for some beer." Bert's reluctant request produced the proper response and, thanks to Caroline, a cold beer was waiting for me when I finally arrived at the big beach. It was already 5:00 so washing up was hurried. Fortunately, Gary knew a warmish spring was waiting for us at the lower end of the beach and when he was done, I took my turn. Dunking, while not exactly pleasant, was bearable without my making a terrible face. It had been an eleven-hour day. Our longest yet—5 miles.

One Group Becomes Two
The upthrust of the Fence Fault is on the upstream side, so leaving our camp was easier than getting there. It looked to me as if there was a way to the top of the Redwall right behind camp and I persuaded Bert to give it a try. I might have gone that way, too, except that Bob and Don wanted to climb

up just inside the drainage. It probably was easier and soon some of those who had started to follow Bert ended up following us. Now we really were two groups—in theory as well as in fact. It was Friday and the others were on their way to the top. Don, Bob, Gary, and I were on our own with whatever leftover food we had managed to squirrel away. We all left camp at 7:30 and our little band of warriors was at the top of the South Canyon descent at 9:30. This spot is well marked and we headed down the trail to the beach. There is an occasional proliferation of trails, which go every which way to ruins and caves, but we threaded our way through the intersections and found the beach with only one backtrack. We were there at 10:00 and the first order of business, after dropping our packs, was to comb the beach for lost cans of beer. Unfortunately, none were found.

A Hard-Won Rest Day

We didn't do much the rest of the day, except for Gary, who went down to Vasey's to get some pictures. Besides the pictures, he also contracted a case of poison ivy. The rest of us just lazed around—we didn't even go to Stanton's Cave. Not even a boat party disturbed our serenity. This was a hard won rest day and we made the most of it.

Bedrock Canyon Exit

We were on our way by 6:15 the next morning and at the top of the Redwall, where we had cached all our extra water, by 6:40. It was two hours to Bedrock Canyon. We overlooked the ducks that would have told us to climb up on the south wall to get above a Supai pour-off in the bed and had to backtrack 0.25 mile. Bedrock comes in just above that pour-off; we turned into it at 8:45 and had a long shady rest before tackling the ascent.

It is unfortunate that the details of the Bedrock Canyon exit route are spread over three 7.5-minute maps. That's the bad news, but the good news is that most of the route is shown on the 7.5-minute Buffalo Tanks quad map. We left the bed of Bedrock about 200 yards inside the canyon and headed up the first suitable indentation—there were cairns. From the bed, the route follows a fault and goes pretty much 1,800 feet straight up. Occasionally you can see a 40-foot natural cairn—about at the 4,800 foot level—in the shape of a mushroom with two other rocks on top like ears. You can also look across Bedrock Canyon and see the extension of the fault cutting its way to the skyline.

After reaching the Esplanade we followed a less steep talus tumble up to a deeply cut gully through the top of the Coconino and the bottom of the Toroweap. An overabundance of small ducks, doubtless placed by hikers eager for a short rest, can confuse you if you let them. The best plan is to ignore them and head for the gully—and shade if you are early enough. Near the top of the gully we took a small ledge out to the right (south) about 150 feet to a small flat area on a point. In the process we moved from the Buffalo Tanks Quad to the North Canyon Point quad. This flat spot is shown on the west edge of the North Canyon Point quad map just north of the 4,040 grid designation. The mushroom rock is here, too.

The Way Out Is *Up, Up, Up*

The principal view up from here is *cliff,* and it will be intimidating unless you trust me. There are plenty of ledges, and the route uses them to zig and zag up the face to a small gully on the east side of the point. There were comforting ducks to guide us as we left the promontory and started up the skyline. This route is not for the acrophobic. A friend of son Stan was climbing up here and dislodged a rock. Looking down to follow its trajectory and observing that it seemed to take forever to make the first bounce shocked the friend into a torrent of tears. She saw herself in a similar endless freefall. Perhaps it is best not to look down. One advantage to a route such as this is that there is no wasted motion and every step takes you closer to the rim than you expect. The result is that upward progress is rapid. We left the bed of Bedrock at 10:00, were at the bottom of the Coconino gully at 10:30, at the promontory at 11:10, and on top at 12:00. Since Bert's car was gone, we concluded that our instructions had been adequate to get the others out, too. It took two more hours on the road to reach the cars and close the loop—without packs. Then we drove back and picked them up.

10 Further Loop Possibilities

On man's place in the Grand Canyon in summer:
"Human beings were invented by water as a device for
transporting itself from one place to another."

TOM ROBBINS, ANOTHER ROADSIDE ATTRACTION

Section 1: Introduction

Great loops are born of great promontories. Loops around Powell Plateau and Walhalla Plateau are great loops—I would even say they are the very essence of loopy-ness. But other great promontories still remain. Before he died, my friend Robert had planned a loop hike around Great Thumb Mesa. This would have been a great hike, showing us, as it would have, familiar places—like Kanab Creek and Deer Creek Falls—from a most unfamiliar angle. In addition, I have also thought much about a loop hike around that greatest of promontories—the Shivwits Plateau.

That is as it should be. Something should be left that is touched by the unknown.

As I prepared to write this chapter, I looked at my copy of the shaded relief map that is sometimes handed out at the park entrance station to see the Canyon as a whole—the scale is approximately 1:400000. What I saw was that the course of the River is basically a W. The lower left point is the Shivwits Plateau, the lower right is the Walhalla Plateau, and the middle is the Great Thumb Mesa. These points are the locations of great loops.

Loops are constructed by finding connections between nearby drainages, and the farther apart the mouths of these drainages are, the more magnificent the loop. One such magnificent loop—the Walhalla Plateau Loop—was conceived of by my examining this very 1:400000 shaded relief map and noticing that the Bright Angel and Nankoweap drainages came within a mile of each other on the rim. It was several years before I found a convenient route off the Kibbey Butte Saddle, but the genesis of the loop was that tiny park handout map.

Some of the loops and loop elements to which I refer in this chapter are also discussed by other authors. Usually, I looked in their indices or tables of contents to find appropriate references. Twice I found ones that were in neither place. The words "not mentioned" used in the listings mean only that the reference desired was not in the index—or table of contents if there was no index. The guidebooks to which I will refer are (alphabetically by author):

Aitchison, Stewart, A *Naturalist's Guide to Hiking the Grand Canyon*, Prentice-Hall, 1985.

Annerino, John, *Hiking the Grand Canyon*, Sierra Club Books, 1986.

Looking downstream to the beach where the Fence Fault crosses the Colorado River. This picture was taken from the top of the Redwall.

Butchart, Harvey, *Grand Canyon Treks: 12,000 Miles Through The Grand Canyon,* Spotted Dog Press, 1997.

Kelsey, Michael R., *Canyon Hiking Guide to the Colorado Plateau,* Kelsey Publishing, 1988.

Section 2: Information for Marble Canyon Loop Possibilities—West Side

Many loops are possible in Marble Canyon—both long and short—and the accompanying schematic diagram, titled Marble Canyon Route Summary, represents my effort to condense the information from which they can be constructed—on the west side.

Numbers, in general, represent transit times, in hours, between adjacent intersections; these times are usually rounded up to the next whole hour. The exception is that a pair of numbers like "6/3" means that the 6 miles required approximately 3 hours. Parentheses, such as, "(6/3)," mean either one, or both, the numbers are estimated. In this particular case the 6 miles are along a road and I estimate hiking speed at 2 miles per hour.

The word rim is, unfortunately, vague but I intend it to mean outside the canyon where the car is, or could be, left. For example, in the Nankoweap case, the car must be left some distance from the saddle, which hikers might legitimately consider the rim.

Loops in the more or less linear stretch of River in Marble Canyon are impossible to construct without segments of cross-country travel on the rim, but the abundance of roads, and the relatively short distances involved, make both prior placement of water caches and subsequent travel reasonably convenient.

The Kaibab National Forest Map for the North Kaibab District will be helpful in finding roadheads in Marble Canyon. This map shows some pertinent BLM land, but not all—it is still 13 highway miles to Marble Canyon Lodge from the east edge of the map. These maps are available from the forest visitor center at Jacob Lake (when open) and from the registration desk at the Jacob Lake Lodge. It is also helpful to have the 7.5-minute maps for Marble Canyon.

When he was accompanying me on the closure of the Rider Canyon/South Canyon Loop, my friend Don Mattox made it quite clear that he thought it stupid to walk on back roads to complete a loop. He favors a mountain bike. Good idea. A word of caution for mountain bike enthusiasts: The highway is narrow, and there is no shoulder to speak of so bikes would not seem to be a good idea along the highway stretches.

It was not my original intention to "force" loops in Marble Canyon. Some, like the Buck Farm Canyon/36.7 Mile Canyon Loop or the South Canyon/Rider Canyon Loop seemed natural enough, but others, like the Cathedral Wash/Lees Ferry Loop seemed contrived. But then I thought, "Why not include them?" No one has to do them and, besides, their inclusion lends a certain completeness to the whole enterprise represented by this book.

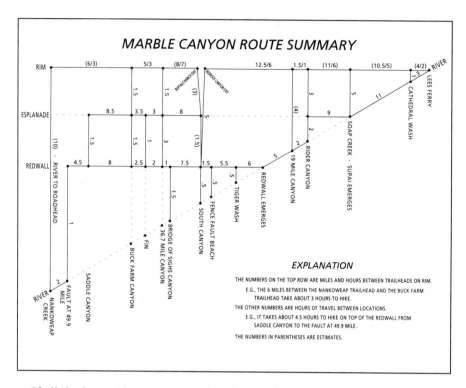

MARBLE CANYON ROUTE SUMMARY

EXPLANATION

THE NUMBERS ON THE TOP ROW ARE MILES AND HOURS BETWEEN TRAILHEADS ON RIM.
E.G., THE 6 MILES BETWEEN THE NANKOWEAP TRAILHEAD AND THE BUCK FARM
TRAILHEAD TAKE ABOUT 3 HOURS TO HIKE.
THE OTHER NUMBERS ARE HOURS OF TRAVEL BETWEEN LOCATIONS.
E.G., IT TAKES ABOUT 4.5 HOURS TO HIKE ON TOP OF THE REDWALL FROM
SADDLE CANYON TO THE FAULT AT 49.9 MILE.
THE NUMBERS IN PARENTHESES ARE ESTIMATES.

If all the loops I have presented, either as done or as possibilities, are considered together, they cover the River from Lees Ferry to Lava Falls, except for the 1 mile segment between Crystal and Tuna Creeks. This can be hiked separately, as an adjunct to a loop, if someone demands complete completeness.

ROUTES FROM RIM TO RIVER

- Cathedral Wash
  Aitchison—68, 70
  Annerino—277
  Butchart—61 (2.7 Mile Canyon)
  Kelsey—179

- Soap Creek
  Aitchison—72, 73
  Annerino—not mentioned
  Butchart—61, 62
  Kelsey—182, 183

- Rider Canyon
  Aitchison—77 to 80
  Annerino—not mentioned
  Butchart—65, 68, 70
  Kelsey—186, 187

Like so many Marble Canyon rim takeoffs—for example, Buck Farm Canyon, 36.7 Mile Canyon, Bedrock Canyon—the Rider rim takeoff, too, begins by going down a steep ravine between the rim and a semidetached piece of rim. Once in the bed of Rider, you will find some obstacles of greater or lesser severity depending on how much and how wet the muds. A major obstacle requires climbing up the sloping north wall and contouring to a duck that seems to lead you farther along the ledge. Don't be misled. Go steeply down at that place.

Be wary of camping on the beach below the top level of driftwood, and be wary, as well, of the mice and ringtails. The mice are brazen enough to pillage in broad daylight. The route upstream begins in the drainage where the Supai emerges and the route downstream begins on the River talus.

- 19 Mile Route
  Butchart 70

- South Canyon
  Aitchison—85 to 87
  Annerino—not mentioned
  Butchart—65, 66, 72, 81, 86, 87
  Kelsey—188, 189

The Buffalo Ranch trailhead gives best access to routes connecting downstream (see the Kelsey reference).

The Bedrock Canyon trailhead gives best access to routes connecting upstream (see Butchart, page 71).

Access to Bedrock Canyon is made via a spur road east from Cane Ranch (labeled just "Cone" on the 7.5-minute map). It leads to a roadhead near the north rim of Bedrock Canyon. Leave the rim off the point south of the "5391T" elevation point. I think it is slightly easier off the east side of the point. Descend to a flat place and contour west to a chute.

- Nankoweap Creek—Tilted Mesa Trail
  Aitchison—88 et seq
  Annerino—252 et seq
  Butchart—83, 90, 100
  Kelsey—192, 193

I have found a small dripping spring on the Tilted Mesa Trail where it rounds the first point below the b in boundary ridge on the 15-minute Nankoweap quad map. Thoughtful passersby have placed small containers to catch the drips so you may find some relatively full. Next water is at Nankoweap.

- Nankoweap Creek—The "Freefall" Route

This route is more direct and more dangerous than the Tilted Mesa Trail, but it gets you to water much more quickly. Take the Tilted Mesa Trail down from the Saddle Mountain Saddle for a short distance—until you are about even with the bottom of the top cliffs. Then head down to your right to a point slightly upcanyon from some ponderosa pines you can see below you in the drainage between Seiber and Marion Points. These pines are almost at the top of the steep talus chute that takes you through most of the Redwall. Across the drainage on the face that goes out to Seiber Point, there is a long narrow avalanche chute extending from the base of the Coconino through to the top part of the Supai. The route to the top of the Redwall is almost in line with that chute. There are only two Supai cliffs of any consequence and the upper one comes soon after you get lined up with the avalanche chute across the way. There are several ways through these cliffs and with a bit of luck you can manage without the necessity of lowering packs. The way is steep with a lot of brush, but eventually you reach the top of the Redwall.

After that you want to work your way down the left-hand side of the drainage to a place where a big spur of Redwall juts out into the drainage several hundred feet. To get to the trees, you can either go out to the end of the spur and down to a ledge or go down the left-hand notch and over to another ledge on the main drainage which leads to a spot where you can scramble down, across, and up to the trees.

Once in the trees, you will find a shelf up against the cliff that leads to a small notch beyond which is a steep ravine filled with loose rocks at the angle of repose. I recommend that only one person descend at a time. Once a friend came upon a helicopter in Upper Nankoweap that was being used to evacuate a hiker with a compound fracture of his leg from having had a rock roll over it. The surest way to find this steep talus ravine from below is to follow the drainage until a big wall at the end of a slot stops you. Then back up 100 yards and you'll find it on stream right.

There is good water at the top of the Bright Angel Shale and more—in the form of a waterfall—up the first big side canyon from the west. Before you get to the creek, there is a spring below a large stand of cottonwoods on a bench visible from quite some distance.

ROUTES FROM RIM TO TOP OF REDWALL

- 36.7 Mile Canyon (access to Bridge of Sighs)
  Aitchison—not mentioned
  Annerino—not mentioned
  Butchart—66, 67, 80, 81
  Kelsey—not mentioned

There are at least two ways into this canyon. Some hikers use a route on the south side of the canyon, but I will describe one on the north that I like better. Take Forest Service Road (FS) 445E and go 2.5 miles past the water trough—Tank 6 on the 7.5-minute Buffalo Ranch quad map—before parking the car. This will put you at Tank 7 on the 7.5-minute Tatahatso Point quad map, but I don't remember ever seeing it. Strike off toward the rim on a bearing perpendicular to the road. What you are looking for, I think, is the bulge of the 5,560-foot contour 0.5 mile east of the western edge of the Buffalo Ranch quad map. There is a small valley—maybe 50 feet wide—parallel to the rim, and you start the descent at the eastern end. Head east diagonally down to the base of a tower and then down talus and small Coconino cliffs to the Supai rim. From here contour east about 0.5 mile; you will see a way to the bed of 36.7 Mile Canyon at the top of the Redwall. There is sometimes pothole water in the bed of this drainage near the Redwall rim.

- Buck Farm Canyon
  Aitchison—not mentioned
  Annerino—279 (River-level access only)
  Butchart—65, 66, 81–84
  Kelsey—not mentioned

To get to the trailhead, take Buffalo Ranch Road, FS 445; when it splits to make a big loop down toward Saddle Mountain, take the left fork. Later, turn left onto FS 445H and follow it a short distance to the rim. The rim takeoff point is about 0.25 mile south of where the road hits the rim. The descent ravine is shown on the 7.5-minute Buffalo Ranch quad map. Lay a ruler down on the map at the upper edge of the words NATIONAL PARK and extend it west to the rim. The ravine is a narrow appendix of 5,840-foot contour on this line at the rim. Go down this ravine; when it descends steeply to a jumble of rocks, you do the same. Climb down the rocks, turn south around the corner at the bottom of the ravine and go diagonally down through the Coconino toward the top of some talus. There is sometimes a small trickle of water where this route finally meets the Esplanade. The way to the Redwall is down the southwest arm of Buck Farm Canyon, which drains the area closer to Hansbrough Point.

ROUTES FROM ESPLANADE TO TOP OF REDWALL

- Fin (see page 258)
  Butchart—87, 1st para

ROUTES FROM REDWALL TO RIVER

- Ravine Opposite Tiger Wash—Mile 26.7
  Butchart—71

The route down to the River in the ravine opposite Tiger Wash begins on the steep slope on the south side of the ravine.

- Fence Fault—Mile 30.4
  Butchart—71, 76

The ways down the fault to the River are described near the end of chapter 9 on the Rider/South Loop. The time given for this descent is half an hour on the Marble Canyon Summary at the head of this chapter. That time applies only to the direct routes—the easy one just inside the drainage on the south side and the steep, scary one off the upstream point. If you contour in from upstream and then descend to the beach, the correct time might be between an hour and an hour and a half.

- Emergency Route to River at 35.7 Mile Canyon
  Also a Prehistoric Route to River, aka Bridge of Sighs Canyon
  Butchart—65, 66, 80 (These pages document his not finding the route,
  though he did find a "permanent" rain pool.)

This remarkable Redwall route to the River was discovered serendipitously
in 1984 by Dave Dawson while another companion was helping Steve Emslie
explore nearby caves for condor remains. Steve's findings are reported in
the April 1986 issue of *Natural History*, pages 10–14. What Dave saw when
he was standing under the Bridge of Sighs were pegs sticking out of the
canyon's north wall. Convinced they were too high to be driftwood, he thought
they might be part of a stairway. What Dave had found is apparently part
of an ancient Indian route through the Redwall. It is an extraordinary route.

When I thought this route would be a nice thing to do, I asked Dave's
father, Robert Dawson, to come with us. This turned out to be a wise move.
We entered Bridge of Sighs Canyon on the south slope of its Redwall rim,
crossed, and climbed down to a cave entrance on the north side. This
entrance is on a small shelf close to the drainage, so it may not be visible
when you climb down the south slope. It is about 3 feet wide and 5 feet high
with soot on the ceiling. We went into the cave 20 to 30 feet—I wasn't meas-
uring—to a room with a hole in the floor. This hole, which was somewhat
less that 2 feet across the long way, was the top of a spiral tunnel leading to
a lower level. I was cautioned to start down by lying on my left side with
my arms over my head. Gravity was on my side and I slid 12 feet or so and
dropped 4 feet to the floor of another cave. Light could be seen; I crawled
toward it some 20 feet to the mouth of the cave. The platform at the mouth
looked like it had been built up by people, and the logs that Dave Dawson
saw are stuck in a crack below it.

From the lower cave we had to climb down a 50-foot cliff to the bed, slithering behind a big rock leaning against the face in the process. Having
reached the bed and gone under the bridge, I thought I was home free; so
it was a surprise to find myself stopped close to the River by a 20-foot chimney. I didn't have to climb down the whole thing, but that was no help. It
was too narrow for me to feel comfortable, and I would need either a fixed
rope or a belay to negotiate it. Fortunately for those depending on me for
water, Robert Dawson took all my water bottles to the River and filled
them. I was sure lucky to have thought of asking him to accompany us.

Across from the Bridge of Sighs is a companion Redwall route to the River
that I have already described in chapter 8. It is likely that there was a rim
to rim route here—down 36.7 Mile Canyon, across to 35.7 Mile Canyon, down
the route I just described, across the River and up the companion route, over
to Tatahatso Wash, and up and out the route there. Dave Dawson's find is
most interesting.

Despite its unusual character, I almost didn't include this Redwall route
to the River. It is difficult and dangerous and requires rock climbing skills;
besides a rope, careful climbers will need a headlamp. Nevertheless, I finally
decided to describe it because, water being as important as it is, it might save
a life in an emergency. I am 6 feet 2 inches tall and thought for a while that

I was not going to make it back up the spiral tunnel—it is a route for short gymnasts. Someone was pulling on me, but my dead weight was too much because I couldn't bend my knees so my feet could change their purchase. Finally, in thrashing around, I found something to push against with my right foot; the rest was easy. Next time, I'll look for that life saving place before I start up.

- Fault at Mile 49.9
  Butchart—83, 90, 96, 97

I have done this route twice from the top and we got a fine view of it from an upstream point. Kayakers have a saying: "When scouting a rapid, you can tell its severity by the intensity of your need to urinate." When I first saw the wall we had to cross, it looked like the Hinterstosser Traverse on the Eiger Nordwand, and my need was so great I nearly dehydrated myself. Fortunately, the task was much much easier than it looked. To get set for the crossing, we contoured around to the drainage coming in from the south—not easy—and went down it to the lip. There we found a duck, and I was much relieved. We were obviously on route. After making the traverse the first time, we went straight down to the bed. That was a bad idea. The talus is at the angle of repose and rolling rocks were all too common. We each took what we thought was a different fall line, but every once in a while someone would have to seek shelter. After the second traverse, we went diagonally down toward the River on game trails. This descent was gentler and safer.

ROUTES ON THE RIM

I have not connected any of the possible loops by hiking across the top except for the Rider Canyon/South Canyon and 36.7 Mile Canyon/Buck Farm Canyon Loops. It seems to me that most of the rim travel—except for parts of Rider to Soap and Soap to Cathedral Wash—can be done on roads where speeds of up to 2.5 miles per hour are possible, even carrying your pack. However, because the distances are relatively short, packs can be left behind to be picked up later and just a day pack used for carrying water.

RIVER ROUTE: LEES FERRY TO NANKOWEAP CREEK

It is not possible to hike along the River all the way from Lees Ferry to Nankoweap; so when I use the term River route, I really mean what I have found to be the route closest to the River.

I have hiked from Lees Ferry to Nankoweap Creek on two occasions—once in hiking from Lees Ferry to Lava Falls and once in hiking from Lees Ferry to Grand Wash Cliffs. These two Marble Canyon segments differed in only one important respect. In 1977 we hiked the Esplanade from South to Saddle Canyons and in 1982 we hiked the Redwall. The good news was that the Redwall route was shorter and easier, and the bad news was that we had to carry our pretrip water caches farther.

The River route from Lees Ferry to Soap Creek is straightforward except for a short bypass required just upstream from Navajo Bridge. This bypass goes up a ramp and then down a 30-foot cliff—steep, but lots of handholds and footholds. Shortly after this bypass, we followed a ramp up under the bridge and came down again just after the bend—at mile 5. This segment, Lees Ferry to mile 5, was a long first day each time.

In 1982 it was also a long first night. Mosquitoes were in full swarm, and we were the only dinner available. It was a hot night in early September and I wore light clothes and socks and put a towel over my head, but it was hard to breathe and I eventually took it off. At frequent intervals during the night, I used it to wipe—and happily kill—the mosquitoes that covered my face. It is quite possible that if the next few nights had been repeats of the first, our hike to Lake Mead might have ended almost within sight of Navajo Bridge.

Below Soap Creek we followed a rising ramp of Supai. There are basically two ramps—low and high. If you follow the lower one, you will have to climb to the upper one no later than mile 13.8. In 1982 we took the lower one and sometimes hiked on the edge so the rocks we accidentally kicked off fell to the River more than 100 feet below. My brother got the attention of some kayakers this way and they shouted and screamed at us, but they couldn't possibly see who we were and we jumped up and down and made gorilla noises back at them. In 1992 we took the higher level and had no such opportunity to knock rocks into the River.

The first time I turned into Rider—in 1977, I was dismayed and disheartened. Everything was shimmering in the heat, and it seemed it would be forever before we could get into the bed. "Forever" in this case was approximately 0.75 mile. Then it was down Rider to the River. The route down Rider Canyon is described in chapter 9.

In '77, with more sand and lower water, we could hike the River talus from Rider downriver to where the Redwall emerges and then follow the Redwall ramp down to South Canyon. There were occasional routes to access to the River and I can still close my eyes and see one of those beaches—an expanse of brilliant white sand followed by a strip of vivid green River against a backdrop of gray-and-white-striped Redwall.

The route down to the beach at South Canyon is at the upper end of the Redwall bench going upriver from South Canyon. Continuing along the Redwall rim gets you to the bed of South at the top of the Redwall narrows. These narrows can be followed to the River, but some downclimbing of chockstones is required. Once, a companion was standing with me on top of one of these chockstones while others were climbing down when, with no hint of warning, he jumped down into the sand. It was at least 12 feet and I yelled at him, "John, what the hell do you think you're doing?" John got up, shook himself a bit, and said, a little defensively, "I thought the sand would be softer." He did not tell us until weeks after we got home that he had broken some bones in his foot. He said he was ashamed to admit he had hurt himself by that stupid jump. But the belated confession at last explained why John was so much slower than the rest of us in climbing out.

I planned a "rest day" at South Canyon in '77 to allow time to find a way to the Esplanade. The idea was to carry as much gear and water as we could up there to make the next day's job easier. It would be two days to a water cache at Buck Farm. The route to the Esplanade we eventually found started up the first major drainage from the south—the one coming in at the 3,320-foot contour, in the northeast corner of the Buffalo Ranch quad. We went up that drainage just under 0.5 mile and worked our way up through the Supai to within about 75 feet of the top. Then we contoured around the point to the east on a bench and climbed to the top in a ravine. There was about 10 feet of pack passing, but that was all. It is unfortunate that the top part of the route, as I remember it, is almost exactly on the border of the Tatahatso Point and Buffalo Ranch 7.5-minute quad maps.

In 1982 we put water caches on the Redwall in both 36.7 Mile and Buck Farm Canyons. This made life a great deal easier. Besides, it is easier to hike on the Redwall than on the Esplanade. The only requirement is to be kind to the cryptogamic soil—aka microbiotic or cryptobiotic soil. This is the "funny black dirt" that abounds on the Redwall in Marble Canyon. It is really a complex community of organisms and what is destroyed by a careless foot can take a hundred years to grow back.

As we rounded South Canyon Point on the Redwall, we had a fine view of Redwall Cavern from an unusual vantage point, and we passed Bridge of Sighs Canyon without knowing anything about the prehistoric Indian route to the River. If we had, we might have at least tried to see the stairs. We camped at 36.7 Mile Canyon and found ample pothole water—enough even for a bath in the biggest pothole. A great virtue of following the River by contouring along on top of the Redwall instead of the Esplanade is that the distance you must go into a major drainage in order to cross it is much less for Redwall travelers than it is for Esplanade travelers.

Continuing on to Buck Farm, we passed what Butchart calls a jug handle arch. Actually, the proper description is more complicated because the "handle" is quite wide and itself has a hole in it. Perhaps the correct name is jug handle arch arch. Just after the arch, on the south side of the drainage coming in from the west at mile 39, is what I call a fin. This is a ridge of triangular crossection coming from the Coconino down through the Supai to the Redwall. Each side of the triangle is perhaps 100 feet and the whole thing is unconsolidated rubble at the angle of repose. Room-sized rocks stick out from the sides like warts, and when we had to cross it in '77 on the Esplanade, we wondered seriously about how much of these rocks stick in. Anyone who plans to use the fin to change levels should not climb directly up or down it. Instead, climb along the crease at the side. If you reach an impasse, climb on the fin at your peril and try to move more diagonally than vertically. The one time I climbed it, we had to move out on the rubble face only once as I remember.

If you have taken the high road downriver from South Canyon, you will need to return to the Redwall level in Saddle Canyon. There is a spring up near the Coconino, but in 1977 it was dry—in fact, Vaseys Paradise was almost dry. In '82 there was some water but we had to go high to find it and it took four of us two hours to get what we needed. How much water you carry from Buck Farm depends on whether you are an optimist or a pessimist. I think pessimists live longer.

From Saddle Canyon to the fault would be a Sunday stroll if it weren't for the last drainage that must be crossed. The fault—intimidating as it is from a distance—is nowhere near as hard as it looked to us that first time. Anyone who finds it very hard is probably lost. The route goes up and down as it crosses the face and is sometimes near—but not at—the edge, but I never had the feeling that if I fell, I was a goner. When we reached the talus at the east side of the face, we followed the game trails down toward the beach. This is better than following the fall line of rolling rocks down to the bed like we did in '77.

After four days away from the River on high thirsty benches and terraces, I felt a profound joy at being once again at water—lots of it. We were there for a late lunch, and its being so beautiful—and so wet—meant we also spent the night. The move down to Nankoweap Creek through the beaver tunnels in the tamarisk was an anticlimatic end to our River journey from Lees Ferry.

The above summary provides information for the construction of a large variety of west-side loops. Here are sketches of five loops that cover the River from Lees Ferry to Nankoweap Creek.

LOOP 1: LEES FERRY TO CATHEDRAL WASH

—Leave car at Lees Ferry and hike along River to Cathedral Wash—time three hours (two hours from end of River Road).

- Hike up Cathedral Wash to pavement—time one hour.
- Hike back to Lees Ferry—estimated time two hours.

LOOP 2: CATHEDRAL WASH TO SOAP CREEK

- Leave car near Cliff Dwellers at the end of a road heading east at mile marker 548.25 (bear left at a corral) and hike or arrange a ride back to where the pavement crosses Cathedral Wash—10.5 miles, estimated time five hours.
- Hike down Cathedral Wash to River—time one hour.
- Hike along River to Soap Creek—time eleven hours.
- Hike out South Fork of Soap Creek to car—time five hours.

LOOP 3: SOAP CREEK TO RIDER CANYON

- Leave car at the roadhead near Cliff Dwellers described in Loop 2 (above) and hike down Soap Creek to River—time five hours.
- Hike along River and take Esplanade bench into Rider Canyon—time nine hours.
- After a round trip to River (time four hours), hike out Rider to rim—time three hours.

- Hike back to car—estimated distance 11 miles, estimated time six hours. (I estimate 6.5 miles to pavement taking four hours and then 4.5 miles to car taking two hours.)
- I do not know where the best place is to cross Rider Canyon on the return.

LOOP 4: RIDER CANYON TO SOUTH CANYON

- See chapter 9

LOOP 5: SOUTH CANYON TO NANKOWEAP CREEK—ALONG REDWALL

- Put in water caches at Redwall level in 36.7 Mile and Buck Farm Canyons via accesses described earlier—two days.
- Leave car at Buffalo Ranch Trailhead and hike down South Canyon to top of Redwall—estimated time four and a half hours.
- Round trip to River—time two hours.
- Hike Redwall to 36.7 Mile Canyon noting Bridge of Sighs Canyon as you pass. If you have time look for stairs—time eight and a half hours.
- Hike to Buck Farm Canyon noting jug handle arch arch and fin as you pass—time four and a half hours.
- Hike to Saddle Canyon—time eight hours.
- Hike to fault at mile 49.9—time four and a half hours.
- Hike across fault and down to River—time one hour.
- Hike along River to Nankoweap Creek—time two hours.
- Hike up Nankoweap Creek and take either the Tilted Mesa Trail or the "Freefall" Route to saddle and thence to roadhead—estimated time ten hours.
- Hike roads back to Buffalo Ranch Trailhead—estimated distance 11 miles, estimated time five hours. This distance is estimated from the Kaibab National Forest Map.

Of the many Marble Canyon loops that are possible, I have done only two. These are the one described in chapter 9, and the one between Buck Farm and 36.7 Mile Canyons. On the latter hike I had the company of a young man who was studying to become an operatic tenor; he has since become a respected specialist in Mozart operas. I particularly remember being charmed by "Il Mio Tesoro" from Don Giovanni. I didn't realize it then, but Mozart tenors must have quite a different voice than, say, Italian tenors.

Section 3: Information for Marble Canyon Loop Possibilities—East Side

ROUTES FROM RIM TO RIVER

- Jackass Wash
  Aitchison—71, 72
  Annerino—277, 278
  Butchart—62
  Kelsey—180, 181

- Salt Water Wash
  Aitchison—74, 75
  Annerino—278
  Butchart—62, 63, 68
  Kelsey—180, 181

- Unnamed wash at Mile 21.7
  Aitchison—not mentioned
  Annerino—278?
  Butchart—74
  Kelsey—not mentioned

This last route is difficult and dangerous. At the worst place, Butchart writes, "One can go left along a narrow ledge to a place where the sandstone is broken." Robert used this route to place a cache for his Pearce Ferry to Lees Ferry hike in 1983, and his words are more dramatic.

"I followed Butchart's description and headed straight down the middle of the drainage. I scouted a few places that seemed to have an easier access, but found the only route was in the middle. Beyond several big pools that can be bypassed on the side I found one constructed bypass of an 8-foot falls. A couple of hundred yards farther and I reached the big drop. The 60-foot drop in the Coconino. H. B. mentions the bypass of this barrier rather casually as 'a narrow ledge to the left.'

"It looked narrow all right. As a matter of fact, I find the term ledge a great exaggeration unless you are a rabbit or a squirrel. At only a few inches wide, I looked at a traverse route that got me thinking twice. It was the only possible way—no doubt. The other side of the fall was a sheer wall. The difficult part of this traverse extended for maybe 50 feet. Then the ledge widened. I could also see the talus I had to reach below the ledge.

"I tried it first without gear. What made me especially cautious was not the size of the surface where I placed my feet, but the loose rocks on top of it. I could have pushed them off but I was afraid if I removed them the 'ledge' would disappear completely. Easy. I could say that to myself on the other side. Except that my slightly shaking legs did not agree. Before hauling the cache across the 'ledge that isn't there,' I wanted to make sure of the route to the talus below. The slope starts about ?0 [a punch hole in Robert's notepaper removed the significant digit] feet below the ledge but the Coconino cliff is broken up here and with a little scouting I found a walking route that required little use of hands. So back up, across the tippy-toe ledge and on to Round 2. To minimize the weight on the loose rocks I carried each container across separately. Each time it became easier. On the last traverse I felt rather secure."

- Shinumo Wash
  Aitchison—81, 82, 83
  Annerino—279
  Butchart—75, 76, 80, 81, 178
  Kelsey—not mentioned

- Eminence Break Route
  Aitchison—not mentioned
  Annerino—not mentioned
  Butchart—76–78, 80, 93, 96
  Kelsey—not mentioned

ROUTES FROM RIM TO ESPLANADE

- Tanner Wash
  Aitchison—not mentioned
  Annerino—not mentioned
  Butchart—65, 68
  Kelsey—184, 185

It is possible to get almost all the way through the Supai in Tanner Wash. At the bottom I was left with 15 to 20 feet of cliff to the debris fan. A peg was pounded into the wall, and a shred of rope remained attached to it. A little experience with setting up rappels could get you to the River, and a little experience with prussiking could get you back up. Not having much of either and not needing the water, we satisfied ourselves with just looking at it.

- Hot Na Na Wash
  (This wash is called Hanaa on the 7.5-minute map.)
  Aitchison—not mentioned
  Annerino—not mentioned
  Butchart—65, 68
  Kelsey—184, 185

Both Butchart and Kelsey mention the possibilities of connecting Salt Water Wash and Tanner Wash, and Tanner Wash and Hot Na Na Wash into loops.

ROUTES FROM RIM TO TOP OF REDWALL

- Tatahatso Wash
  Aitchison—not mentioned
  Annerino—not mentioned
  Butchart—76
  Kelsey—not mentioned

- Route at Mile 32.6
  Described in detail in chapter 8. This may be the route mentioned by
  Butchart, page 76, line 10.

- Route at Mile 35.7
  Butchart, page 66. He mentions a route across the River from the Bridge
  of Sighs.

This route also figures in the Tatahatso Wash/Eminence Break Loop described
in chapter 8.

Section 4: Loop Possibilities between Shinumo Creek and Lava Falls

LOOP: CIRCUMAMBULATION OF RAINBOW PLATEAU

- Down White Creek (North Bass Trail) to junction with Shinumo Creek.
  Aitchison—130, 131, 132
  Annerino—254-258
  Butchart—183, 184
  Kelsey—198,199

When the trail leaves the White Creek drainage, the loop route continues
on down the creek.

- Up Shinumo Creek, through Merlin Abyss, to fault ravine going north/
  northwest just east of peak 7131.
  Aitchison—not mentioned
  Annerino—not mentioned
  Butchart—181
  Kelsey—not mentioned

A bypass is required at the Flint junction to get around a big pool in the creek.
A chockstone blocks the way just inside the fault ravine, but it can be
climbed—use the log on a rope trick if all else fails. When a buttress divides
the drainage, take the right hand branch. Climb the Supai when you can.
Above the eastern Supai wall there is a grove of ponderosa and as Mattox
and I approached it at evening, we heard a sound I first mistook for the erratic
sighing of wind. In a few moments it dawned on us it was the sound of gurgling water. A short stream wound its way through the pines, and we camped
on the soft needles. The stream was still there a few years later.

- To the rim and back to Swamp Point.

There are several breakdowns in the Coconino. The principal obstacle is brush. I recommend gloves for pulling yourself up through it. You will probably reach the road somewhere in the neighborhood of Swamp Lake. From there is it about 3 miles back to Swamp Point. A mountain bike will be helpful.

LOOP: STAIRWAY CANYON TO LAVA FALLS

- Down Lava Falls Trail to River
  Aitchison—151, 152, 153
  Annerino—299
  Butchart—207
  Kelsey—210, 211

- Along River up to Stairway Canyon—no obstacles

- Up Stairway Canyon (see chapter 5) to Esplanade

- Hike back on Esplanade to car via Tuckup Trail
  Aitchison—145-150
  Annerino—not mentioned
  Butchart—not mentioned
  Kelsey—208, 209

Section 5: Loop Possibilities in Western Grand Canyon

The 1:400000 shaded relief map shows the Shivwits Plateau to have the same vulnerability to being caught by a loop as the Walhalla. Surprise Canyon drainages lead up to a long stretch of the west side of the Shivwits nearly connecting to an unnamed canyon draining the east side. A smaller scale map shows this to be 209 Mile Canyon. Three other loop possibilities that never occurred to me until I specifically looked for them on the aforementioned map are between Whitmore Wash and Parashant Canyon across Whitmore Point; between Granite Park Canyon and an unnamed drainage that turned out to be 193 Mile Canyon; and between Spencer Canyon and Bridge Canyon. Some, or all, of these peripheral loops may not work out, but at least they show up as possibilities.

LOOP: WHITMORE CANYON TO PARASHANT CANYON

- Down Whitmore Wash to River
  Aitchison—157, 158, 159
  Annerino—not mentioned
  Butchart—208 et seq.
  Kelsey—212, 213

- Down Parashant to River
  Aitchison—160, 161, 162
  Annerino—not mentioned
  Butchart—208-ff
  Kelsey—212, 213

- Along River—10.5 miles, straightforward but some of it is slow.

- Across top—Kelsey's map show a road across Whitmore Point almost 20 miles up Parashant Canyon. There may be a crossing before that.

LOOP: 192 MILE OR 193 MILE TO GRANITE PARK CANYON

- Granite Park Area
  Butchart—237, 238

LOOP: 209 MILE CANYON TO 214 MILE CANYON

- Down 209 Mile and up 214 Mile
  Butchart—213-215

LOOP: BRIDGE CANYON TO SPENCER CANYON

- A subsidiary loop within Spencer is also possible—Milkweed to Meriwitica
  Aitchison—not mentioned
  Annerino—300
  Butchart—244-251
  Kelsey—214, 215, 216, 217

LOOP: 209 MILE CANYON TO SURPRISE CANYON OR SEPARATION CANYON

- Up Surprise Canyon
  Butchart—221-ff

- Up Separation Canyon
  Butchart—219
  Arizona Highways, September 1991, page 12 et seq.

From the maps I inherited from Robert, it appears much easier to go up Separation to the rim than up Surprise. Surprise Canyon tributary drainages have many chockstones, and the words "rope needed" appear frequently.

- Along River

Several of us, Robert, brother Al, son Stan, niece Sara, friend Marcy Olajos, and I, hiked along the River from 209 Mile to Surprise Canyon in 1982 as part of a longer hike. The distance is 40 River miles, and it took us seven days. Only one night was a dry camp. A little of the distance could be traversed at River level, a little more on top of lava cliffs, but the bulk of it, after the Tapeats emerged at Mile 215, was on the Tonto.

- Across the Shivwits Plateau

Robert's route up Separation Canyon connects with his route down 209 Mile Canyon within 0.5 mile, while his route up Surprise Canyon requires 5 to 10 miles depending on which arm you come up. His map notes say Rodger Tank was dry in December 1979 and the smaller of the Kelly Tanks was also dry. The larger one was covered with ice on that December afternoon. The problem with the crossover is to get from last water in one canyon to first water in the other. The road to Kelly Tank is in poor condition and when you get there it is about 120 miles back to the gas station according to Roger Mitchell's book, *Grand Canyon Jeep Trails I, North Rim,* La Siesta Press, 1977.

Section 6: Loops on an Expedition Scale

A fine loop would be to go from Lees Ferry to Phantom Ranch, cross a bridge, and head back upstream to Lees Ferry on the other side. This would, I guess, take from five to six weeks—plus time to put out the caches. It will also require permits from the Navajo Indians. Another loop, similarly conceived, would be to hike down the Whitmore Wash Trail, hitch a ride across the River and hike up to Phantom, cross a bridge, and hike back to Whitmore Wash on the other side. This hike would require a permit from the Havasupai Indians. A logical conclusion to this series of loops is to add a third—Whitmore Wash to Pearce Ferry. In this way the River is divided into three segments of approximately 90 miles each with each segment the core of a major loop.

Anyone considering these possibilities may wish to read Robert Benson Eschka's journal which is on file at the Study Collection at Grand Canyon National Park. In 1982–83 Robert executed a mammoth hike from near Green River, Utah, to Pearce Ferry on river right and then, four months later, continued from Pearce Ferry to Moab, Utah, on river left. In the course of doing this hike, Robert obviously hiked the length of the Grand Canyon on both sides, and his journal can be very helpful to anyone trying to travel lengthwise through the Canyon.

Robert dreamed of a Canyon hike of extraordinary proportions and made it come true. I, too, managed, with the help of my brother, to realize my dream of a through-Canyon hike. I hope this book will help make a dream hike of your own come true.

About the Author

Born in Berkeley, California, in 1925, George Steck grew up in a family who appreciated the outdoors. His grandparents were especially fond of the mountains of California and, to this day, George uses their cook kit on his backpacks. After moving to New Mexico with his wife, Helen, and two sons in 1955, he got his first taste of the canyon country around the Colorado River on a 1956 Sierra Club float trip through Glen Canyon. The are so impressed him that he immediately bought an inflatable raft. For six summers, George took Helen and friends on two-week float trips through that beautiful canyon.

George began hiking in the Grand Canyon after the diversion tunnels at Glen Canyon Dam were closed. He consistently spent four weeks a year exploring Grand Canyon on his own expeditions and with his family and friends. These annual adventures culminated in 1977 in a six-week hike from Lee's Ferry to Lava Falls with sons George and Stan, a niece, a nephew, and two other friends. In 1982, he made an eighty-day expedition from Lee's Ferry to Grand Wash Cliffs at Lake Mead, with his brother, Allen, and friend Robert Benson, as well as other friends who hiked sections.

He is the author of *Grand Canyon Loop Hikes I* and of *Grand Canyon Loop Hikes II*—published together in this book, *Hiking Grand Canyon Loops*.

George resides with his wife in Albuquerque, New Mexico.

WHAT'S SO SPECIAL ABOUT UNSPOILED, NATURAL PLACES

Beauty   Solitude   Wildness   Freedom   Quiet   Adventure

Serenity   Inspiration   Wonder   Excitement

Relaxation   Challenge

There's a lot to love about our treasured public lands, and the reasons are different for each of us. Whatever your reasons are, the national **Leave No Trace** education program will help you discover special outdoor places, enjoy them, and preserve them—today and for those who follow. By practicing and passing along these simple principles, you can help protect the special places you love from being loved to death.

THE PRINCIPLES OF LEAVE NO TRACE

- Plan ahead and prepare
- Travel and camp on durable surfaces
- Dispose of waste properly
- Leave what you find
- Minimize campfire impacts
- Respect wildlife
- Be considerate of other visitors

Leave No Trace is a national nonprofit organization dedicated to teaching responsible outdoor recreation skills and ethics to everyone who enjoys spending time outdoors.

To learn more or to become a member, please visit us at www.LNT.org or call (800) 332–4100.

Leave No Trace, P.O. Box 997, Boulder, CO 80306